BABY BOOMERS OF COLOR

Baby Boomers of Color

IMPLICATIONS FOR SOCIAL WORK POLICY AND PRACTICE

Melvin Delgado

 COLUMBIA UNIVERSITY PRESS   NEW YORK

COLUMBIA UNIVERSITY PRESS
Publishers Since 1893
New York   Chichester, West Sussex

cup.columbia.edu

Library of Congress Cataloging-in-Publication Data

Delgado, Melvin.
  Baby boomers of color : implications for social work policy and practice / Melvin Delgado.
    pages cm
  Includes bibliographical references and index.
  ISBN 978-0-231-16300-2 (cloth : alk. paper) — ISBN 978-0-231-16301-9 (pbk. : alk. paper) —
ISBN 978-0-231-53842-8 (e-book)
  1. Minority older people. 2. Baby boom generation. I. Title.

HV1451.D45 2015
305.2—dc23

2014014340

Columbia University Press books are printed on permanent and durable acid-free paper.
This book is printed on paper with recycled content.
Printed in the United States of America

c 10 9 8 7 6 5 4 3 2 1
p 10 9 8 7 6 5 4 3 2 1

Cover design: Noah Arlow
Cover art: © Christopher Robbins / Getty Images

References to Web sites (URLs) were accurate at the time of writing.
Neither the author nor Columbia University Press is responsible for URLs
that may have expired or changed since the manuscript was prepared.

THIS BOOK IS DEDICATED TO DENISE, LAURA, AND BARBARA

CONTENTS

MY EXPERIENCE WITH WRITING HAS taught me that no book ever evolves precisely as planned, and this one is certainly no exception. My initial intent was to focus on baby boomers of color and the cultural assets they bring to their families, communities, and the country at large. I wanted to highlight the strengths of this population, which are often ignored in the national discourse or characterized in terms of needs and issues (what I refer to as a *deficits perspective*). I also wanted to emphasize the potential of the social work profession to serve this population. A strengths or assets perspective is not new to social work.

Early reviewers of the book prospectus encouraged me to include the ongoing policy debates over Social Security and Medicare and how these programs would impact (and be impacted by) baby boomers of color. I was initially prepared to touch upon this, as well as concerns over the "tsunami-like" economic havoc baby boomers are about to wreak upon our financial and health care systems. I was not eager to devote much attention to this; I preferred to focus on my analysis of baby boomers of color from an *assets* or *capacity enhancement* perspective. However, to fully discuss the forthcoming financial and health challenges that baby boomers of color face, I had to delve into the economic literature far more than I anticipated and, quite frankly, felt comfortable with. I tried to capture the major points in sufficient detail, but not so deeply that the reader is drowned in financial analyses. I have endeavored to make this material "reader friendly," but I am not sure that I have succeeded.

Part 1 of the book focuses on why baby boomers—particularly those of color with low wealth—present such challenges to our financial and health care systems and to those in the helping professions, especially social work, that are the focus of this book. These chapters have a heavy emphasis on a deficit perspective, which is quite contrary to my original intent in writing this work. Further, it is impossible to examine the current state of boomers of color without also addressing how racial discrimination has played an instrumental role in shaping the challenges they face as they enter their retirement years.

Part 2, however, shifts to an analysis of the many assets brought by baby boomers of color and (I hope) offers a counternarrative to the more negative prevailing views of this population. The reader will have a sociocultural-economic-political comprehensive view of boomers of color and, as a result, will be in a stronger position to understand the national debates on deficits and debts and how boomers have been cast as a key element in this "crisis." Part 3 considers the economic crisis that is projected to be caused by boomer retirement and how it will bankrupt Social Security and Medicare, which has taken central stage in social policy debates about what needs to be done to avoid this nation-undermining event.

BOOK GOALS

Four goals have guided the development of this book:

(1) To provide a current and projected detailed sociodemographic picture of baby boomers of color (African American, Asians/Pacific Islanders, Latino/as, and Native Americans/Alaskan Natives) against a backdrop of baby boomers in general;

(2) to aid social workers and others in the helping professions develop an understanding and appreciation of the unique rewards and challenges that baby boomers of color provide health and social service systems now and in the future;

(3) to present social policy, research, and practice implications of baby boomers of color; and

(4) to provide an assets perspective that is uniquely tailored to the unique characteristics of boomers of color and their cultural backgrounds, with implications for the structuring and delivery of social work services to this population cohort.

These four goals are woven throughout this book in an attempt to provide a comprehensive and in-depth view of boomers, with an emphasis on those of color. To do so, the book draws upon literature and research from an interdisciplinary perspective.

BOOK OUTLINE

This book consists of three parts, eleven chapters and an epilogue. Part 1, "Setting the Context," provides the reader with a multifaceted introduction to various perspectives on baby boomers in general, and those of color in particular. In part 2, "Cultural Assets," the reader is grounded in a new paradigm for viewing boomers of color, based upon strengths and community assets. Part 3, "Implications for Policy, Practice, and Research," presents a variety of ways we can address the needs of baby boomers of color that tap into social work values, particularly social justice and empowerment.

Finally, as I began researching this book, I anticipated that there would be limited research literature on baby boomers of color—but I was not prepared for the extent of the dearth that I found. My sincere hope is that this book spurs additional research that will do justice to this crucial subject in the years to come.

I would like to acknowledge the assistance provided by Christopher Chapin, Jenee Fortier, Dory Ziperstein, Boston University School of Social Work research assistants.

BABY BOOMERS OF COLOR

PART 1

Setting the Context

1

Overview

THERE ARE NUMEROUS WAYS TO determine the extent to which a society is "advanced": such as the longevity of its citizens and/or the quality of life and respect they are shown in older adulthood (Cook & Hatzell, 2012; Ghilarducci, 2008). While medical achievements have greatly improved the former, the latter is still highly variable. It has been argued that quality of life for baby boomers is dependent upon three factors: adequate income (Hudson, 2010), quality health care (King et al., 2013; Olson, 2013; Powel, 2013), and affordable housing (Cook & Hatsall, 2012; Gonyea, 2005; Villa, Wallace, & Huynh-Hohnbaum, 2005–2006). The challenges of providing each of these to the baby boomer cohort (and particularly to boomers of color) will be discussed throughout this book.

Concerns about how to serve a rapidly growing older population have been building over the past several decades—long before the start of the recent recession (Lynch, 2010). Almost thirty years ago, Longman (1985) published an article titled "Justice Between Generations: Unless a Number of Trends Are Soon Reversed, the Baby Boomers Are Headed for a Disastrous Retirement." Satcher (1996) also emphasized that the needs of older adults, particularly baby boomers of color, would require careful planning and that ignoring this cohort would be dangerous for the nation's financial stability and well-being. The recession that began in 2008 has magnified concerns over the feared financial drain that wil be caused by baby boomers.

Baby boomers are entering old age at a particularly precarious political and economic time in the nation's history (Hudson, 2009a; Pruchno & Smyer, 2007). There is general agreement about the seismic changes that will occur when boomers retire, and the vast majority of them are negative (Schieber, 2012; Strack, Baier, & Fahlander, 2008). Nolan (2009) predicts that boomer retirement will result in an entitlement crisis (the depletion of Social Security and Medicare), a fear echoed by many others who worry that boomers will stress our health care and Social Security systems in a way that we have never before had to contend with (Ohlemacher, 2011; Reuteman, 2010). These fears have been exacerbated by the recession, which forced many boomers to turn to Social Security earlier than anticipated because of long-term unemployment and financial crises (Johnson and Wilson, 2010a, b). "The oldest of the 78 million Americans born during the post–World War II baby boom generation are turning 65 this year, while the share of the population older than 85 is growing even faster. The flood of elderly Americans is putting severe financial stress on programs that benefit older citizens" (Greenblatt 2011, p. 577)

Nolan (2009) and others also predict a workforce crisis. "Along with overburdened retirement plans and overcrowded early-bird buffet bars comes yet one more worry as the flood of Baby Boomer retirements begins. The overwhelming majority of American businesses are not prepared to deal with the coming loss of so many experienced workers" (Belsky, 2012). This anticipated mass exodus of baby boomers from employment will be noted particularly at the top tiers of the workforce (Alba, 2009) and in specialized occupations: it is estimated, for example, that half the nation's air traffic controllers reached the mandatory retirement age of fifty-six in 2011 (Goldsmith, 2008). Similarly, Richardson (2011) projects severe shortages of nurses due to baby boomer retirement.

Concerns over the health needs of an aging boomer population are another area of trepidation; there is great concern over whether our health care system, particularly Medicare, will be adequate to meet the mental and physical health needs of older adults. Some critics charge that the discussion of medical issues reduces the totality of boomers and other older adults to their medical status (Estes, Biggs, & Phillipson, 2003).

This chapter will introduce the baby boomer generation and examine why boomers are poised to wield such a significant impact.

THE SIZE OF THE BOOMER GENERATION

The sheer magnitude of the estimated 81.5 million boomers in the United States makes them a population to reckon with—as well as the most closely watched, studied, and marketed-to generation in history (Croker, 2007;

Jacobsen et al., 2011; Keeter, 2008). The baby boom generation increased the overall population of the United States by 44 percent in a short period of eighteen years (Goldsmith, 2008). The boomer generation is 50 percent bigger than the "silent" generation that preceded it. Baby boomers are the largest generation in the history of the country, thus worthy of considerable national attention (Frey, 2010; Gillon, 2004; Goldsmth, 2008). As an economic engine, boomers are unmatched: they have generated an estimated $3.7 trillion in earnings, as compared to $1.6 trillion for the silent generation at the same age (Beinhocker, Farrell, & Greenberg, 2008).

"We are often accused of being a self-centered, narcissistic 'me' generation. But the truth is we are important because there are just so many of us. It is the phenomenon often metaphorically referred to as 'the pig in the python,' as this gigantic 'bulge' in the population moves from one stage of life to another. It is because of our numbers that we have overwhelmed every institution along the way" (Croker, 2007, p. xii). This is a generation that stressed maternity wards when they were born, filled classrooms in schools and universities to capacity, and competed like few previous generations for jobs and housing, for example (Light, 1988).

Other countries are also grappling with the issues raised by aging populations; Boomer International estimates that there are 450 million baby boomers worldwide. But this book will largely focus on the American boomer population and its impact on American policies and programs.

THE BIRTH OF THE BOOMERS

A brief historical overview of how and why the baby boomer generation developed will help us better understand current circumstances and challenges. Developing a historical interpretation of a social phenomenon is always challenging; to paraphrase Voltaire, "history is the lie that we can all agree on." Nevertheless, there is value in seeking the origins of the term *baby boomer* and following its evolution over time.

The birth of the boomer generation was arguably the result of the interplay of several significant social forces (Greenblatt, 2007). First, the Great Depression acted as a disincentive to childrearing due to the severe economic hardships suffered by so many adults, creating a pent up demand for children that could only be realized when improved economic circumstances created a degree of certainty and hope. World War II followed and served as another hindrance to the national birth rate by causing social uncertainty and taking many men away to battle. Birthrates finally accelerated dramatically through the 1950s as a result of an expanding economy and optimism about the future. The gross national product more than doubled during this period, from $227 billion in 1940 to $488 billion in 1960. This newfound economic prosperity resulted in increased educational attainment (thanks to programs such as the G.I. Bill, which encouraged college attendance among those of poor and working-class backgrounds), increased household income, and increased home ownership rates (thanks in part to V.A. loan guarantees). All these forces combined to create a climate conducive for raising a family, and led to an unprecedented birth upsurge in the country. Incidentally, comparable forces were also at work in other nations.

It is important to pause and point out that these governmental benefits afforded ex-veterans were not accessed or enjoyed by ex-veterans of color, resulting in significant racial inequalities due to racism impacting their economic and human capital (Alschuler & Blumin, 2009; Herbold, 1994–1995; Onkst, 1998). An intersectionality perspective on boomers of color highlights persistent lifetime low wealth status, which translates into compromised health, low formal educational attainment, and the social ills associated with residential segregation (T. Brown, 2012; Robinson, 2010–2011).

Their inability to obtain housing guaranteed loans, and their lack of access to housing outside of their ethnic and racial neighborhoods due to discriminatory practices, severely limited their accumulation of wealth (Boustan & Shertzer, 2011; Murray, 2008; von Hoffman, 2011). Woods's article, titled "ALMOST 'NO NEGRO VETERAN . . . COULD GET A LOAN': AFRICAN AMERICANS, THE GI BILL, AND THE NAACP CAMPAIGN AGAINST RESIDENTIAL SEGREGATION, 1917–1960" (Woods 2013) does an excellent job of chronicling how this discrimination unfolded regarding African Americans and the gallant efforts to counteract this racism.

Although eligible for these loans, banks refused to give them (Littrell et al., 2013). Racial discrimination even occurred in situations where the ex-veteran clearly had the financial resources to move into White surburbs (Monholtan, 2010). This, in turn, prevented the parents of boomers of color from acquiring equity in their homes, which could be tapped for equity loans, retirement, and inheritance for their children (Valls & Kaplan, 2007).

Not accessing the educational benefits of the G.I. Bill, in turn, too, severely limited ex-veterans of color from entering careers that were well paying, with appropriate benefits, and physically less taxing (Mencke, 2010; Rosales, 2011). The long-term wealth and health consequences are addressed in chapters 5 and 6. Their ability to transfer wealth to their children, and today's boomers of color, has placed them at a distinct disadvantage when compared to their white, non-Latino counterparts. Racially segregated and unequal schools are a direct consequence of segregated housing patterns (Bonastia, 2010).

There are numerous other interpretations of the forces that led to the boomer generation. One perspective emphasizes the importance of rising male incomes and falling female incomes as a result of female job displacement when men returned from the war, relegating women to traditional roles as mothers and housewives (Macunovich, 2000).

The origin of the term *baby boomers* is open to debate (Doyle, 2005). Thompson (2008) traces it back to the middle to late 1940s: "The news media quickly noticed a sharp rise in childbirths that began in 1946, after Germany and Japan succumbed. *Time* and *Newsweek* magazines both ran baby boom features in 1948, although not in-depth ones. Time treated the story as a short business item, noting that '2.8 million more consumers' were added to the population, and quoted the National Industrial Conference Board: 'The significance to businessmen can hardly be overestimated.'" (Internationally boomers have other names; in Britain they are referred to as The Bulge and in Canada they are called Boomies.)

It is important to situate the boomer generation within the context of those before and after. Bernstein (2010) observes that this is the first time in American history that five generations are in the labor market: (1) the World War II generation born between 1925 and 1945; (2) the baby boomer generation (1945–1964); (3) Generation X, born between 1965 and 1980; (4) Generation Y, sometimes referred to as Millennials, born between 1981 and 2000; and (5) Generation 2000 (post 2000).

Not surprisingly, the 1980s and early to mid 1990s witnessed a proliferation of publications on the topic of baby boomers in the United States. America started to look at this generation in a different light, both with admiration as well as from an alarmist perspective. Two publications stand out during this period due to their significance for how they helped to spur national awareness about baby boomers, bringing together a statistical and cultural picture of this generation.

Landon Jones's *Great Expectations: America and the Baby Boomer Generation* (1980) played a pivotal role in bringing baby boomers to national attention in the early 1980s. Jones is widely credited with popularizing the phrase *baby boomer,* drawing attention to how this generation played a significant national role in the shaping of fashion, politics, education, lifestyles, and business styles and behaviors. Jones also addressed the influential forces of the Great Depression and World War II setting the stage for the birth of this generation, which was discussed earlier. Light's *Baby Boomers in Retirement: An Early Perspective* (1993) provided a detailed statistical examination of baby boomer's financial well-being upon retirement and raised serious questions about how well this generation would do upon retirement. This Congressional Budget Office statistical portrait represented what many would argue is the first, and most comprehensive, economic analysis of boomers.

Hudson and Gonyea (2012) contend that boomers entering older adulthood will represent a conceptually distinct cohort from that of their parents and grandparents, entering a new political landscape and "fracturing" their singular political image and power, compromising their ability to shape old-age related agendas.

ALL BOOMERS ARE NOT ALIKE

Jones (1980) chronicles the way in which baby boomers became the first cohort specifically labeled and targeted by Madison Avenue and its role in popularizing this term. Treating an entire generation as a monolithic entity is a dual-edged sword. On one hand, it serves to help create a collective identity that facilitates sociological and political analyses of a group of individuals sharing a significant demographic variable. Conversely, the use of a singular label blurs important between-and-within group distinctions. Variations within the boomer generation are greater than the variations between generations, making broad generalizations difficult, if not dangerous, to make (Cote & Allahar, 2007). There may be an extreme difference, for example, between a boomer who served in the Vietnam War and one who protested America's military engagement there. Other significant differences can arise related (but not limited) to age, gender, sexual identity, socioeconomic status, race, and ethnicity. Some of these factors will be briefly explored here.

Age

There are dramatic differences between boomers born in 1946 and those born in 1964. To distinguish between them, terms such as *younger boomers, leading edge boomers, first cohort,* or *trailing edge boomers* are often used to describe those from forty-five to fifty years of age, whereas *second cohort* and *older boomers* are used to describe those from fifty-one to sixty-four (MetLife Mature Market Institute, 2010). Developmentally, these two groups of boomers are at distinctly different phases in the life cycle, and to combine them does a disservice to them and their families. Faith Popcorn, as quoted in Croker (2007, p. 13), questions the wisdom of grouping a population cohort that spans an eighteen-year period: "How can there be a group that's forty and sixty? How can there be a group that's having babies and getting married and the other size of it is going through menopause and trying to retire? That's impossible."

Race and Ethnicity

For all the discussion of the boomer cohort in general, little if any attention has been paid to the racial and ethnic subgroups within it: "although it's hard to believe that 11 percent of this most heralded generation could have slipped by without much analysis, the nation's 9 million black baby boomers have managed to do just that" (Wellner, 2001, p. 1). When we describe boomers in colorful terms such as *silver tsunami, silver century,* or *gray warriors,* we tend to focus on the "graying" rather than the "browning" of this population (O'Neill, 2009; Roberts, 2008).

There is a desperate need to include race and ethnicity when examining the boomer cohort (Campbell, 2005). Making the invisible visible is a critical first step in ensuring that socially just treatment is given to baby boomers of color. It is ironic to realize that, although baby boomers in general have been prized by marketers and advertisers in recognition of their tremendous financial clout (Street, 2009), baby boomers of color have remained invisible from a marketing perspective and from economic, social, and political perspectives as well (Stanford, Yee, & Rivas, 2009; Wallace & Villa, 2009).

Baby boomers of color face two concurrent challenges: (1) they have been subsumed under the general dialogue on baby boomers and thus become invisible and, (2) the few times that they are specifically addressed, they are often viewed as an added burden because of their unique cultural and linguistic needs (Treas & Carreon, 2010).

Sexual Orientation

Unfortunately, lesbian, gay, bisexual, and transgender boomers are largely invisible in the gerontological literature even though they represent at least ten percent of this population group (Knochel, Quam, & Croghan, 2011). Social support among lesbian and gay boomers (Baker, Herdt, & de Vries, 2006; Gabrielson, 2011; Neustifter, 2008) takes on even greater importance when they are thrust into social situations where their sexuality is frowned upon by the dominant group (Neville & Henrickson, 2010).

Scholars have addressed baby boomers from a variety of cultural, sociological, and political perspectives (see for example Dumas & Turner, 2009; Gilleard & Higgs, 2007; Phillipson, 2007). Yet, even though baby boomers have been the subject of considerable attention in the scholarly literature, there is still a serious lack of a coherent theoretical base to allow a more sophisticated grasp of this generation (Lipschultz, Hilt, & Reilly, 2007). One of the first steps in achieving this degree of clarity is to view this generation in terms of its subgroups to avoid simplistic generalizations. "Given its relative size and influence on U.S. consumer markets, surprisingly little formal, quantitative segmentation work has been conducted on Baby Boomers. The question remains: how to right-size the huge Boomer cohort? How many segments would capture the important, often subtle, nuances?" (Anderson & Kennedy, 2006, p. 2).

AGEISM AND THE BOOMER GENERATION

How population groups are conceptualized and described in media messages and scholarly research is very important in shaping national attitudes and expectations. The labels we attach to people, events, or situations bring with them tremendous power. This is especially true when discussing our view of the elderly. While old age was once seen as synonymous with mental and physical decline, social isolation, and obsolescence, the boomer generation is redefining older adulthood. Along with impressive medical gains in the length of life, boomers are exploring how to improve the quality of life as well.

The term *ageism* was first introduced by Dr. Robert N. Butler and popularized in his Pulitzer Prize–winning book *Why Survive? Growing Old in America*. The study of ageism is relatively recent (Brownell, 2013; Butler & Berret, 2012; Finkelstein & Truxillo, 2013; Macnicol, 2009; Roscigno, 2010).

> The advent of a possible means to delay aging and extend longevity is a great intellectual and social as well as medical achievement. The added years of life that is available for so many is requiring that we as a society change obsolete mind-sets and attitudes about growing old. The social contract of old age, even the inner life and the activities of older persons, is now subject to review and revision. The very words we use to describe people are undergoing greater variability.
>
> (Butler, 2011, p. 7).

The concept of "benevolent ageism" has emerged in the past to capture a perspective toward older adults that is paternalistic, but no less insidious.

Unfortunately, still, many boomers will grapple with discrimination against older adults. "When it comes to ageism, do baby boomers really need a new consciousness movement? Haven't we already 'been there, done that' with women's liberation and gay rights? You bet we do, and we need it pronto. Not only is the adoption of anti-aging messages pervasive in our society destructive to our psyches, it bears dangerous ramifications for us economically, socially and politically" (Osborn, 2012).

One response to ageism is to attempt to resist or subvert the ageing process. Turner finds the boomer quest for eternal youth not surprising in light of recent advances of rejuventive medicine: "The ageing of the baby boomer generation brings to an end a significant and perhaps peculiar period of history. Having enjoyed wealth and social success, it is hardly surprising that this generation wants to retain its social influence through rejuvenative medicine. . . . The lifestyle of the Baby Boomers thus denies both ageing and death, embracing lifestyles that emphasize continuing activity, youthfulness and success" (Turner, 2009, p. 41). These advances have opened up a bold new world, pursuing what is possible to delay aging and its effects on the human body. It is estimated that the anti-aging industry in the United States generated $88 billion in 2010 (Newton, 2011), and will increase in the coming years.

Budrys comments on our national obsession with youthfulness: "As we all learned in grade school, America, specifically Florida, was 'discovered' by explorers searching for the fountain of youth. . . . Five hundred or so years later, many of us are still not willing to give up the quest. If anything, we seem to be even more determined in our pursuit of the secrets leading to perpetual youth. What spurs on this quest is the fact that we can all see that some people do, in fact, age better than others" (Budrys, 2003, p. 1).

The ability to afford anti-aging products and services, as well as expensive medical and surgical treatments that can improve the quality of life, is tied to social class and economic wealth and accentuates the differences between those boomers who can afford such luxuries and those who cannot, often resulting in stigmatization because they "look their age" or worse (Joyce & Loe, 2010; Rexbye & Povlen, 2007; Rosanova, 2010). The great divide that currently exists between the privileged boomer and the unprivileged boomer will only increase in the foreseeable future. Nowhere is this more pronounced than when discussing boomers of color because of their compromised health and financial situation due to their race and discrimination at the national and the local level.

Perry and Wolburg sum up what it means to be a boomer in a culture that favors youth: "To be an aging consumer in a youth culture means facing several challenges, including maintaining self-esteem in the face of negative media portrayals, redefining the meaning of being sexually active, coping with vulnerability, planning for retirement and investing for the final years" (Perry & Wolburg, 2011, p. 365).

The *critical gerontology* perspective can be used to question basic assumptions concerning baby boomers and other older adult groups (Estes et al., 2009a, b). The critical gerontology school utilizes both macro and micro interdisciplinary levels of analysis, bringing a social activist agenda that is guided by social justice principles and themes (Estes, Biggs, & Phillipson, 2003). Critical gerontology thus represents a lens through which age-related concepts, such as productive aging, anti-aging, healthy aging, and successful aging, can be critiqued (Polivka, 2006).

Productive aging, broadly defined, refers to older adulthood that is vibrant, with a combination of meaningful work (whether employment, volunteering, civic engagement, or other activity), social connections (family, friends, neighbors), hobbies and activities, and health. Productive aging can encompass a multitude of perspectives and arenas, and is best understood within a cultural context (Delgado, 2008; Mui & Shibusawa, 2008). The 1980s witnessed the emergence of *productive aging* as term and concept. The 1990s and early 2000s, in turn, saw the reemergence of the term *active aging*, largely as the result of the work done by the World Health Organization's integrative knowledge related to social determinants of health.

Hilton and colleagues (2012) found in a study of Latin Americans that perceptions of successful aging consisted of several key factors: a focus on a positive outlook, importance of living in the present, the need to enjoy a sense of community, and reliance on spirituality and family for creating a sense comfort and meaning as they age. They also found, however, that worries about finances were ever present in their respondents' lives.

Not surprisingly, Yan, Silverstein, and Wilbur (2011) found that aging anxiety was greater among baby boomers who were older, less healthy, less educated, and of lower income. Boomers with less personal contact with older adults, and less knowledge about the aging process, also displayed greater anxiety than counterparts with more contacts and knowledge. The authors suggest a greater use of research informed public education campaigns to promote accurate perceptions about aging and increasing opportunities for younger people to interact with older adults, thereby increasingly the likelihood of comforting age-related stereotypes. Media images of boomers and older adults are generally quite skewed. Consequently, we must be ever vigilant about pointing out ageist media images.

There is conceptual confusion as to what constitutes productive aging (Hilton et al., 2012). Dillaway and Byrnes (2009) offer a sociopolitical critique of the emergence of successful aging paradigms (Hutchison, Morrison & Mikhailovich, 2006; Ouwehand, de Ridder, & Bensing, 2007; Urban Institute, 2006).

Productive aging is sometimes reduced to a focus on postponing retirement and delaying retirement benefits as a way of saving the country from financial disaster (Estes, Biggs & Phillipson, 2003). This limited definition almost always focuses exclusively on those employed in white collar professions. From this narrow viewpoint, the concept of productive aging and its various manifestations can result in criteria that are irrelevant to low-income boomers of color. However, when conceptualized within a cultural context, the concept of productive aging values their active participation within the lives of their immediate and extended families as well as within their respective communities. An older adult does not necessarily need to remain employed in order to feel valued.

This chapter has introduced the baby boomer generation and outlined various economic, political, and social forces that impact baby boomers. It also briefly addressed the lack of attention to boomers of color—a gap this book will attempt to fill. There are numerous arguments being put forth to advocate for or against services to boomers. Each of these arguments will be presented in subsequent chapters and each rests upon a set of values and assumptions about how the nation should address boomers as they enter older adulthood and retire.

2

Two Perspectives on Baby Boomers

BABY BOOMERS OF COLOR CAN be best analyzed when contextualized within the current debate about baby boomers in general (White, 2013). Are boomers considered a national asset or a drain on our resources? More specifically, how will boomers impact Social Security and Medicare in the next twenty years as they retire and enter older adulthood (Papadimitriou, 2007)?

It is this author's view that baby boomers of color represent a vast and largely untapped resource in this country; a tremendous often overlooked source of economic, human, cultural, and social capital. However, it is difficult to consider the positive contributions of boomers (regardless of their ethnic and racial background) if society at large views them from a deficit perspective. This chapter will examine two philosophical or political perspectives—*generational equity* and *intergenerational equity*. Each viewpoint takes a dramatically different view of the financial interactions and obligations between generations and thus offers different "solutions" to the economic problems we face. Each of these perspectives embraces a set of values and beliefs that are explicit and implicit and that wield prodigious influence on views pertaining to the role of society in maintaining a "safety net."

There can be no denying the extent of those problems. It is estimated that baby boomers will be on Social Security approximately one-third of their lives if current longevity patterns do not dramatically change (McKernan, Steuerle, & Lei, 2010). Medicare costs are expected to increase by 80 percent to $929 billion between 2010 and 2020, and program enrollment is expected to grow from 47 million to 80 million in 2030, even accounting for deaths during that period (Wolf, 2010).

Clearly, difficult choices must be made to ensure the solvency of these critical systems. The language used to discuss those choices plays an important role in shaping public attitudes and, ultimately, achieving solutions that are either socially unjust or just, with profound implications for the boomer generation in general, but more so for those boomers who had lifetimes of low-wage employment, which many boomers of color experienced.

The power to shape debates is often a power that gets overlooked: "The debate over the future of Social Security, usually presented as a financial issue or an issue of affordability, is really a debate about societal values and the balance between how much risk should be addressed through individuals and individual families and how much risk should be addressed through social mechanisms such as social insurance" (Kingson, Corman, & Torre-Norton, 2009, p. 95).

THE BOOMERS AND THE SOCIAL SECURITY "CRISIS"

Before we address possible solutions to save the future of Social Security, we must understand the underlying problem. Some economists and analysts fear that baby boomers will bankrupt Social Security—and the nation in the process. A World Bank report entitled *"Averting the old age crisis"* (1994) advocated for pension privatization, and considered the current "pay as you go" approach unsustainable (Turner, 2009). The ratio of workers to retirees needed to maintain the Social Security system could not be maintained, it argued, as boomers entered retirement in massive numbers. Boomer retirees are expected to increase by 3 percent per year, while the number of workers entering the workforce will be less than 1 percent. The ratio of employed workers to retirees will decrease from 3.4 to 2.3 in 2030. This is a significant drop that greatly diminishes the base of workers paying into Social Security. Some analysts fear that the Social Security surplus will gradually disappear and be completely gone by the year 2041 (Meyer, 2009).

The debates about Social Security solvency and budget deficits are summarized by Hagemejer:

> In times of economic downturn, revenues earmarked from contributions or taxes to finance social security programmes fall, while expenditure—due to the increased number of beneficiaries—rises. The countercyclical behaviour of social security expenditure is its inbuilt feature as a source of automatic stabilizer of individual incomes and aggregate demand. However, funding for increased expenditure does not come automatically (beyond existing reserves of those social security systems which keep such contingency reserves) and may come from either reallocation of existing public spending, increased contributions and taxes or from an increase in public financing deficit.
>
> (Hagemejer, 2009, p. 2)

The year 2010 witnessed the passing of a critical milestone in the history of Social Security, and one dreaded by many in governmental circles: for the first time, payouts exceeded pay-ins. The economic recession played an important role; a large number of boomers elected to apply for Social Security early because of unemployment, and the decrease in the number of workers paying into the Social Security Trust Funds (Walsh, 2010).

Fremstad suggests that alarmists have painted a skewed picture of boomer impact on Social Security upon their retirement:

> Some people point to this pay-as-you-go financing structure and claim that the retirement of the baby boomer generation will trigger a crisis in Social Security. This is simply untrue. To ensure that Social Security had sufficient resources to pay for the retirement of the baby boomer generation, changes were made to Social Security in the 1980s to create a surplus in the Social Security Trust Fund. Current projections suggest that Social Security will be able to continue paying full benefits without even drawing on these surplus funds until 2023. After that, payments from current workers and the surplus funds will be sufficient to pay full scheduled benefits to retirees through the year 2038.
>
> (Fremstad, 2011, p. 10)

Other critics suggest that predictions of the demise to Social Security do not take into account an expanded demographic base through immigration. To some, that suggests a potential solution. Turner (2009) suggests that the economic solution to the "aging problem" in developed societies is to import labor from developing nations and thus increase the labor market with workers who would be expected to pay into Social Security for a long period of time before they start collecting on their investments. Myers (2007, 2009) similarly argues for the forging of a "new social contract" between immigrants and baby boomers. Baby boomers would benefit from enactment of laws favoring newcomers and their children; they, in turn, will pay and help support these cohorts through contributions to taxes, Social Security, and employment in services that cater to baby boomers and other older cohorts. This perspective, however, is not without controversy since it involves rapid changes in the country's racial and ethnic composition.

It is important, here to consider the subject of undocumented workers and their significant contributions to the trust funds. The generational equity advocates completely overlook the contributions of the undocumented to Social Security, even though this group will not be eligible to receive payments upon reaching retirement age (Delgado, 2007).

Immigrant non-citizens need to be differentiated from those who are undocumented. The former refers to individuals who have a legal status in the United States through an appropriate visa; the latter, are not legally allowed to reside here. They, however, may still pay into Social Security. For example, approximately half of the Social Security payments on the part of undocumented workers is the result of using a Social Security number belonging to someone else (borrowed), or an invented name. Others, in turn, obtained a card while on a temporary work visa, and then stayed past the expiration date. Only those individuals who "lent" their Social Security number will see any potential benefits.

In 2007, it was estimated that undocumented workers had contributed between $120 billion and $240 billion, or 5.7 percent to 10.7 percent of the Trust's total assets, which were $2.24 trillion. (Hoy, 2010; Shumacher-Matos, 2010). In fact, they made a contribution of $12 billion in 2007, with an estimated 66 percent of all undocumented workers (5.6 million) paying Social Security taxes that year. Consequently, any debate about "fairness" cannot overlook the subject of fairness for a group to contribute to Social

Security but not expect to get any benefits in return, or public acknowledgment, for that matter.

Other critics argue that calculations of Social Security shortfalls are predicated on an economy that is not expected to dramatically expand in the near future. But other experts argue that an expanding economy has the potential to accommodate the projected financial needs of boomers, with a non-consequential impact on the nation's fiscal health (Goldsmith, 2008; Turner, 2009). Further, the Social Security Administration attributes future shortfalls in the trust funds to lower birthrates (from three to two children per woman) which not all analysts agree with.

It is predicted that the anticipated shortfalls to the Social Security program will be stable after 2035:

> Currently, the Social Security Board of Trustees projects program cost to rise by 2035 so that taxes will be enough to pay for only 75 percent of scheduled benefits. This increase in cost results from population aging, not because we are living longer, but because birth rates dropped from three to two children per woman. Importantly, this shortfall is basically stable after 2035; adjustments to taxes or benefits that offset the effects of the lower birth rate may restore solvency for the Social Security program on a sustainable basis for the foreseeable future. Finally, as Treasury debt securities (trust fund assets) are redeemed in the future, they will just be replaced with public debt. If trust fund assets are exhausted without reform, benefits will necessarily be lowered with no effect on budget deficits.
>
> (Goss, 2010, p. 111)

I want to end this section by emphasizing an important point made by the Commission to Modernize Social Security (2011, pp. 31–32) concerning the national debt and Social Security: "[Embedding] Social Security reform within a discussion about debt reduction . . . implies that Social Security benefits must be restructured in order to help alleviate the nation's debt burden. This narrative is false. By law, the Social Security program cannot contribute a single penny to the nation's debt. . . . Benefits cannot be paid if the trust funds run out of money. Thus, it is highly misleading to include decisions about Social Security's future in negotiations or conversations focused on reducing the national debt."

Beinhocker, Farrell, and Greenberg (2008, p. 10) put forth an optimistic perspective on the future of Social Security: "In short, demographics need not be destiny. Government and business leaders who start acting now to change policies and practices can lessen the negative impact of the boomers' aging and help tens of millions of households enjoy a more secure retirement. The boomers have reinvented themselves and society throughout their lifetimes. They can reinvent aging and retirement too."

As this quote demonstrates, how one analyzes the boomers and their impact upon Social Security greatly depends on the lens through which we view older adults and their relationship to younger generations. We will now examine two vastly different perspectives.

THE GENERATIONAL EQUITY PERSPECTIVE

The generational equity perspective pits one generation against another in a bid for the nation's resources. It argues that every generation must be responsible for itself, thus prizing individualism and self-sufficiency; reliance on the next generation is a type of Ponzi Scheme (an image popularized by Governor Rick Perry of Texas in his quest for the Republican nomination for president in 2012). This perspective is often endorsed by conservative organizations and think tanks; the Cato Institute, for example, is one of the biggest advocates of Social Security reform (Gokhale, 2011). Critics of this school of thought use the terms *neoconservative* or *neoliberal* to characterize it (Polivka, 2011).

Williamson, McNamara, and Howling (2003) identify five arguments for renegotiating Social Security programs that appeal to the generational equity perspective: (1) most older adults are economically secure; (2) affluent older adults are getting more than their fair share of society's resources; (3) older adults enjoy unfair advantage over working-age adults; (4) current policies are unsustainable because of pending baby boomer retirement; and (5) each generation should be responsible for itself and it is unfair to rely upon generations that proceeded.

A 2012 article in the *Economist* titled "Sponging Boomer" sums up the generational equity argument: "ANOTHER economic mess looms on the horizon—one with a great wrinkled visage. The struggle to digest the swollen generation of ageing baby-boomers threatens to strangle economic growth. As the nature and scale of the problem become clear, a showdown between the generations may be inevitable."

Tankersley (2012) elaborates upon many of the points made by proponents of generational equity:

> Ultimately, members of my father's generation—generally defined as those born between 1946 and 1964—are reaping more than they sowed. They graduated smack into one of the strongest economic expansions in American history. They needed less education to snag a decent-salaried job than their children do, and a college education cost them a small fraction of what it did for their children or will for their grandkids. One income was sufficient to get a family ahead economically. Marginal federal income-tax rates have fallen steadily, with rare exception, since boomers entered the labor force; government retirement benefits have proliferated. At nearly every point in their lives, these Americans chose to slough the costs of those tax cuts and spending hikes onto future generations.
>
> (Tankersley, 2012)

Many generational equity proponents besides Tankersley have described the baby boomer generation as "selfish" and as displaying a total disregard for the needs of the generations that follow in their footsteps. The tone and the assumptions embedded in the generational equity argument reveal a deep and disturbing resentment about the boomer generation that is probably unprecedented in this nation's history (Garstka, Hummert, & Branscombe, 2005).

Interestingly, however, a 2010 USA Today poll found that 57 percent of respondents described boomers as "giving," as opposed to 37 percent who thought of them as "selfish" (Jayson, 2010). The MacArthur Foundation (2009) reviewed public attitudes in the United States toward older adults and concluded that there was no evidence that showed intergenerational conflict over entitlements for older adults. On the contrary, there was strong support for those entitlements. The framing of social discourse through a focus on age warfare essentially pits age cohorts against each other (Vespari, 2009).

Ozawa and Lee (2011, p. 15) analyzed social spending and found that "it is clear that the American system of social spending is tilted toward the elderly. This finding does not necessarily argue that the United States should spend less on the elderly for the sake of children." Proponents of generational equity often refer to the research by Samuel Preston (1984), which showed that older adults have been improving in economic well-being while children have not—thus shaping the discussion in a zero-sum manner, with winners and losers.

Street and Cossman, however, found "a greater percentage of elderly citizens favor increased education spending compared to increased Social Security spending, while younger Americans express higher levels of support for increased Social Security spending than do elderly citizens. We find little empirical support for the negative connotations of generational equity as it applied to support for U.S. social spending" (2006, p. 75).

Policy makers and political analysts often invariably stress that baby boomers present dramatic and unprecedented financial challenges for the nation once they enter retirement (AARP, 2004a; Leal & Trejo, 2010). Academics, too, tend to approach the topic in a similar fashion. Phillipson and colleagues (2008), for example, undertook a content analysis of 431 articles about baby boomers from the AARP database. They found that economics and finance constituted the largest category of articles; most focused on the financial strain that boomers would pose if major changes in Social Security and Medicare were not undertaken in the near future. This reinforces a deficit perspective on boomers and essentially reduces them to a financial number.

As examples, consider the following two quotes on the Boomer generation.

Last October Earlesville, Maryland resident and former 7th grade teacher and nutrition consultant Kathleen Casey-Kirschling, touted for decades as "Baby-Boomer Zero" or "First Boomer," filed for Social Security benefits. Sixty-one year old Casey-Kirschling was born in Philadelphia, Pennsylvania at midnight, Jan.1, 1946—the first official baby boomer. Her filing for benefits was a momentous occasion for her and a frighteningly symbolic event for the nation. Casey-Kirschling's filing is believed by many in government to be the financial straw that will ultimately break the camel's back. She represents the first of the World War II war babies to begin drawing from dollars that have not existed since Lyndon Johnson's Great Society.

(Ryter, 2008)

A more macro perspective is captured by the second article:

> Do you hear that rumble in the distance? That is the Baby Boomers—they
> are getting ready to retire. On January 1st, 2011 the very first Baby Boom-
> ers turn 65. Millions upon millions of them are rushing towards retirement
> age and they have been promised that the rest of us are going to take care
> of them. Only there is a huge problem. We don't have the money. It sim-
> ply isn't there. But the millions of Baby Boomers getting ready to retire are
> counting on that money to be there. This all comes at a really bad time for
> a federal government that is already flat broke and for a national economy
> that is already teetering on the brink of disaster.
>
> (EducationNews, 2010).

It is estimated that over 50 percent of federal expenditures not involving defense and debt interest are devoted to older adults (Penner, 2008b).
Growth in the older adult population and a corresponding increase in
Social Security, Medicare, and Medicaid is expected to result in an increase
of 3.5 percent of the gross domestic product by 2030 (Penner, 2008a). The
federal budget, in essence, is graying (Uhlenberg, 2009).

Brownstein brings the political ramifications of this propensity to the
fore: "Overall, the tilt toward the elderly over the young in federal priorities remains strong.' Look at where American money is going today. We
are investing in the past, not in the future—which is education, research
and development, infrastructure,' [said] former Republican Rep. Tom
Davis. . . . 'We're General Motors, when you take a look at where the investments in this country are today. And how do you compete globally with
that?'" (Brownstein 2010, p. 3). Comparing older adults to an antiquated
organization is quite telling.

THE INTERGENERATIONAL EQUITY PERSPECTIVE

As opposed to generational equity, the intergenerational equity perspective (sometimes also called intergenerational solidarity or intragenerational
equity) emphasizes the importance of valuing all generations. "The social
insurance approach rests on an understanding that generations depend
on each other; they are interdependent. It gives concrete expression to
values supporting mutual aid and the obligations to care for our families,

our neighbors, and ourselves. Consequently, the values at stake and moral choices embedded within social insurance policy discussions require explicit recognition and discussion. Indeed, as social insurance policy discussions proceed, it will be important to not lose sight of this moral dimension of the social insurance approach, which is a cornerstone of our society and its values" (Kingson, Cornman, & Torre-Norton 2009, p. 107).

Those favoring the intergenerational equity position acknowledge that Social Security needs modest adjustments to both help ensure its viability for future generations and also to redress unfairness built into the system. However, they insist that we as a society must not lose sight of social justice and moral justifications (Cianciolo, 2009; Rogne, 2009). Current efforts to dismantle Social Security, as we know it, run counter to the United Nation's global "social protection floor" initiative to protect the most vulnerable to economic and social risks (Bonnet, Ehmke, & Hagemejer, 2010).

Proponents of an intergenerational equity perspective offer more expansive solutions when it comes to determining how to care for aging boomers.

> The economic burden of aging in 2030 should be no greater than the economic burden associated with raising large numbers of baby boom children in the 1960s. The real challenges of caring for the elderly in 2030 will involve (1) making sure society develops payment and insurance systems for long-term care that work better than existing ones, (2) taking advantage of advances in medicine and behavioral health to keep the elderly as healthy and active as possible, (3) changing the way society organizes community services so that care is more accessible, and (4) altering the cultural view of aging to make sure all ages are integrated into the fabric of community life.
> (Knickman and Snell, 2002, p. 849).

An intergenerational equity perspective values interdependence versus independence and stresses the importance of collective well-being as opposed to individual well-being. Shared risk and obligation is favored over individual risk and reward. The family as a whole, for example, is more important than any one individual within the family. Any definition of success brings in collective, as opposed to individual, dimensions.

"Individualism pertains to societies in which the ties between individuals are loose: everyone is expected to look after themselves or herself and his or own immediate family. Collectivism [interdependence] as its opposite pertains to societies in which people from birth onwards are integrated into strong, cohesive in-groups, which throughout people's lifetime continue to protect them in exchange for unquestioning loyalty" (Hofstede, 1991, p. 151). Reciprocity, as a result, forms the cornerstone of the intergenerational equity school (Grossman, 2009).

Cooperation and interdependence, or collectivism, are cultural values that can be found among African Americans, Asians/Pacific Islanders, Latino/as, and Native people (Delgado, 2007; Davis & Waites, 2008; Ruiz & Carlton-LaNey, 2008). Consequently, an intergenerational equity perspective is often well received in these communities because of its historical tradition.

Stanford, Yee, and Rivas address the role importance of a social contract in the intergenerational equity position: "Some are of the opinion that government should not play a role in supporting individuals and that individuals should be totally self-reliant. However, absolute self-reliance is rarely possible, largely because communities are designed to be interdependent to improve productivity and survival of every member" (Stanford, Yee, & Rivas, 2009, p. 180).

Steuerle (2011) raises a similar argument concerning the meaning and role of a social contract in serving as a moral compass for this nation: "America needs to look at all the elements of our nation's social contract—those created deliberately and those that arose by accident—and question whether they forward our goals of social justice and progressively as well as make the best use of our most valuable resource, our people."

Other critics charge that the generational equity argument is based purely on economic grounds and totally ignores the social and cultural contributions that all generations make to our society. Baby boomers cannot be measured solely in terms of their economic costs (Bessant, 2008). Walker and Fong (2010) argue for broadening the discourse on relations between the generations to include both macro and micro perspectives. This expands the discussion to include social and cultural aspects (Butts & Lent, 2009).

SOCIAL SECURITY REFORM

Social Security solvency has been the focus of increased public attention, largely fueled by the national recession, baby boomer impending retirement, and the 2012 national presidential election. Some say that calls for reform started as early as 1977 (Svihula & Estes, 2009; Williamson, McNamara & Howling 2003). However, since 2004 the discussion has increased in significance (Campbell & King, 2010; Hollister, 2009). Efforts to reform Social Security fall under what is sometimes referred to as the politics of retrenchment, as governments actively seek ways of redefining their social contract and safety nets in efforts to cut costs and, in the process, also disenfranchise segments of their populations they consider "budget busters."

The debate on reforming Social Security has resulted in at least five substantive approaches being discussed singularly, or in combination, with each other (Bloom & McKinnon, 2010; Diamond & Orszag, 2003; Kurtzleben, 2011; Sperling, 2005; Yasar, 2009). The following five possible responses can be thought of separately or in various combinations and permutations:

(1). Raising the Retirement Age: Increased longevity has brought with it altered financial calculations for older Americans' income needs (Pritchard & Potter, 2011) as well as the suggestion to raise the current age at which people can begin to collect Social Security and Medicare benefits. Every major baby boomer group is projected to live longer than the previous generation and set new longevity records in the process. The current early retirement age of sixty-two and the full retirement age of sixty-six to sixty-seven (depending upon one's year of birth) does not reflect our increased life expectancy.

Congress has set the new retirement age to sixty-eight; this will transpire in 2027. This change to sixty-eight, instead of the current sixty-seven, would reduce the anticipated Social Security shortfall of $5.3 trillion by 23 percent. It could be reduced by 33 percent if the retirement age were increased to seventy (Ohlemacher, 2011). The Congressional Budget Office notes that gradually increasing the retirement age from sixty-seven to seventy for Social Security and Medicare benefits will result in $380 billion in savings in the first ten years, and will reduce the debt by 20 percent within twenty-five years and by 33 percent within thirty years (Hill, 2012). The size of the economy, in turn, will increase by 1 percent ($150 billion) within the first decade and 3 percent within fifty years.

Unfortunately, not every racial/ethnic group has benefited equally by the improvements in life expectancy over the past several decades. The postponement of retirement only serves to increase the benefits of retirees when they eventually do retire. Also, not everyone will be able to retire later because of disabilities and/or being in positions that are physically demanding. In addition, employers may not want to keep older workers because of cheaper labor costs associated with hiring younger workers. There are distinct boomer subgroups that will be at a distinct disadvantage in any effort to further increase retirement age.

(2) Altering Cost of Living Adjustments: Historically, cost of living adjustments to Social Security were tied to the Cost of Living Adjustment Index, as a means of helping retirees maintain a standard of living that would not be threatened by runaway inflation (Béland, 2007). It acknowledges the importance of maintaining a certain level of income relative to costs.

The failure to index Social Security benefits to inflation would eventually require periodic steps to increase payments to take inflation into account (Cashell, 2010). However, tying increases to other measures that are lower, for example, would result in a significant reduction in expenditures over time, but not allow retirees to keep up with annual inflation rates. This would further compromise what may be a precarious financial situation, particularly for recipients heavily dependent on Social Security. As a consequence, this proposed reform would severely undermine the financial well-being of retirees who either totally, or significantly, rely on Social Security for their income, many of whom are of color and have long histories of low wage earnings that have resulted in few financial assets (Acs & Nichols, 2007). The formula for determining Social Security benefits can be changed to reflect the longer longevity of retirees with higher incomes and longer life expectancy (*New York Times* editorial, 2013a).

(3) Means-Testing Benefits: The development of a measure to take into account all sources of an individual's income is referred to as means testing. Means testing has a long, often disturbing, history in the United States because it has been used to separate the "worthy" from the "unworthy" to receive governmental aid (such as public assistance).

Having wealthy retirees not receive Social Security, even though they have paid for it over the years, is one possible solution, although it has not gotten the same level attention as some of the other reform options (Coile & Gruber, 2007; Munnell, 2008). A means-tested approach could help ensure that those retirees most dependent upon Social Security can continue to receive it and those with other financial resources either do not receive it at all or at a reduced amount relative to their need.

A means-tested approach is similar to paying insurance: one pays into it but hopes never to need it. In April 2011 three Republican senators proposed a plan that raised the retirement age and also proposed means-testing for retirees making more than \$43,000 a year (Adams, 2011). The increase in retirement age, coupled with the reduction in benefits, would substantially reduce future deficits in the trust funds.

Means testing, although economically attractive, is counter to the fundamental premise upon which Social Security was founded—you pay into the system, and you have every right to expect to receive from the system (Holstein, 2009). Further, Kurtzleben (2011) argues that means testing Social Security may make it seem like a "welfare" program and thus be stigmatizing, altering the historical nature of Social Security as a program that has enjoyed almost universal acceptance. One possible, less stigmatizing alternative might be to tax Social Security benefits. In this scenario, all who are eligible to receive Social Security do so, but those recipients having other sources of income can be expected to pay greater taxes.

The political feasibility of signing means-testing reforms into law may be very arduous, unless it is part of a broader strategy. This type of reform, however, would spare boomers, particularly those of color, with lifelong low-wage histories.

(4) Increasing the Payroll Tax Cap: Social Security taxes are based on a maximum amount of earned income that can be taxed in a given year. In 2013, workers were expected to pay 6.2 percent on a maximum of \$113,700 in wages. Wages above the maximum amount (which gets adjusted yearly) are not taxed. (The Medicare hospital insurance program, however, does not have a maximum cutoff, and employees pay 1.45 percent on all of their salaried earnings.)

Not putting a ceiling on earnings, or increasing the current ceiling, could result in a significant increase in tax revenue (Commission to Modernize Social Security, 2011). It is estimated that the anticipated \$5.3 trillion Social Security shortfall over the next seventy-five years could be erased by having an increase in payroll tax of 1.1 percent on both employees and employers (Ohlemacher, 2010). The Commission to Modernize Social Security (2011) recommends increasing the payroll tax by one-twentieth of a percent over a twenty-year period, helping to reduce the anticipated seventy-five-year shortfall by 1.39 percent and thereby minimizing financial hardships on the current labor force. In essence, some adjustments related to Social Security benefits and financing hold much merit in addressing anticipated future shortfalls (Aaron, 2011).

However, not putting a limit on contributions and then turning around and putting a limit on benefits, results in privileged workers paying considerably more into the trust funds than they could ever expect to get back. Increasing the ceiling and/or tax rates will take money out of the economy that will limit consumer spending. Further, increasing the tax or eliminating the earnings cap could be considered a disincentive to continue to work, although it would spare those boomers with lifelong low wages.

(5) Privatizing Social Security: Of all the options suggested thus far, this one has generated the most discussion and debate. It was advocated during President Bush's second term, but there was great political resistance in Congress from both Democrats and Republicans. In late 2011, presidential candidate Newt Gingrich proposed a modified version of privatization. Employees would have the option of taking the employee portion of the payroll tax and putting these funds into private savings accounts (similar to 401(k) plans). There would be a guaranteed minimum level of benefits as a means of offsetting market volatility. These funds, in turn, could be passed on to an estate once the individual passes away. The employer portion, however, would still be paid to the Social Security program (*Boston Globe,* 2011). The organization Third Way, a critic of the current system, has proposed offering those under the age of thirty an option to open up private retirement accounts in lieu of participating in Social Security (Center for a Responsible Federal Budget, 2011).

Critics argue that such an individualized approach puts retirees at increased financial risk during economic downturns, as we saw during the 2008 recession. There are no guarantees that the stock market will be able to return suitable profits on investments; in fact the money could be reduced significantly, or lost, in the future.

Baby boomers of color, many of whom are low-income and low-wealth retirees, are especially vulnerable to such a strategy because they do not have savings and/or have limited access to employer pension plans. Tanner (2001, p. 2), although a major advocate for privatization of Social Security, acknowledges this: "The debate over Social Security reform is vital to all America, but no group has as much at stake as do African Americans." I would add that low-income Asians, Latino/as, and Native Americans share the same concerns. Social Security reform cannot ignore racial and ethnic factors, although it is supposed to be race and gender neutral (Commission to Modernize Social Security, 2011). Baby boomers of color will be severely impacted by almost all the suggested reforms, since they are very dependent upon public funding.

Kurtzleben (2011) and others also question how such a system would operate, particularly for those retirees currently receiving Social Security.

How would they be supported in their retirement if a significant portion of the upcoming generation opts out of Social Security in favor or individualized retirement accounts? The Center on Budget and Policy Priorities, too, has raised this concern with a potential gap in funding (Gabriel, 2011).

These five reforms or various manifestations will continue to be debated in the near future (*New York Times,* 2013b). Each is predicated upon an embrace of a set of values about the role of society in meeting the needs of its citizens who are near retirement or have retired (Svihula & Estes, 2006). And, as mentioned previously, none of these reforms takes a "best case" scenario by envisioning an expanding economy, dramatic increases in birth rates, or immigration, which will go a long way toward easing, if not eliminating, the solvency crisis. An increase of several decimal points in the growth domestic product over a ten-year period, for example, makes a tremendous economic difference (Favreault & Nichols, 2011; Kotkin & Ozuna, 2012; Su, 2007).

Longman argued almost twenty-five years ago that "what becomes of Social Security, Medicare, and other retirement programs in the future is not an issue for senior citizens. It is an issue for their children and grandchildren to decide, before time runs out" (1985, p. 81). I, and others, would argue that it is an issue for all age groups to decide, and no one group must be disenfranchised in the process.

Walker contextualizes efforts to reform Social Security and Medicare in the United States against a backdrop of similar efforts in Europe:

> The creation of Europe's social insurance systems represented the heyday of the continent's welfare states, but in the 1990s, they became prime targets for reform as a general wave of neoliberalism [what we refer to as neoconservativism] engulfed policy makers in all countries. Although specific national reforms have followed their own paths and there is considerable variation between them, the common trend among European countries is unmistakable. A scaling back of social insurance coupled with an increasing role for both social assistance and private provision.
>
> (Walker 2009, pp. 302–303)

What happens in the United States will undoubtedly be noticed and discussed by other countries who are struggling with their own social insurance programs.

VALUES UNDERPINNING SOCIAL INSURANCE REFORM

There are a set of values that underpin the arguments for or against social insurance and older adults in this and other countries. These values, not surprisingly, help guide the arguments made by the generational and inter-generational equity schools regarding Social Security and Medicare.

The following five values have been addressed in various forms through-out this chapter, but will be emphasized in this section: (1) individualism versus collective responsibility, (2) working-age adults are society's most valued generation, (3) generational contributions to society are measured by economic output, (4) social contracts are negotiable, and (5) small is beautiful. These values are not all of equal weight and importance, yet in combination they provide a powerful rationale for undertaking policy decisions with profound long-range implications.

(1). Individualism versus collective responsibility: As mentioned earlier in this chapter, the importance of the individual versus the collective good is the core value put forward by generational equity proponents. A focus on individualism emphasizes self-sufficiency, which is deeply rooted in Ameri-can lore (Coates, 2011). However, this value is antithetical to many groups of color who culturally subscribe to a collective value.

Turner typifies this perspective: "Despite the cogency of the GI [gen-erational interdependency] criticism, it is nevertheless the case that the GE [generational equity] lobby has been successful, because the simple logic of its appeal to individualism resonates with the neoliberal climate that was sustained after the departure of political leaders like President Regan and Prime Minister Thatcher. The appeal to responsibility and personal choice against mandatory measures remains a potent aspect of the view that gen-erational interests are on a collision course" (Turner, 2009, p. 86). Turner's conclusion highlights the influence that individualism has in shaping dis-course on many different social issues, including Social Security. Individu-als, in this view, should assume all risks and rewards concerning their future economic well-being. The privatization of retirement accounts is thus an agreeable policy from this viewpoint.

On the other hand, opponents such as Starr value the collective shar-ing of risks to ensure economic well-being: "Social Security protects people against a variety of risks to ensure them a basic floor of income in old age and to enable many people who have struggled all of their lives to look forward to a decent standard of comfort and dignity when they retire. It would be a crime to take that away from them" (Starr 2005). In this view the privatizing of retirement funds would devalue the basic concept of a guaranteed minimum income for older adults.

(2) Working-age adults are society's most valued generation: Proponents of generational equity value working-age adults as making the most important contributions to this society; they should not be burdened with the responsibility for the generation that preceded them.

"It does not matter if Senior Citizens have accumulated greater wealth that provides retirement income or manage only on Social Security. Once a person stops working (retires, is laid off, etc.) beyond what that individual does for her/himself, someone else has to provide the goods and services that person requires. Ultimately, the cost of providing for Senior Citizens is borne almost entirely by the productive component of the country's productive labor force (i.e., those who are employed)" (Pritchard and Potter, 2011, p. 25).

The mere idea that any generation is more or less worthy than any other is undemocratic and effectively pits groups against each other in the process. Overvaluing working-age adults further marginalizes those in society who cannot hold full-time employment or cannot do so over a sustained period of time because of a host of factors (such as disabilities, for example). Further, "work" in this instance often really refers to those fortunate enough to gain employment in sectors requiring high levels of formal education who have private pension plans. In other words, there are "worthy" and "unworthy" working-age adults. This value totally ignores the work that transpires in the informal economy (Delgado, 2011), for example.

(3) Generational contributions to society are measured by economic output: The generational equity school stresses the value of economic contributions to the exclusion of social and cultural contributions. This is a very narrow interpretation of the value of human contribution to society and is unsustainable in a democracy and antithetical to social work. Even the most capitalistic of enterprises cannot stand by profit alone; it must consider the economic, social, and political consequences of the work it performs.

One argument made by proponents of postponing retirement is that those who continue to work enjoy physical and mental benefits along with improved finances (McManus, Anderberg, & Lazarus, 2007). That argument, however, is predicated on workers who are not in physically demanding or dangerous employment, and, as noted throughout this book, many boomers of color fall into this precarious category.

Arguments that emphasize economic output ignore many other contributions that boomers make: the caregiving role they often play in helping their children and parents, for example. Volunteering is another way in which boomers can improve their communities. As will be discussed further in part 2, boomers play influential roles within their families and communities that cannot, and should not, be monetized to determine their value.

(4) Social contracts are negotiable: Boyce (2000) puts forth a conceptualization of social vulnerability that can be viewed from two dramatically different values perspectives: (1) wealth based—those who pay more deserve more—and (2) rights based—each individual has an inherent right to exist regardless of their economic circumstances. The first approach speaks for itself. The second approach is a signature element of democratic societies and gets conceptualized as a social contract and operationalized through social policies such as Social Security and Medicare.

The social contract helps to ensure that individuals have an opportunity to live with minimal disruption in their basic human needs across the lifecycle (Coates, 2011). In essence, there is an understanding that some individuals are in a position to help and some are in a position to need assistance at some point in their lives. Those needing assistance must not be stigmatized for doing so. However, if social contracts are easily renegotiated, or broken, it means that they are not worth the paper they are printed on.

(5) Small is beautiful: many neoconservative-led Social Security reform efforts argue that government is too large and therefore has too great an opportunity to "meddle" in an individual's life and pursuits. This value, of course, is not limited to social insurance programs; it also gets raised when considering policies related to the environment, education, energy, transportation, housing, and even the military.

Social insurance programs, however, not only involve a substantial portion of governmental funds but are also symbolic, a testament to what a nation believes in as basic living standards for its citizens. Efforts to move Social Security, for example, out of the public domain and into the private domain through individualized retirement accounts represents a fundamental shift in how we view the role of government in caring for its most vulnerable citizens. Unfortunately, Social Security reform has become the "poster child" of this movement to privatize government functions.

These five basic core values present a comprehensive picture of how the generational equity school is trying to control the discourse on social insurance programs and the policies that are being advanced as possible solutions to the "pending disaster" awaiting this country. The arguments based on these values seriously undermine the most vulnerable boomers, which are most likely those who are low income and of color, as the reader will see in the succeeding chapters. Nevertheless, these efforts to reform Social Security are part of a broader movement to alter the social contract and reduce the power and influence of government to help ensure that basic financial and health needs go unmet for a significant sector.

The debate about the financial future of the nation seems to rest solely, and unfairly, on the backs of baby boomers. Scapegoating this generation, as evidenced by the arguments put forth by those in the generational equity school, does a disservice to a very complicated set of factors influencing this nation's economic well-being. Intergenerational equity proponents have tried to broaden the argument to include the important social, political, cultural, and economic role boomers can play. Their efforts have not been successful in this author's opinion.

Federal Reserve Board chairman Bernanke poses a critical question regarding baby boomers and the fiscal future of the nation: "If, as a nation, we were to accept the premise that the baby-boom generation should share at least some of the burden of population aging, what policy choices might be implied?" (Bernanke 2006, p. 2). The answer to this question will not only impact baby boomers but also their families, communities, and the nation as a whole. Further, the answer must be grounded within a sociopolitical context, with a requisite set of values that either undermine or reenforce a social contract.

The following chapter provides a demographic grounding to highlight how the boomer generation has evolved and the demographic trends that are projected to unfold in the next several decades. Demographic data plays an influential role in national debates and policy choices. Demographics will also play a role in shaping how helping professions strategically address this emerging population cohort in the next four decades.

3

Baby Boomer Demographic Profile and Trends

DEMOGRAPHICS PLAY A DISTINCT AND influential role in helping to paint a picture of the multifaceted composition of this country, and particularly so in the case of baby boomers (Wilmoth, 2010). How demographic data get collected and interpreted depends upon a variety of factors, including the political lens through which they are viewed, as noted in the last chapter (Booth, 2006; Perry, 2009; Wray, 2006).

Demographic data often fail to appeal to many professionals, because the numbers offered are rarely grounded within the stories of those they portend to describe; they are faceless. A statistical profile is just that, providing a one-dimensional view of a very complex picture of our social ecology. Nevertheless, this data will help us develop a more comprehensive understanding of baby boomers in general and greater insight into boomers of color and their place within the constellation of boomers and the nation as a whole.

This chapter will discuss baby boomers in terms of age distribution, geographic location, and racial and ethnic breakdown, as well as some other important demographic parameters. This contextualization sets the foundation for the following chapter, which will focus on specific racial and ethnic boomer groups, and helps highlight similarities and differences within and between boomer groups.

DEMOGRAPHIC PROFILE

According to the 2010 U.S. Census, baby boomers represent 26.4 percent of the United States population, or an estimated 81.5 million people, up from 62 million in 2000, and an increase of 31.5 percent since 2000 (Howden &

Meyer, 2011). Their sheer size makes them this world's largest boomer cohort. Ten thousand boomers will turn sixty-five every day over the next ten years (Cohn & Taylor, 2010); 3.5 million boomers will turn fifty-five each year. (These statistics do not take into account undocumented boomers.)

In 2006, approximately 8,000 boomers started turning sixty years of age each day, which translates into one every 8 seconds, 56,000 per week, or 2,912,000 per year (Greenblatt, 2007). On January 1, 2011, it was estimated that 10,000 baby boomers a day turned sixty-five years old, and this trend is projected to continue to well into 2030. In the beginning of 2011 approximately 13 percent of the nation's population was sixty-five or older, and by 2030, when the last of the baby boomers turn sixty-five, that rate will be 18 percent, representing an almost 50 percent increase in the nation's older adult population (Barry, 2010).

Bernstein and Edwards (2008, p. 1) examine demographic projections related to older adults and provide important data on projected trends in the next four decades: "In 2030, when all of the baby boomers will be 65 and older, nearly one in five U.S. residents is expected to be 65 and older. This age group is projected to increase to 88.5 million in 2050, more than doubling the number in 2008 (38.7 million). Similarly, the 85 and older population is expected to more than triple, from 5.4 million to 19 million between 2008 and 2050" (Bernstein & Edwards, 2008, p. 1). Baby boomers are largely responsible for this significant numerical increase (Ortman & Guarneri, 2009; Vincent & Velkoff, 2010).

The baby boom period did not witness an even distribution of baby births: 1957 produced the greatest number of boomers (4.3 million); 1946 had the fewest (3.47 million). In 1945, which some argue was the "real" beginning of the baby boomer generation, there were 2.8 million births. During the period of the 1930s to early 1940s, births averaged between 2.3 and 2.8 million (Rosenberg, 2011). Early to mid boomers (1946–1954) represent 11.1 percent of the national population, with older adults aged sixty-five or older accounting for 12.3 percent of the population (Johnson & Wilson, 2010b).

HOUSEHOLD COMPOSITION AND MARITAL STATUS

Interestingly, minimal attention has been focused on the changes to marital status upon retirement, even though retirement often brings with it dramatic changes in relationships (Wickrama, O'Neal, & Lorenz, 2013).

Household composition and marital status provide important information for the successful planning for baby boomer retirement. Lin and Brown (2012), for example, specifically address the socioeconomic status of boomers who are unmarried as they face older adulthood. They point out that one-third of baby boomers were unmarried, with the majority of these being either divorced or never married, and 10 percent were widowed.

The socioeconomic profile of unmarried boomers is quite dismal when compared to their married counterparts: "Unmarried Boomers faced greater economic, health, and social vulnerabilities compared to married Boomers. Divorced Boomers had more economic resources and better health than widowed and never-married Boomers. Widows appeared to be the most disadvantaged among Boomer women, whereas never-married were the least advantaged among Boomer men" (Lin & Brown, 2012, p. 153).

MORTALITY/LIFE EXPECTANCY RATES

National demographic predictions involve three key variables: death, birth, and immigration rates. Each is based upon a set of assumptions that wield considerable influence on predictions. The dynamic interactions between these three factors, in turn, determine the growth of a nation's population over a period of time.

Federal Reserve Board chairman Bernanke commented on the mixed blessings of national high longevity and low fertility rates: "Even a practitioner of the dismal science like me would find it difficult to describe increasing life expectancy as bad news. Longer, healthier lives will provide many benefits for individuals, families, and society as a whole. However, an aging population also will create some important economic challenges. For example, many observers have noted the difficult choices that aging will create for fiscal policy makers in the years to come" (Bernanke, 2006, p. 1).

Mortality rates are a statistical measure of the number of deaths in a population. This rate takes into account the size of the population group at a given period of time, usually applied to a unit of analysis of one thousand or one hundred thousand individuals per year (Kochanek et al., 2011). According to the Centers for Disease Control and Prevention, mortality rates between 2006 to 2009 decreased for all age groups, with those ages one to seven years old experiencing the greatest decrease (6.7 percent), and boomers (fifty-five to sixty-four) experiencing the smallest decrease

(0.9 percent) (Kochanek et al., 2011). Those aged sixty-five to seventy-four (3.4) and seventy-five to eighty-four (4.9) experienced more dramatic decreases than boomers.

The United States mortality rate, in turn, is closely tied to life expectancy rates. Life expectancy refers to a measure of remaining life for an individual at a particular age and is closely related to age specific death rates. In 2009, life expectancy at birth was 78.2 for the total country, or an increase of 0.2 years from 75.5 in 2008 (Kochanek et al., 2011). White, non-Latinas had the highest life expectancy of any group with 80.9 years, and White, non-Latino males had the second highest rate with 78.6. African American females (77.4) and males (70.9), however, had significantly lower life expectancies.

Life expectancy rates are best appreciated within a historical context. Life expectancy in this country has increased more over the past thirty years than the two-hundred-year period from 1750 to 1950, with an individual expecting to live until age eighty (Transgenerational Design, 2011). This increase in life expectancy among boomers is at the heart of generational equity proponents who fear that Social Security and Medicare will continue to experience strain because someone retiring at age sixty-two can expect to spend almost twenty years drawing on these funds. An increase in life expectancy translates into greater Medicare and Social Security economic costs (Cox, 2008).

The MacArthur Foundation explains why policy makers may under estimate the financial ramifications on the nation:

> The aging of the baby boom generation, the extension of life, and progressive increases in disability-free life expectancy have generated a dramatic demographic transition in the United States. Official government forecasts may, however, have inadvertently underestimated life expectancy, which would have major policy implications, since small differences in forecasts of life expectancy produce very large differences in the number of people surviving to an older age. . . . The cumulative outlays for Medicare and Social Security could be higher by $3.2 to $8.3 trillion relative to current government forecasts.
>
> (Olshansky et al., 2009, p. 842)

The projected costs are considerable.

GEOGRAPHICAL DISTRIBUTION

Much attention has been paid to where boomers are living and where they wish to retire, with important social, political, and economic consequences for those geographical areas. There are numerous states, particularly those with more temperate climates, that wish to attract boomers because of the economic resources they bring. A 2012 national poll of baby boomers found that any community able to attract three-tenths of 1 percent of this group to relocate there will realize an economic boom of $1 billion a year (Consumer Federation of the Southeast, 2012). This potential for mobility, however, brings with it challenges related to social-economic planning at the local level, with a particular impact on the housing market and support services.

Older baby boomers that are aged fifty-five to sixty-four and much closer to retirement than their younger cohorts, for example, are not equally distributed throughout the country regionally or by state (Frey, 2007, 2009, 2010, 2011; Rogerson & Kim, 2005). The term *gerontic enclaves* has emerged as a means of identifying geographical areas of the country where over one-third of the population consists of older adults. As noted in table 3.1, in 2010, there were small differences in the fifty-five to sixty-four age groups across the major regions of the country.

In 2006, five states accounted for almost 36 percent of the nations' baby boomer population: California (8,809,000 or 11.5 percent), Texas (5,637,000 or 7.3 percent), New York (5,081,000 or 6.6 percent), Florida (4,647,000 or 6.0 percent), and Pennsylvania (3,373,000 or 4.4 percent) (U.S. Census Bureau, 2009). However, these are not the top five states with the highest percentages of baby boomers: Vermont (30.1 percent), Maine (29.8 percent), New Hampshire (29.7 percent), Montana (28.7 percent), and Connecticut (28.1). The New England region dominated this category. There is uneven but universal growth in boomers across the country (Frey, 2007).

Not surprisingly, states with populations of color sixty years and older follow an almost similar distribution (U.S. Administration on Aging, 2011a, b) with California (2,163,000 or 37.8 percent), Texas (1,159,000 or 33.0 percent), New York (978,000 or 27.2 percent), Florida (965,000 or 23.0 percent), and Virginia (286,000 or 21.4 percent) rounding up the top five states from a numerical perspective. However, Hawaii (75.1 percent), New Mexico (40.0 percent), Maryland (29.0 percent), and Mississippi (27.4)

TABLE 3.1 Population 55 to 75 by Region and Percent of the Total Population by Region (Numbers in thousands: civilian noninstitutionalized population)[1]

SEX AND REGION[2]	ALL AGES		UNDER 55		55 TO 59 YEARS		60 TO 64 YEARS		65 TO 74 YEARS		75 YEARS AND OVER		55 YEARS AND OVER		65 YEARS AND OVER	
	NUMBER	PERCENT	NUMBER	PERCENT	NUMBER	PERCENT	NUMBER	PERCENT	NUMBER	PERCENT	NUMBER	PERCENT	NUMBER	PERCENT	NUMBER	PERCENT
Both sexes	304,280	100.0	230,272	75.7	19,172	6.3	16,223	5.3	20,956	6.9	17,657	5.8	74,008	24.3	38,613	12.7
Northeast	54,654	100.0	40,451	74.0	3,574	6.5	3,058	5.6	3,820	7.0	3,751	6.9	14,203	26.0	7,571	13.9
Midwest	66,096	100.0	49,677	75.2	4,331	6.6	3,608	5.5	4,560	6.9	3,920	5.9	16,419	24.8	8,480	12.8
South	112,312	100.0	85,164	75.8	6,904	6.1	5,914	5.3	8,096	7.2	6,234	5.6	27,148	24.2	14,330	12.8
West	71,218	100.0	54,980	77.2	4,363	6.1	3,643	5.1	4,481	6.3	3,751	5.3	16,238	22.8	8,232	11.6
Male	149,485	100.0	115,707	77.4	9,318	6.2	7,667	5.1	9,735	6.5	7,058	4.7	33,778	22.6	16,793	11.2
Northeast	26,555	100.0	20,189	76.0	1,684	6.3	1,451	5.5	1,811	6.8	1,420	5.3	6,366	24.0	3,230	12.2
Midwest	32,510	100.0	25,004	76.9	2,143	6.6	1,693	5.2	2,122	6.5	1,547	4.8	7,505	23.1	3,669	11.3
South	54,921	100.0	42,586	77.5	3,323	6.1	2,770	5.0	3,713	6.8	2,529	4.6	12,335	22.5	6,242	11.4
West	35,500	100.0	27,928	78.7	2,168	6.1	1,753	4.9	2,089	5.9	1,562	4.4	7,572	21.3	3,652	10.3
Female	154,795	100.0	114,564	74.0	9,854	6.4	8,556	5.5	11,221	7.2	10,599	6.8	40,230	26.0	21,820	14.1
Northeast	28,099	100.0	20,262	72.1	1,889	6.7	1,607	5.7	2,009	7.1	2,332	8.3	7,837	27.9	4,341	15.4
Midwest	33,586	100.0	24,672	73.5	2,188	6.5	1,915	5.7	2,439	7.3	2,373	7.1	8,914	26.5	4,812	14.3
South	57,392	100.0	42,578	74.2	3,582	6.2	3,145	5.5	4,382	7.6	3,705	6.5	14,814	25.8	8,088	14.1
West	35,718	100.0	27,052	75.7	2,195	6.1	1,890	5.3	2,391	6.7	2,189	6.1	8,666	24.3	4,581	12.8

[1]Plus armed forces living off post or with their families on post.

[2]Regions are described in the CPS glossary of subject concepts at www.census.gov/population/www/cps/cpsdef.html.

Source: U.S. Census Bureau, Current Population Survey, Annual Social and Economic Supplement, 2010. Internet release date: June 2011.

would rank among the states with the highest percentage but not the actual number of boomers of color (U.S. Administration on Aging, 2011b).

Not all cities share the baby boomer population equally either. Denver, for example, is considered the baby boomer capital of the United States with 32.8 percent of its population in this age category, even though Colorado is not a state with a high number of boomers. Santa Fe, New Mexico, and Anchorage, Alaska, are ranked second and third in percentages of their boomer population, and neither of these states has high percentages of boomers either.

How baby boomers of color are distributed within states also varies (Frey, 2010). San Francisco, for example, based on a dated 2000 census, shows their baby boomers to be more of color than that of the rest of California and the nation. This city has a baby boomer population that consists of Asians/Pacific Islanders (30 percent), Latino/as (12 percent), and African Americans (8 percent). Its Asian baby boomer population is considerably higher (33 percent) than that of the nation's Asian boomer population of 4 percent (Jensen & Little, 2008). In 2010 the following five states had the highest number of Asian baby boomers (Ethic Technologies, 2012): (1) California (478,959) led the nation, followed by New York (154,425), New Jersey (73,858), Florida (59,559), and Illinois (55,545). It is no accident that four of the states with the largest Asian population were located on the coasts. The size of Asian boomer populations can be felt throughout all sectors targeting older adults and the communities they wish to either stay in or move to.

FUTURE PROJECTIONS

Population projections have the United States population at 438 million in 2050, up from 296 million in 2005, with 82 percent of this increase due to immigration; one in five Americans (19 percent) will be an immigrant in 2050 compared to one in eight or 12 percent in 2005 (Passel & Cohn, 2008). However, as the reader will see in the following section, immigration, which is a key factor in demographic projections, is also highly sensitive to economics and political climate.

Kotkin and Ozuna, of the conservative think thank Cato Institute, highlight the importance of immigration to the nation's future posterity and security: "Immigration represents a key factor in determining whether the United States can avoid long-term stagnation and maintain a leadership role in the world economy. Overall we should be less concerned about too many newcomers than with the consequences of drastically reduced rates of immigration" (Kotkin & Ozuna, 2012, p. 56). A poor economy and an unwelcoming political environment will diminish projected increases. The reverse is also true.

By 2061 this country will have an older adult cohort that is primarily of color: "The baby boom generation may be the last made up of a non-Hispanic white majority population. The younger generations are much more diverse, with higher shares of Hispanics, African Americans, and Asian Americans in each successive cohort" (Jacobsen et al., 2011, p. 15). Thus how well we as a nation address the current needs and expectations of boomers of color, as well as those who are low income, homeless, and uninsured, will serve as a precursor to how well we address them fifty years from now (Wright, 2005). An investment today will reap considerable returns in the future.

In 2009, adults aged sixty-five and older numbered close to 40 million or 12.9 percent of the United States population (Transgenerational Design, 2011). In the future the older adult population will increase dramatically and predictably. It is estimated that by 2030 older adults over the age of sixty-five should peak at 71.5 million or 20 percent of the nation's total population (Gillick, 2009).

These demographic predictions represent quite a contrast when compared with this nation's older adult population in the late 1930s, when those sixty-five years and older numbered 7 million and represented 5.4 percent of the country's population (Transgenerational, 2011).

Johnson, Toohey, and Wiener provide an assessment of boomer long-term care needs through use of demographic projections into the future and paint a picture that can be considered alarming under the best of circumstances:

> The demand for long-term care services will surge in coming decades when the baby boomers reach their 80s. Declining family sizes, increasing childlessness, and rising divorce rates will limit the number of family caregivers. Rising female employment rates may further reduce the availability of family care, increasing the future need for paid home care. This study projects to 2040 the number of people ages 65 and older with disabilities and their use of long-term care services. The simulations show that even under the

most optimistic scenario long-term care burdens on families and institutions will increase substantially.

(Johnson, Toohey, & Wiener, 2007, p.1)

These predications, in similar fashion to any demographic based predic-
tion, are based upon a set of assumptions, or values, which can be subject to
social forces that can alter outcomes. There is value in using demographics
to predict the future. However, much can happen to alter the future for the
better or for the worse. Consequently, it is best to consider demographic
predictions carefully and embrace a willingness to change opinions as data
become available.

INCARCERATED BOOMERS AS A SPECIAL POPULATION GROUP

We rarely think about baby boomers, or older adults in general, in prison
(Rikard & Rosenberg, 2007). Yet the number of boomers and older adults
in the nation's prison system is considerable, and their presence is increasing. (Note that in the prison system, anyone aged fifty and over is classified
as an older adult.) It is estimated that inmates aged fifty-five years or older
are increasing at a faster rate than the groups' share of the population at
large (Williams, 2012). It is estimated that state and federal prisons have
26,200 inmates over the age of sixty-five, and the 124,000 who are older
than fifty-five has increased by 400 percent between 1995 and 2010 (Belluck, 2012). Those over the age of fifty-five have grown by over 600 percent when compared to the rest of the prison population (Human Rights
Watch, 2012; Williams, 2012). This age group increased by 282 percent
between 1995 and 2010 in state and federal prisons. California, for example,
has 13,000 inmates aged fifty-five year and older (Belluck, 2012).

The impact of the nation's correctional system has been disproportionately greater on people of color, and that has historically been the case for
all age groups. In the case of boomer of color inmates, their incarceration
has compromised their families and communities by depriving them of
contributing (social and financial) adults who are predominantly male
(Alexander, 2012; Delgado, 2012).

The number of inmates serving life sentences is 10 percent of the nation's
1.6 million prisoners, while another 11 percent have sentences over twenty

years in length, making aging prisoners a cohort to reckon with from a health perspective (Belluck, 2012).

Incarcerated boomers face a unique set of challenges (Haugebrook et al., 2010). Health care costs related to medications, special diets, special assistance (walking canes, braces, or wheelchairs), medical (physical and mental) conditions, trauma, and those with terminal diseases are considerably higher than those of the general prison population. Inmates who are undocumented or have PTSD from military combat experience additional stressors that compromise their well-being while in prison (Haugebrook et al., 2010). It is estimated that Alzheimer's disease is growing between 200 to 300 percent faster among inmates than the general population (Belluck, 2012). For all those reasons, the cost of housing older adult prisoners is estimated to be three times that of younger inmates (Price, 2006). Prisons, it should be emphasized, were never designed to serve as geriatric facilities (Human Right Watch, 2012).

The increase in costs and numbers of boomer inmates has raised serious discussions about how best to meet their needs in an increasingly overtaxed prison system. One expert, Jamie Fellner, highlights this dilemma (Williams, 2012, p. A12): "Age should not be a get-out-of-jail-free card, but when prisoners are so old and infirm that they are not a threat to public safety, they should be released under supervision. . . . Failing that, legislatures are going to have to pony up a lot more money to pay for proper care for them behind bars." In Florida, for example, prisoners aged fifty and older accounted for 16 percent of the prison population, but 40 percent of all episodes of medical care and almost 48 percent of all hospital stays (Human Rights Watch, 2012). Releasing them from prison, however, does not make their health care costs go away. Instead, these costs are shifted to other sectors of government and the community they are being released to (Delgado, 2012).

WORD OF CAUTION

A word of warning is needed regarding the foibles of demographic predictions. Demography, after all, is not destiny. Munro and Zeisberger (2010) highlight the challenge of predicting the future: "Our ability to forecast degrades rapidly the further out we predict. Even if we do manage to accurately forecast an event, the magnitude and consequences of that event usually astonish us. On the rare occasion where we manage to accurately forecast the event, its magnitude and consequences, our timing is invariably off—sometimes by many years. Yet we still seek the advice of economists, technicians and academics, knowing full well their documented inability to forecast with greater accuracy than chance would allow."

Predictions are subject to a wide range of unanticipated events that can significantly alter projected outcomes. Natural disasters, for example, can result in high mortality rates, mass influx of newcomers, and significant increases or decreases in fertility rates, all of which wield considerable influence on demographics. The Great Depression and World War II are other examples that resulted in dramatic changes in decreased birthrates for the nation. Nevertheless, demographic projections have merit that must be acknowledged, although not without a healthy degree of caution.

Stein comments on the relative ease of projecting demographic trends and offers a caveat for policy makers: "Demographic forecasts are fairly straightforward. Absent famine, plague or war, everyone entering the labor force over the next 15–25 years is already born, as is everyone retiring over the next 65–70 years. Factor in life expectancy and forecasting demographic developments is comparatively easy. Nevertheless, forecasters sometimes get it wrong. The two main factors that currently tend to throw out forecasts are birth rates and migration" (Stein, 2008, p. 23).

Projecting demographic profiles well into the future is, at best, a dangerous task, but one that we cannot avoid engaging in for the country to be better prepared for a significant demographic shift: "Predicting the future is fraught with risk—the ever-present danger of being embarrassed by the unfolding of actual events. Nevertheless, people seem morbidly fascinated by forecasters and our frail art. Compelling visions of the future have a self-fulfilling aspect. That is because expectations are a powerful engine of behavior change, perhaps the most powerful of all" (Goldsmith, 2008, p. 178). Although Goldsmith's concerns about projecting demographic changes well into the future require that, when doing it, we do so with a great deal of caution, there certainly is value in projecting and planning accordingly. The value of a best scenario, worst scenario, and most likely scenario in viewing demographic trends has appeal for a social-planning perspective. Effective development of each of these scenarios necessitates an in-depth understanding of trends and how explicit and implicit values help us decipher these data.

Wilmoth and Longino Jr. (2006), for example, address the high degree of diversity within older adult populations, making broad predictions of limited value if these differences are not taken into account. McCulloch, Lassig, and Barnet (2012) argue that there is also wide diversity among White, non-Latino/a older adults that must not be overlooked in a rush to draw conclusions on boomers.

Demographics play an influential role in helping to shape the destiny of a nation, and these data lend themselves to speculating and even predicting what the future of a nation holds in store. Further, demographic profiles and trends provide important information that can help shape a nation's policies and programs and do so in an anticipatory manner to minimize hardships to its citizens. Nevertheless, demographics can be shaped by unforeseen events. Further, the type of data we focus on is greatly influenced by the biases in what a nation considers important or unimportant.

There is no question that baby boomers are a significant demographic group and that this nation has paid and will continue to pay close attention to it in the foreseeable future. How this attention gets translated into programs and policies that increase the well-being of boomers will have a profound impact on these individuals, their families, and the communities they reside in. This chapter has provided baseline demographic data on boomers in general to help ground the reader for perspective on policies and programs. The following chapter provides readers with a more nuanced appreciation of the boomer generation and the complexities of generalizing for an entire generation of 81 million members. Special attention will be paid whenever possible to boomer newcomers to this country because they represent an even more invisible group within a largely invisible boomer of color cohort.

4

A Demographic Focus on Baby Boomers of Color

BABY BOOMERS OF COLOR ARE generally not discussed in scholarly reports and publications; they are typically subsumed under the general rubric of "baby boomers," making data difficult, if not impossible, to obtain, limiting the development of a comprehensive understanding of their status. Yet these data are important, particularly for social work and other helping professions that embrace diversity and cultural competence (Torres-Gil & Lam, 2012). This lack of data is a testament to their invisibility and results in challenges for developing policies, programs, and services that take into account their profiles.

The socioeconomic status of boomers of color is significantly different from that of the general boomer population, and thus they require different services from social workers and other helping professionals. As noted earlier, the consequences associated with racism have compromised their economic well-being. This chapter will help introduce various demographic facets of baby boomers of color.

A NOTE ABOUT DEMOGRAPHICS

While it is helpful to understand the racial and ethnic composition of baby boomers of color, it is important to emphasize that such an analysis does not include other distinctions such as English language skills, acculturation level, formal educational attainment, and religious/spiritual beliefs and practices, to note but several critical factors. Each of these factors wields considerable influence on boomer of color participation in the labor force and their experiences outside of work. In combination, they dramatically shape a different existence from that more commonly experienced by White, non-Latino/a boomers. Demographic data provide a limited and less nuanced picture that would benefit from a qualitative understanding of the lived experiences of baby boomers of color even more.

"There is a tendency among policy makers and academicians to fail to embrace the heterogeneity of the boomers when considering the aging of the generation. It is a mistake to do so" (Mutchler & Burr, 2009, pp. 40–41). An inability to have a nuanced understanding of boomers of color translates into a narrow if not stereotypical portrait of them. Wallace and Villa (2009) challenge us to go beyond a surface examination of boomers to see how diverse this population group really is—and how it is increasing in diversity.

Further, demographic data rarely provide faces and stories that help contextualize the way in which differences within boomer categories emerge and influence their decision making concerning finances and retirement. The challenge for the social work profession is to go beyond broad statistical categorization and delve into the nuances of these groups. This speaks to the use of qualitative research to supplement data gathered from quantitative methods such as those employed by the U.S. Census Bureau. Mind you, there is a place for quantitative data regarding boomers of color. However, a comprehensive understanding is not possible without the information that qualitative data can provide concerning the lived experience.

RACIAL AND ETHNIC DISTRIBUTION

According to the 2011 U.S. Census, no racial or ethnic group of color has more than 10 percent of its population in the boomer category, with Asians/Pacific Islanders (9.8 percent) having the largest percentage of boomers, followed by African Americans (9.0 percent), Latino/as (6.1 percent), and American/ Alaskan Natives (0.9 percent) (U.S. Census Bureau, 2009; Hellmich, 2009). Although each of these groups is very distinctive in background, they do share having a lived experience of racially segregated communities.

It is important to note that these four general groupings consist of numerous subtypes. Latino/as, for example, can consist of twenty-one different backgrounds, with varying histories of residence in this country.

Asian and Pacific Islanders, in turn, consist of ten subgroups. These subtypes may not appear as significant for outsiders. However, within group differences can be as significant as between group differences, particularly when taking into account phenotype.

Demographic projections for older adults of color are quite striking. Between 1999 and 2030, older adults of color sixty-five years old and older will increase by 217 percent, compared to 81 percent for older White, non-Latino/as. African American older adults will increase by 128 percent, Asian American will increase by 301 percent, and Latino/as by 322 percent. American Indian and Alaska Native elders will increase by approximately 193 percent (Golick, 2008). According to the U.S. Census Bureau, White, non-Latino/as aged sixty-five years or older will decline by 11 percent while those of color will increase dramatically during this period: African Americans will increase by 25 percent, Latino/as and Asians will almost double in size (Voelker, 2010).

If we extend the predictions to 2050, the numbers become even more striking. Older adults of color aged sixty and older are projected to number almost 37 million or 36.3 percent of the total aged sixty and older population (U.S. Administration on Aging, 2011c). Latino/as will represent the largest group of color with 16.64 million, followed by African Americans (10.988 million), Asians (7.45 million), American Indian/Alaskan Native (717,000), and Native Hawaiian/Pacific Islanders (176,000). These increases are due largely to baby boomers entering the ranks of older adulthood (Dolan, 2010).

NEWCOMERS AND UNDOCUMENTED BOOMERS OF COLOR

These statistics also do not include boomers who are undocumented, even though they may be longtime residents in the United States and are overly represented in certain regions of the country, and because of segration, certain communities will have a disproportionate number. The undocumented category is particularly important for Latino/as and Asian/Pacific Islanders. Undocumented baby boomers, as a result, face unprecedented challenges. As they enter older adulthood, their invisibility will work to their detriment when they are not included within discussions about how best to meet the increased demands of boomers in the immediate future.

Immigrant boomers of color are an important group to analyze and understand. The national debates about immigration reform are a testament to their significance in the nation's political landscape. It is estimated that 12 percent of early boomers (those born 1946–1955) and 15 percent of late boomers (those born 1956–1964) are immigrants to the United States (Campbell, 2005; El Nassar, 2010). There are approximately 8 million Latino/a baby boomers who came to this country early in their adult life.

> Our results suggest that immigrants from different parts of the world experience very different labor markets and retirement outcomes, with workers from less-developed countries earning less, working in very different jobs, and ultimately receiving lower Social Security benefits and retirement incomes. While time in the United States does tend to narrow the gap between immigrants from less-developed countries and both their counterparts from more-developed countries and natives, pronounced differences remain. Among immigrants from less-developed countries, legal status differences are associated with a large fraction—but not all—of the disadvantage relative to natives.
>
> (Favreault & Nichols, 2011, p. 3)

As a consequence, foreign born boomers often do not share similar living circumstances or goals for retiring. Being newcomers to this country has certainly shaped their work experiences, and there is no reason to think that it will not shape their retirement experiences either (Favreault & Nichols, 2011).

Tovar describes the fate of foreign-born Latino/a baby boomers (but the description could apply to other racial/ethnic groups just as easily):

> When they left their homelands, many of them had the idea that they would make lots of money and someday return to their country for good. Upon arrival, they experienced a culture clash, which was to be expected. What they didn't know then, and may still not know, was that when they finally return home, they'll experience another. The severity will depend on the amount and duration of times they've visited over the years, but it'll be a culture clash all the same. Somewhere along the way, amid the business of raising a family and going to work, they became Americans (and not just on paper), whether they want to admit it or not. They're used to a different kind of lifestyle now, one that may conflict with the lifestyle they will

lead back in their own country. Let's face it: they aren't the same risk-taking twenty-something year olds that arrived here decades ago. They've become set in their ways, as people tend to do. They've changed, and their native countries have as well. When the time comes, what are they going to do? . . . The choice they made back then couldn't have been easy, and this one may or may not be so simple, depending on individual circumstances. If you're expecting a mass exodus of Latino boomers in the next few years, you might be very disappointed. They are more American than they think.

(Tovar, 2011)

Tovar (2011) raises a series of challenges facing newcomer boomers, and each has profound implications for their well-being and ability and willingness to retire. Lum and Vanderaa (2010) advance a commonly accepted argument that immigrating to the United States is a stressful event, even if the immigrants are relatively young when they do it. The process of immigration is stressful, as are circumstances that await them once they enter into the country. This accumulation of stressful events compromises their physical and mental health as they enter older adulthood and their economic prospects as they enter retirement age.

Acculturation stress is ever present in the lives of newcomers of color, regardless of their age, and this will translate into unique older adult experiences (Pumariega & Rothe, 2010). Mui and Kang's (2006) study of acculturation stress and urban Asian immigrant (Chinese, Korean, Indian, Filipino, Vietnamese, and Japanese) older adults found those with higher acculturation stress to also have higher levels of depression. Trauma related to the migration process, particularly for those who are undocumented, plays a role in how they approach retirement. The concept of acculturation stress does not take into account how racial charateristics increase or decrease this form of stress, however.

McDonald (2011) argues that current theories on aging, family, and immigration are inadequate because they do not capture the impact of immigration structurally and connect this phenomenon on social, psychological, and familial levels or how physical aging is perceived and experienced. The complexity of aging and immigration requires a long-term view and an integrating framework. Further, immigration and aging tend to be viewed through a deficit perspective, thereby limiting our grasp of how this process unfolds.

Favreault and Nichols identify a set of factors that shape immigrant boomer experiences with Social Security: "Many factors—including earnings, marital history, disability history, and age at benefit claiming—shape all workers' experiences with Social Security. But immigrants' experiences depend on several additional factors, especially the age of entry to the United States, the number of years in covered employment, and the duration of residence in the United States, all of which are likely to differ across cohorts, place of birth, and legal status" (Favreault & Nichols 2011, p. 2).

Bhattacharya and Shibusawa (2009), in a rare article examining baby boomers and older adult immigrants, bring up a different aspect of acculturation stress: those who arrive and settle in their respective ethnic communities have the opportunity to adjust and cope more successfully as compared to those who do not. Thus the community in which boomers of color live takes on significant influence in shaping their experiences; they, in turn, also are cast into positions of influencing their surroundings.

The American Association of Retired Citizens' (2004b) survey of Latino/a baby boomers, for example, found that 41 percent of Spanish dominant Latino/as, compared to 31 percent who were English dominant, were concerned about economic hardships in retirement and were almost twice as likely (46 percent versus 25 percent) to expect to struggle economically. Socially, Spanish language–dominant respondents were more likely (35 percent), when compared to those who are English dominant (19 percent), to view retirement as a time of increased isolation from society. Their world essentially becomes that much more circumscribed within their families and communities, particularly for those who had to leave these confines to venture to work in English-dominant arenas (Schrauf, 2009).

Similar differences were found on knowledge of Social Security, health, and longevity. Not surprisingly, English-dominant Latino/as were more optimistic (78 percent) than those who were Spanish dominant (50 percent) about retirement. Their ability to socially navigate their way through society is greatly enhanced because of their language proficiency. Language dominance (speaking, writing, reading, and comprehension) is a critical factor in socially navigating retirement, just as it is in navigating social and health services. This finding may have implications for other newcomer groups who do not have English as their dominant or preferred language.

An examination of the "never" beneficiaries (those who never collect Social Security, such as late-arriving immigrants, infrequent workers, those who die before they receive benefits, and noncovered workers), a group rarely mentioned in the popular media and academic sources, finds that newcomers who arrived at age fifty or later represent 55 percent of this category (Social Security Administration, 2011a). Latino/a and Asian baby boomers are disproportionately represented among this group, further compromising their social-economic transition into older adulthood. For example, in 2005 it is estimated that almost 50 percent (2.2 million) of all Latino/as aged forty-five to fifty-four were born outside the United States, with many arriving in the 1970s and 1980s (Fry et al., 2005). These boomers experience a different United States when compared to their counterparts who were born and raised in this country.

GEOGRAPHIC DISTRIBUTION

The geographic distribution of baby boomers of color across and within states is also worth analyzing. "The demographic future of the nation relies heavily on its youth and the areas where they reside, and the challenge in the decades ahead will be to balance their needs with the needs of baby boomers and seniors who are aging-in-place every where" (Frey, 2011, p. 1).

In 2008 almost 60 percent of Asians, Hawaiians, and Pacific Islander older adults lived in three states (Administration on Aging, 2010a): California (40.5 percent), Hawaii (9.6 percent), and New York (9.2 percent). African Americans, however, had a wider national distribution, with 50 percent living in eight states (Administration on Aging, 2010b): New York (9.1 percent), Florida (7.1 percent), California (6.5 percent), Texas (6.4 percent), Georgia (6.1 percent), North Carolina (5.5 percent), Illinois (5.4 percent), and Virginia (4.4). Finally, 70 percent of Latino/a older adults resided in four states (Administration on Aging, 2010c): California (27 percent), Texas (19 percent), Florida (16 percent), and New York (9 percent).

The close association between geographical distribution and historical ports of entry into the United States should not come as any great surprise. Baby boomers of color will, in all likelihood, retire in place, and "place" invariably refers to low-income and low-wealth urban communities where many have lived all their lives. The long-term implications of racially segregated policies and practices continue to influence boomer of color well-being as they approach and enter retirement age. Unlike their more wealthy counterparts, most will not have the option of relocating to retirement communities, suburbs, rural areas, or warmer climates. The possibility of uprooting and leaving behind their families, social networks, and the key institutions upon which they rely is not an attractive option. Cultural values that stress familial obligations and reciprocity may also play a significant role in their choice of retirement location.

GRAYING AND BROWNING

The boomer generation is best understood within the context of two powerful and distinct demographic trends in the United States: the nation is graying (getting older) and also becoming more diverse ethnically and racially, that is, browning (Frey, 2007; Johnson & Borrego, 2009). Torres-Gil and Lam (2012) call the convergence of these major trends, along with increased longevity, a "perfect storm" for the nation.

Brownstein sums up:

> In an age of diminished resources, the United States may be heading for an intensifying confrontation between the gray and the brown. Two of the biggest demographic trends reshaping the nation in the twenty-first century increasingly appear to be on a collision course that could rattle American politics for decades. From one direction, racial diversity in the United States is growing, particularly among the young. Minorities now make up more than two-fifths of all children under the age of 18, and they will represent a majority of all American children by as soon as 2023. . . . At the same time, the country is also aging, as the massive Baby Boom Generation moves into retirement. But in contrast to the young, fully four-fifths of this rapidly expanding senior population is white.
>
> (Brownstein, 2010, p. 1)

The graying of America has certainly gotten its share of attention. The median age for the nation as a whole in 2012 was 37 years, which represents a significant increase from 35.3 years in 2000 (U.S. Census Bureau, 2000). Latino/as had the lowest median age with 27, followed by Asians with 29, and African Americans with 32. The number of adults aged 65 and older has increased from 12.4 percent in 2000 to 13 percent (39.6 million) in 2009 (U.S. Census Bureau, 2011a). In 2010, older adults of color represented 20 percent of all older adults. However, they are projected to increase to 42 percent by the year 2050. That same year will have all older adults accounting for 88.5 million, or 40 percent, doubling by 20 percent of the nation's population in 2010. In 2050, boomers of color will represent 40 percent of the older adult population, doubling from 20 percent in 2012. Contrary to popular opinion, more than half (55 percent) of all adults aged sixty-five and older were employed in 2009, numbering 6.5 million, and representing 16 percent of the nation's labor force (U.S. Census Bureau, 2011a). They are expected to number 11.1 million in 2018 because the recession has compromised their ability to retire.

The browning of the nation represents another major demographic wave. Latino/as are the largest and fastest growing group of color in the United States with 50.5 million in 2010 representing 16.3 percent of the nation's population (U.S. Census Bureau, 2011b). Those with Mexican backgrounds (63 percent) are the largest Latino/a subgroup, followed by Puerto Ricans (9.2 percent), Cubans (3.5 percent), Salvadorans (3.3 percent), and Dominicans (2.8 percent). Latino/as are projected to number 132.8 million residents by 2050.

African Americans are the second largest group of color and numbered 41.8 million in 2009, representing 13.6 percent of the nation's population (U.S. Census Bureau, 2010). They are projected to reach 65.7 million residents or 15 percent of the total population by 2050.

Asian/Pacific Islanders are the third largest group, with a population of 17.3 million in 2010 or 5.6 percent of the total population (U.S. Census Bureau, 2011c). Those of Chinese descent numbered 3.8 million, representing the largest subgroup, followed by Filipinos with 3.2 million, Asian Indians (2.8 million), Vietnamese (1.7 million), Koreans (1.6 million), and Japanese (1.3 million). Asian/Pacific Islanders, in turn, are projected to increase to 40.6 million in 2050. Finally, American Indian and Alaska Natives numbered 5.2 million in 2010, representing the fourth largest group of color, making up 1.7 percent of the nation's population. They are projected to increase to 8.6 million, or 2 percent of the total population, by 2050 (U.S. Census Bureau, 2011d).

Boomers must be viewed within the ethnic/racial demographic composition and distribution across the country, along with the projected trends, in order to better understand their socioeconomic and sociocultural position in this society's mosaic and why discussions concerning this nation's older adult population take on great significance for communities of color, particularly those that are highly concentrated in this nation's urban centers. Fong (2001), well over a decade ago, projected serious challenges Asian baby boomers would face in the future as they entered older adulthood because of their invisibility. Jackson (2010), too, makes similar observations about biracial individuals by looking into the future and raising profound implications of biracial baby boomers that do not conform to conventional identities regarding race and ethnicity.

This chapter on boomer demographics has sought to fill in some of the blanks on the preceding boomer demographic chapter by highlighting similarities and differences between and within boomer racial and ethnic groups. Clearly, there is still much more that needs to be done to fully capture the various differences within groups. Not unexpectedly, boomers of color are not homogeneous in composition. Their heterogeneity, however, will only continue to increase in the next three decades, further challenging the nation and helping professions seeking to reach and serve them as they enter retirement and older adulthood.

Boomers of color, however, are best understood and appreciated within the broader context of how this nation is not only graying but browning. This process of national demographic transformation has escaped public attention even though both trends are widely covered in the popular press and academic circles. Nevertheless, these two trends have been treated separately, with the press and academia for the most part failing to understand their significance for baby boomers. When they come together in analysis, it raises a series of policy and service questions that would not emerge if they were treated separately.

This chapter has also provided a glimpse into the complex world of demographic profiles and trends regarding ethnic and racial boomer groups. These groups share much in common but also present significant within and between group differences. Each of the major boomer groups addressed in this chapter presents nuances that best can be understood within the context in which they live and the role of acculturation in the lives of those who are newcomers to this country (Treas, 2008).

The following chapter continues this discussion by focusing on their health within the national context of debates pertaining to current and projected costs. Demographics play an influential role in these debates because of how boomers will increase medical spending through sheer numbers. These health care debates will focus on Medicare, but the presence of health disparities brings an added dimension to this discourse.

5

Health Needs

HEALTH, REGARDLESS OF THE AGE group being discussed, is a complex topic with significant social-cultural considerations necessitating a multifaceted socioecological perspective. This chapter focuses on several different dimensions related to the health of the baby boomer cohort. Boomers of color will be highlighted whenever data are available, although, as mentioned earlier, such specific research is rare, making a nuanced analysis difficult. Yet a health portrait of boomers of color will emerge in this chapter.

Buckley poses a series of questions that must be answered to meet the challenges posed by baby boomers: "The entry of the baby boomer cohort into later life will have a significant impact on a range of services, particularly those related to health, hence it is essential that policy makers understand the needs of this large cohort. What are the things which constrain or facilitate their ability to age well? How different are baby boomers to previous cohorts and how diverse are they as a group? Diversity is a key factor and is likely to be considerable given the extended time period used to define this cohort" (Buckley 2008, p. 75).

This chapter also presents a profile of current and projected health care needs and financial costs of baby boomers, with particular attention paid to debates about Medicare. How the nation addresses these health care and cost challenges will play a significant role in the well-being of this cohort (Alemayehu & Warner, 2004; Bishop, 2009; Centers for Disease Control and Prevention, 2007; Martin et al. 2009). Just as with Social Security, debates over Medicare raise profound ethical questions about intra- and intergenerational tradeoffs in how we spend health care money (Crippen & Barnato, 2011).

Pritchard and Potter highlight the complexity of baby boomer health care: "One overarching relationship drives healthcare expenditures upward and increases the demand for Social Security: the ongoing interactive process of improving healthcare (that leads to ever greater demand for further healthcare improvements and higher healthcare costs) which, in turn, leads to the payment of Social Security benefits to greater numbers of Senior Citizens for longer periods as their longevity increases. This is a pressing economic and societal issue" (Pritchard & Potter, 2011, p. 26). The increased number of cancer survivors, for example, typifies this dilemma (Parry et al., 2011).

HEALTH DISPARITIES AND RACISM

This is a proper juncture to pause and set health (physical and mental) disparities and boomers of color against a backdrop of how racism plays a critical role in creating these disparities. An in-depth discussion is clearly beyond the scope of this section and this volume. However, it would be irresponsible of the author not to raise this as a serious concern and set the stage for this chapter without addressing the subject of racism, as was done early in this book regarding the G.I. Bill, the Veteran Loan Program, and residential segregation.

Health disparities can be defined "as systematic, plausibly avoidable health differences adversely affecting socially disadvantaged groups" (Roux, 2012). This simple definition, however, has profound implications for boomers of color and their well-being. Health disparities and boomers of color, for example, get compounded by the role of stress (Griffith, Ellis, & Allen, 2013). The help-seeking process gets shaped by past experiences and concerns about potentially negative future experiences, further exacerbating their health status (Greer, Brondobo, & Brown, 2014; Wagner et al., 2011).

The health statistics and conditions that will be addressed later on in this chapter will paint a picture of a generational cohort that is entering retirement with a less than ideal state of health. There is a close and profound relationship between race, racism, and health (Brondolo, Gallo, & Myers, 2009). Further, the introduction of socioeconomic class brings an added dimension that makes it impossible to separate it from race (Kawachi, Daniels, & Robinson, 2005). Thus, as the reader examines boomer of color health conditions and sees the dramatic differences they experience when compared to their White, non-Latino/a counterparts, the role of racism must not be lost.

DEFICIT PERSPECTIVE ON BOOMER HEALTH

A deficit perspective on health undermines boomers of color in their search for social justice and needed services, and it is arduous, if not impossible, to separate a deficit perspective from racism. Kwate and Meyer's summary of the knowledge base on race and health related to African Americans sets the stage for health disparities and boomers. "Recent theoretical and empirical studies of the social determinants of health inequities have shown that economic deprivation, multiple levels of racism and neighborhood context limit African American health chances and that African Americans' poor health status is predicated on unequal opportunity to achieve the American Dream" (Kwate & Meyer, 2010, p. 1831).

A deficit perspective on boomer health often gets operationalized in two ways: (1) fiscally and (2) by viewing health conditions that are typically associated with advancing age as inevitable. Deficits, health care costs, and needs, are all closely intertwined in this view. The picture painted by deficit proponents in chapter 2 essentially depicts baby boomers as economic drains with limited opportunity or ability to financially contribute in their old age. These boomers are cast as burdens, or as a "surplus population," long past their prime.

Furthermore, the medical (disease-based) model is still the primary approach used to discuss health. The prominence of a medical model complicates discussions of baby boomer health. The medical model's emphasis on a patient's health problems is not empowering in philosophy or approach. Viewing illness as an individual phenomenon (rather than casting it as a family or community need) is another limitation associated with the medical model. The medical model is also antithetical to culturally competent practice, further reducing the potential to tap boomer of color cultural assets in service delivery.

Refocusing on boomer patient strengths necessitates an understanding of how assets influence overall health and wellness (Rotegard et al., 2010, p. 513). This chapter will broaden the discussion by grounding health and health care within a values standpoint that is familiar to social workers and facilitating the use of a social justice set of values.

HEALTH CARE COSTS (CURRENT AND PROJECTED)

Medicare is America's single largest health insurance program, and has provided health care to older adults for over 42 years (Potetz & Cubanski, 2009). The current and projected health care cost of boomers, unfortunately, is often the only topic that gets discussed in the media and public policy circles, thereby eschewing a broader range of dialogue on health and vulnerable boomer groups (Borger et al., 2006; Garrett & Martini, 2007; Martini et al., 2007; Truffer et al., 2010). These debates rarely highlight, for example, how American corporations owe $450 billion in pension commitments, and $350 billion in post-retirement health care promises that are unfunded (Goodman, Herrick, & Moore, 2006). The debate is almost squarely focused on the public sector (Morgan, 2010).

Health plays a critical role in the well-being of individuals and their families and communities; reducing this subject to dollars and cents does a tremendous disservice to boomers in general and the health field itself. However, this disservice is magnified for boomers of color who have had lifetimes of low-wage employment and, for many, correspondingly low-quality health care. Their potentially compromised state is further compounded by the fact that low-income boomers and older adults have a propensity to report multiple chronic illnesses (Blackburn, 2010).

Calls to privatize Medicare have not received the same level of public attention as those to privatize Social Security. Nevertheless, these efforts will no doubt increase in visibility in the near future (Geyman, 2006). Discussions of Medicare and Medicaid reform, just like those concerning Social Security, will be shaped largely from a financial perspective (Chernew, Goldman & Axeen, 2011; Holahan, 2009; Morgan, 2010). This view is likely to be fueled by generational equity–inspired arguments, to the detriment of subgroups that are marginalized and vulnerable (Browdie, 2011).

Nusbaum summarizes three general perspectives on the projected costs of an aging national population with direct implications for boomers and the country:

The first of these factors, the numbers of middle-aged Americans poised to become elderly in the next several decades, is essentially an immutable quantity. The second factor, the cost of caring for each episode of illness, has received much attention during the health care debates of recent months, with a variety of strategies (such as use of electronic health records to guide care, measures to avoid duplicative laboratory tests, and increased resources to ferret out healthcare fraud) being proposed to make health care delivery more cost effective. The third factor of the equation, which has gotten much less attention, is the average level of baseline health of the older individual, which in turn drives the average amount of care that needs to be delivered to a given older individual per year.

(Nusbaum, 2011, p. 1)

Each of these factors brings a set of assumptions predicated upon a wide range of social-economic-political considerations and values. Consequently, arriving at a fixed or stationary cost is best thought of as an educated guess rather than an absolute numerical figure.

In 1990 Medicare accounted for 3.5 percent of the federal budget, but in 2011, approximately 20 years later, it accounted for almost 15 percent (Chernew, Goldman, & Axeen, 2011). The health care share of the Gross Domestic Product is expected to reach 20.3 percent by 2018, which is largely the result of boomers receiving Medicare (Sisko et al., 2009). In 2006, boomers had an average health care spending per capita of $4,863, the second highest of any age cohort, with those sixty-four and over having the highest at $8,776, or six times that of eighteen to twenty-four year olds, for example (Pritchard & Potter, 2011).

Medical spending among baby boomers is almost twice that spent by those between the ages of thirty-five to forty-four (Cawthorne, 2008), raising concerns about how these costs will escalate dramatically once boomers age into older adulthood and encounter illnesses usually associated with advanced age, further taxing the Medicare budget. The National Cancer Institute (Mariotto et al., 2011), for example, estimates that by 2020 it will cost $158 billion to treat cancer—possibly $207 billion because of improved survival rates. These costs and projected increases are largely the result of baby boomers.

It is useful to note that immigrant contributions to Medicare have often been overlooked in the debate about Medicare costs or immigration reform. Immigrant contributions to Medicare between 2002 and 2009 accounted for $115 billion. However, those who were American born accounted for a deficit of $29 billion during this period (Tavernise, 2013). In other words, immigrants were paying into Medicare at a time when the system was experiencing increased demands.

The life expectancy of baby boomers of color becomes a critical factor in determining the lifetime costs of Medicare, just like it does for Social Security, as covered in chapter 3. In 2010 the average life expectancy was eighty-two for all men and eighty-five for all women. Latino men aged sixty-five in 2010 can expect to live to age eighty-five, with Latinas living to age eighty-nine (Social Security Administration, 2011b). Life expectancy among Asians and Pacific Islanders for men is eighty-five and eighty-eight for women (Social Security Administration, 2011d). African American men have the lowest life expectancy with seventy-nine; for African American women it is eighty-three (Social Security Administration, 2011b). The projected increase in costs has led many to call for Medicare reform: "Medicare will be a perennial point of contention in politics in the coming decade, as the number of beneficiaries is projected to grow by one-third to 65 million" (Pear, 2012, p. A11).

The projected "crisis" in Medicare expenditures, however, has less to do with baby boomers and more to do with health care costs rising at a greater rate than inflation (Binstock, 2010). It is unfair to focus on spiraling Medicare costs in isolation from the spiraling costs of the entire health care system (Yasar, 2009). Bishop notes that the baby boomer generation has not caused exceedingly high health care costs as it has moved through the age continuum and should not be expected to do so in older adulthood: "the aging of the population will not in itself have a major impact on the growth of the total health expenditures—the blame for uncontrolled health sector growth falls elsewhere" (Bishop, 2009, p. 95).

As already noted, efforts to reduce costs by getting beneficiaries to assume a larger portion of the costs will have a disproportionate impact on low-income and low-wealth baby boomers of color who are the least capable of assuming these additional expenses.

Current projections of health care costs will prove particularly troubling for low-income baby boomers as their share of income spent on health care is projected to increase from 21 to 39 percent between 2010 and 2040 (Johnson & Mommaerts, 2010b; Wheary & Meschede, 2010). The projected increase of out of pocket health care costs translates into 60 percent of the growth in older Americans' real household income between 2010 and 2040, effectively consuming important funds that can be used to pay housing and food-related expenses, for example. This increase, incidentally, translates into $14,000 per year in health costs for 10 percent of the older adult population (Johnson & Mommaerts, 2010b) and is a considerable sum when talking about boomers and older adults on fixed incomes.

Wister puts forth a counterargument to the alarmist school on boomer health and costs:

> Yet, to contend that baby boomers will break the health care or pension systems, or that they will cause a "pandemic of chronic illness," creates a debate that invariably leads us away from what is really important: detailing the complexities of the health dynamics of the baby boomers as they age. The only conclusion of certainty is that significant investment into further basic research, as well as health promotion and population health initiatives, is not only warranted, but imperative, if we are to improve the health of the nation while adapting to the nuances of population aging in the new millennium.
>
> (Wister, 2005, p. 199)

Wister (2005) stresses the importance of increasing our understanding of boomer health and the need to promote initiatives specifically targeting boomers as a separate cohort. Hughes and colleagues (2011) and Hebert (2012) advocate for health promotion initiatives that target boomer and older adult workers and the importance of prevention.

It is appropriate to end this section with a quote by White. Although made almost two decades ago, its relevance is still current:

> During the 1990s, the claim that an aging population constituted a long-term "crisis" became a policy cliché. This assertion became particularly popular among elite journalists and academics in the United States. . . . I will argue that, as a matter of both policy and ethics, policymakers and citizens need not worry about the implications of aging for medical costs. Aging of the population has some effect on health costs, but a much smaller effect than those factors that are both more susceptible to manipulation and pose less difficult ethical dilemmas. The aging of the population does pose economic and budgetary challenges, but the contribution of health care costs to this equation is relatively minor; policymakers would do better to focus on other concerns such as pension expenses and participation

in the workforce. For these reasons; the health care costs of an aging population do not justify changes in health policy that would not otherwise be
appropriate.

(White, 2004)

White's call for reason and calm on health costs, along with the potential
of the Affordable Health Act's potential impact on cost reductions, seems
reasonable based upon the potential damage to the health of boomers and
older adults of unreasoned costs to Medicare.

HEALTH NEEDS AND DISPARITIES

The literature on baby boomers and their current and projected health care
needs is extensive and likely to increase (Cangelosi, 2011). This attention,
however, reflects the national concerns with costs. Unfortunately, boomers
of color have not been the focus of extensive health care research, thereby
limiting our understanding of their needs and strengths.

This section will present a great deal of data on a wide range of health
issues and concerns. A 2011 national poll asked baby boomers to rank
their health fears: cancer was listed first, followed by Alzheimer's disease
and dementia and heart disease (Neergaard, 2011b). Certainly these conditions have received tremendous attention in the media. However, there are
countless other illnesses and diseases that are very prevalent among boomers but generally undiscussed.

Collins and colleagues (2006) list a series of baby boomer health care
challenges: "Over 60 percent of adults ages 50 to 64 who are working or
have a working spouse have been diagnosed with at least one chronic health
condition, such as arthritis, cancer, diabetes, heart disease, high cholesterol,
or hypertension . . . as aging baby boomers face increasing health problems,
unstable health insurance coverage and medical bill and debt problems are
creating barriers to needed care, raising alarms about the ability of the U.S.
health system to cope with the future health care needs of Americans."

Yeo identifies additional issues with which the health care system will
have to contend: "Challenges to high-quality ethnogeriatric care include
disparities in health status and health care, differences of acculturation
level and other characteristics within the populations, language and limited
English proficiency, health literacy, culturally defined health beliefs and

syndromes, and specific beliefs and preferences about long-term and end-of-life care" (Yeo, 2009, p. 1278).

Disparities in health care access among people of color, including preventive health services, are extensively documented (Talavera-Garcia et al., 2013). Health disparities among boomers result from an interplay of socioeconomic status, gender, and racial/ethnic (Angel & Angel, 2006; Kim, 2011). However, health disparities are even further evident among those boomers and older adults of color with disabilities and mobility impairments (Jones & Sinclair, 2008). Thus the concept of multiple jeopardies emerges, resulting in greater health disparities and challenges (Truman et al., 2011). Reaching and serving boomers with multiple chronic conditions is a difficult challenge for our health care system (Norris et al., 2008). Davis and Roberts (2010), for example, have studied liver disease, particularly in the case of boomers who are obese, and what it means for the health care industry. Liver disease is the twelfth leading cause of death in the United States. However, boomers have higher rates of hepatitis B and C, increasing the likelihood of death by primary liver causes.

The lack of access to quality health care results in health disparities and eventually creates greater costs to the taxpayer, not to mention pain, suffering, and possibly early death for those of color (as in the case of diabetes, for example; see Liburd, 2010). As another example, African Americans and/or those who do not have a college education are less likely to receive surgery for hip and knee replacements, resulting in disproportionate levels of pain and disability (Steel et al., 2008). These individuals also are more likely to work in jobs that are physically demanding, further exacerbating their pain and compromising their health.

The health sector overall will face numerous challenges in meeting the needs of boomers, and in areas that the general public rarely thinks about (Hospital Home Health, 2008). For example, the availability of blood transfusions is rarely addressed in the professional literature but is likely to be an issue, particularly as the number of boomers undergoing operations increases in frequency as they age (Benjamin & Whitaker, 2011). The projected increased demand for organ transplants has also escaped public attention (Sheffrin, 2013). An increase in demand for cardiac care is another example (Beveridge, 2011). Hampton (2008) predicts that emergency room departments will witness dramatic patient increases because of baby boomers, resulting in overcrowding and compromised care for all patients. Finally, McDaniel and Clark (2009) discuss the mental health needs of baby boomers as new adult orphans and how this life event can destabilize their lives, leading, for example, to depression.

Even the topic of climate change and its potential impact on boomers has escaped attention, though it will play a critical role in well-being:

> A range of physiological and socioeconomic factors make older adults especially sensitive to and/or at risk for exposure to heat waves and other extreme weather events (e.g., hurricanes, floods, droughts), poor air quality, and infectious diseases. Climate change may increase the frequency or severity of these events. . . . Older Americans are likely to be especially vulnerable to stressors associated with climate change. Although a growing body of evidence reports the adverse effects of heat on the health of older adults, research gaps remain for other climate-related risks. We need additional study of the vulnerability of older adults and the interplay of vulnerability, resilience, and adaptive responses to projected climate stressors.
>
> (Gamble et al., 2013, p. 15)

Addressing the health care needs of baby boomers, particularly those who are of color and have experienced health disparities, is a daunting task (Delgado, 2008; Devi, 2008; Robert Wood Johnson Foundation, 2007). The intersection of race and class wields a powerful influence on health-seeking patterns and access to quality health care when they do, in fact, receive it. Waidman (2009) estimates that health disparities among African Americans and Latino/as, compared to their White, non-Latino/a counterparts, resulted in additional health expenditures of $23.9 billion in 2009, with Medicare accounting for $15.6 billion and private insurers paying an extra $5.1 billion. However, when examined over the course of a decade, it is almost $337 billion, with projections having this figure more than double by 2050 as these two groups enter older adulthood.

Over the following pages, we will examine some of the key health and mental health issues faced by, and/or feared by, baby boomers: diabetes, hypertension, depression, falls, obesity, disabilities, gambling, hepatitis C, HIV/AIDS, substance abuse and prescription medication, and violence. While this is by no means a comprehensive list, it does introduce the reader to some of the key health issues faced by boomers of color as they enter older adulthood.

Diabetes: Diabetes is a worldwide health condition with an estimated 194 million adults having this diagnosis. This number is projected to increase dramatically to 233 million by 2025 (Pavkov et al., 2010). The risk of diabetes increases with age; thus the growing boomer population is the key reason for the increase in diagnoses. Diabetes is the leading cause of blindness, end-stage kidney disease, and amputations in the United States (ScienceDaily, 2009). In 2012 diabetes-attributed deaths in the United States numbered 246,000 (Wilson & Dengo, 2013).

The costs of drugs for treating diabetes increased by 200 percent between 2001 ($6.7 billion) and 2007 ($15.5 billion). The direct and indirect costs (which refers to absenteeism, lost wages and reduced productivity, etc.) were $245 billion in 2012, up from $174 billion in 2007 (Wilson & Dengo, 2013). It is estimated that by 2034 the number of individuals in the United States with diabetes will almost double from 23.7 million in 2009 to 44.1 million in 2034, with spending increasing by 300 percent from $113 billion to $336 billion during this period (ScienceDaily, 2009).

The dramatic demographic growth projected in the United States during the 2005 to 2050 period will witness increases in diabetes largely fueled by people of color aged seventy-five and older, with African Americans/Blacks (606 percent) and Latino/as (481 percent) playing significant roles in these increases (Pavkov et al., 2010). It is estimated that 8 percent of boomers suffer from obesity and diabetes, with African Americans being more prone to this dual diagnosis (Ahn, Smith, & Dickerson, 2012). Health-seeking patterns, in turn, are influenced by health beliefs and exposure to racism. as in the case of African American women, for example (Wagner et al., 2011).

Hypertension: Hypertension or high blood pressure is prevalent among baby boomers (Centers for Disease Control and Prevention, 2005; Miller, Berra & Long, 2010). It was estimated that in 2005 50 percent of boomers (fifty-five to sixty-four years) had hypertension, up from 41.7 percent in 1988–1994 and 49.5 percent in 1999–2002; women experienced the greater increase (11.3 percent versus 4.6 percent for men) and have higher rates with 53.9 percent when compared to men with 45.0 percent (Brookes, 2005). According to the Centers for Disease Control and Prevention (2013), high blood pressure costs taxpayers $51 billion annually in direct medical costs ($47.5 billion) and lost productivity ($3.5 billion).

Hypertension can result in many possible medical complications (*New York Times*, 2012): aortic dissection, brain damage, blood vessel damage (arteriosclerosis), congestive heart failure, chronic kidney disease, heart attack, hypertensive heart disease, peripheral artery disease, pregnancy complications, and vision loss. It is associated with heart attacks, strokes, and chronic heart failure (Centers for Disease Control and Prevention, 2013).

African Americans are at greater risk of hypertension when compared to White, non-Latino/as, for both men and women. African American men (43.0 percent versus 33.9) and women (45.7 percent vs. 31.3 percent) have the highest rates among people of color. The role of diet and lack of ready access to healthy foods in food deserts associated with the segregated neighborhoods in which they live, for example, is the result of racism and classism (Peters, 2004). However, a review of the empirical literature found the relationship between racism and hypertension to be weak (Brondolo et al., 2011). On a positive note, Mexican American men (27.8 percent) and women (28.9) have the lowest levels when compared to African Americans and White, non-Latino/as (Centers for Disease Control and Prevention, 2013).

Depression: It is estimated that 8 million older adults, including boomers, or 20 percent, have a mental health condition, with depression being a key condition (Bartels & Nasjund, 2013; Eden et al., 2012). One estimate has one in five women aged in their fortiess and fiftiess on an antidepressant, and 10 percent of all Americans (Rabin, 2013).

Early life psychiatric history and cognitive challenges (childhood health, psychiatric history, and lack of access to quality health services) have prolonged life consequences and will wield influence on boomers and older adults during this life stage. Consequently, the cumulative consequences of these early life experiences place boomers of color at risk for psychiatric and cognitive problems (Brown, 2010). Untreated depression has been found to be associated with increased mortality from co-occuring medical causes among older adults (Llorente, Nathaniel, & McCabe, 2012). The prevalence of major depression among native-born people of color, when compared to foreign born, sets the stage for depression taking a significant toll among this group (Gonzalez et al., 2010).

Falls: Falls are considered the leading cause of injuries among those sixty-five and older in the United States. Falls can result in numerous physical, psychological, and financial consequences, may cause chronic disabilities, and may result in long-term care (Centers for Disease Control and Prevention, 2012).

In 2005, according to the Centers for Disease Control and Prevention (Clark, 2008), baby boomers had a rate of nonfatal deaths from falling of 1,970 per 100,000 for those fifty to fifty-four and fifty-five to fifty-nine, and 2,090 for those sixty to sixty-four. The rates increase systematically upward throughout the remaining age groups to a high of 10,752 for those aged eighty-five and over. Almost 50 percent of this nation's 1.6 million nursing home residents experienced a fall (Frolik, 2012). Falls are the number one reason why those over the age of forty-five visit emergency rooms, and almost 250 die every week (O'Brien, 2007).

Obesity: Baby boomers are considered the heaviest generation in this nation's history. It is estimated that 36 percent of boomers can be classified as obese as compared to 26 percent of older adults and 25 percent of younger cohorts. Individuals who are overweight or obese cost 34 percent more in Medicare benefits than those who are not, due to the health conditions associated with excessive weight (Byers, 2006; Jaslow, 2011; MetroSouth Medical Center, 2011; Neergaard, 2011b; PRLOG, 2011): various forms of cancer, respiratory problems, sleep apnea, infertility, Type II diabetes, hypertension, liver/gallbladder disease, osteoarthritis, and coronary heart disease, to list but a few (MetroSouth Medical Center, 2011). The relationship between eating habits, smoking and alcohol use, and body mass index highlights the interrelationship between various habits and the way they influence baby boomer obesity (Worsley, Wang, & Hunter, 2009). Overweight and obesity are also closely tied to arthritis, heart disease, diabetes, and high blood pressure (Jaslow, 2011). Obesity and arthritis together can lead to increased rates of disability, particularly among men (Reynolds & McIlvane, 2009). Obesity is widely considered to be a significant cause of premature mortality in the United States (Buckley, 2008; Mehta & Chang, 2009). Obesity and its deleterious health consequences have disproportionate impact on boomers of color (American Federation for Aging Research, 2005).

Alzheimer's Disease: Alzheimer's disease (AD), as well as other forms of dementia, has a major impact on baby boomers of color (Alzheimer's Association, 2004a). A decline in cognitive functioning represents one of the greatest fears baby boomers have about approaching older adulthood.

According to the Alzheimer's Association (2012), AD is the sixth leading cause of death in the United States. There are an estimated 5.5 million people in the United States, and 35 million worldwide, who have AD (Diamandis et al., 2011). It is estimated that one in eight boomers will be diagnosed with AD during their lifetime (Robinson, 2010). The incidence of AD doubles every five years after the age of sixty-five years. Consequently, as boomers enter older adulthood, the prevalence is expected to reach 30 to 60 million in the United States by 2050 (Diamandis et al., 2011), raising important financial, personal, and health care implications.

Onset of AD among Latino baby boomers has been found to start seven years earlier than their White, non-Latino counterparts (Belluck, 2008; Marcus, 2010). Latino/as are 1.5 times more likely, and African-Americans 2 times more likely than their White, non-Latino counterparts to get Alzheimer's disease (Alzheimer's Association, 2010). One projection has AD increasing from 200,000 Latino/as in 2004 to 1.3 million in 2050, or a 600 percent increase (Alzheimer's Association, 2004b). Interestingly, African Americans and Latino/as with AD may have longer survival rates when compared to White, non-Latino/as with AD (Mehta et al., 2008). African Americans have been found to have high rates of vascular disease, resulting in heart attacks and strokes, and risk factors for AD (Alzheimer's Association, 2010).

Language barriers, mistrust of researchers, lack of outreach by the medical community, and cultural beliefs have all hampered a better understanding of AD among baby boomers of color who are not English dominant and their families (Mahoney et al., 2005; Neary & Mahoney, 2005). Zhan (2004), for example, addresses the role of stigma, cultural factors, and the lack of information targeting Chinese Americans with AD. Alzheimer's disease cannot be understood among racial and ethnic groups without cultural and community contextualization (Avalong, 2004; Connell et al., 2009; Weiner, 2008).

The interplay of family and culture is important from a caregiving perspective. Cultural beliefs can hinder dementia treatment by attributing the symptoms to a normal aging process, fate, God's will, a form of mental illness, or a curse, for example (Dilworth-Anderson, Gibson, & Burke, 2006; Montero-Rodriguez, Small, & McCallum, 2006; Wang et al., 2006), necessitating that any form of assessment take into account culture and community. The need for cultural awareness and research on this group must increase (Dilworth-Anderson & Cohen, 2006), especially given the overall projected increase among those with AD (Apesoa-Varano, Baker, & Hinton, 2011).

Disabilities: Boomers of color, particularly those of who are low income and low wealth who have achieved older adulthood, face increased risks for mental and physical disabilities. Consequently, there is a tremendous need to reform Medicare to be more responsive to their needs (Iezzoni, 2006a, b). Smith, Rayer, and Smith (2008) project that by 2050 21 percent of the nation's households will have at least one member with some form of disability. African American and Latino older adults are more likely than White, non-Latino/as to develop disabilities, largely attenuated by socioeconomic and health differences (Dunlop et al., 2007). First- and 1.5-generation Latino/as had higher rates of disabilities when compared to those of the second generation (Jones, 2011).

There are 40 to 50 million people in the United States with some form of disability, and this number is projected to increase with boomers entering older adulthood (Leveille et al., 2009; Scommegna, 2013; Seeman et al., 2010), particularly among those who are of color and low income. Among baby boomers, those with disabilities (indicating needing help with personal activities) still fall under 2 percent (Martin et al., 2010). However, disabilities among boomers of color are higher when compared with their White, non-Latino counterparts. Those boomers of color experiencing disability may also experience racial and age discrimination, all of which combined increase their challenge in receiving culturally competent health care (Schwab & Glissman, 2011) and the need for advocates to ensure that their rights are not violated.

Gambling: The reader may wonder why gambling is included in the category of health issues. Two aspects regarding gambling impinge on the health of boomers and older adults, although this topic has not received very much attention in the literature: (1) gambling as a form of addiction and (2) the use of money to gamble can come at the expense of buying necessary medicines and nutritious foods.

Gambling has increased across all fifty states and includes various forms, with casino, bingo, and lottery tickets being the most popular (Ariyabuddhiphongs, 2011; Delwiche & Henderson, 2013; Wick, 2012a). The size and economic power of the baby boomer cohort makes this population group particularly attractive to the casino and gaming industry (Jeon & Hyun, 2012).

Baby boomers and seniors constitute over 60 percent of all active gamblers and those of color represent fewer than 10 percent (*Gambling News,* 2009).

It is estimated that those over the age of sixty-five represent between 39–45 percent of casino patrons (Wick, 2012b).

Hepatitis C: Hepatitis C is most often contracted through the use of injection drug abuse or risky sexual behavior. Hepatitis C is the twelfth leading cause of death in the United States; between 2.7 and 3.9 million people are infected (Davis & Roberts, 2010; McCombs et al., 2011).

A 2007 CDC study found that there were fifteen thousand deaths due to hepatitis C, with 75 percent occurring among boomers (Neergaard, 2012). Further, it is estimated that 45–85 percent of individuals with chronic hepatitis C virus are unaware that they have it (Ngo-Metzger, Ward, & Valdiserri, 2013); thus it is often referred to as the silent epidemic.

In May 2012 the Centers for Disease Control and Prevention recommended that all boomers born between 1945 and 1965 be tested for hepatitis C (Aleccia, 2012). Boomers, specifically, were targeted because it is estimated that 75 percent of all those infected fall into this age group (Conaboy, 2012). This recommendation created a controversy, and opponents highlight three primary reasons (Conaboy, 2012): (1) costs (testing and treating infected boomers will result in health care costs of an estimated $19 billion), (2) the health benefits of early treatment are not clear, and (3) treatments can have serious physical and emotional side effects.

Some boomer subgroups are particularly at risk for having contracted hepatitis C: male boomers are twice as likely as females to be infected and boomers of color, particularly African Americans and Mexican Americans, have the highest rates of infection, particularly when compared to white, non-Latino/as (2.89 percent). Liver-related mortality rates have been systematically underestimated among people of color (Asrani et al., 2013), increasing the significance of this disease within high-risk groups.

HIV/AIDS: Popular opinion holds that HIV is a disease that primarily affects the young, not older adults. In truth, HIV knows no age limits (Emanuel, 2014; Tangredi et al., 2008).

As the 77 million baby boomers that brought us the sexual revolution inexorably age, they will face a striking paradox. The ignorance, prejudice, and silence about sex and sexuality they fought so hard to upend are still alive and well in old age. We are a people reluctant to contemplate sex and aging together in the same thought, and even more reluctant to speak of it. Yet experience and emerging evidence indicate that such reticence can have significant implications for the health, rights, safety, and well-being of the large and growing older population in ways that are just becoming clear.

(Connolly et al., 2013)

Evans (2011) reports on how HIV has continued to increase among African American baby boomers. It is estimated that one in six people (11 percent) with AIDS in the United States is at least fifty years or older (Health Watch, 2002; Mack & Ory, 2003). In New York State, for example, almost 50 percent of those with HIV are now fifty years or older, with almost 75 percent of them living alone (Leland, 2013). More specifically, AIDS among African American boomers aged fifty years or older accounted for 11 percent in this racial group through 2000 (Health Watch, 2002), with tremendous implications for prevention and early intervention initiatives. It is estimated that between 10 and 15 percent of new HIV/AIDS cases are diagnosed among those fifty years old and older (Health Watch, 2002; Levy, 2005).

One study found that approximately 50 percent of African American and Latino boomers and older adults perceived themselves at some degree of risk for contracting HIV (Ward et al., 2011). Castro (2010) raises concerns about the influence of stigma and disclosure among baby boomer gay Latino men with HIV/AIDS, and how this status will take on greater importance as boomers enter older adulthood, with potential deadly consequences for their sexual partners.

Jacobs and Kane (2010) highlight HIV-related stigma among midlife and older women in general, and specifically among those of color, and how it impacts their ability to receive needed support and services. Rosenfeld, Bartlam, and Smith address the impact of HIV/AIDS on male boomers from a cohort perspective, as well as the challenges of developing a holistic picture of their lives. "Regardless of HIV status, all gay male Baby Boomers are aging in a context strongly shaped by HIV/AIDS. For this sub cohort within the Baby Boom generation, the disproportionately high volume of AIDS deaths among gay men aged 25–44 years at the epidemic's peak (1987–1996) created a cohort effect, decimating their social networks and shaping their personal and social lives during the epidemic, throughout their life course, and into later years" (Rosenfeld, Bartlam, & Smith 2012, p. 255). They advocate for the use of a life course perspective to better understand how male gay boomer later life is deeply influenced by the intersectionality of historical events, personal biography, and social and community ties.

Lastly, Cahill and Valdez summarize many of the key challenges boomers with HIV/AIDS will face as they enter older adulthood with this disease: "At present, the health care infrastructure is ill-equipped to handle the unique treatment and care needs of HIV-positive older adults. The long-term effects of antiretroviral use are still being discovered and have been associated with a number of comorbidities. Stigma presents challenges for those in need of services and health care, and can significantly affect mental health and treatment adherence" (Cahill & Valdez, 2013, p. e7).

Effective prevention and treatment of HIV/AIDS is not possible until we face our biases about sex among boomers and older adults. Boomers must feel comfortable discussing their sexual behaviors and attitudes with health professionals, and it is equally important for professionals to raise this topic with boomers (Lodge & Umberson, 2012).

Substance Abuse and Prescription Medication: Substance abuse among those 55+ is projected to increase as boomers enter this life stage, making it a significant health issue (Briggs et al., 2011; Clay, 2010; DiNitto & Choi, 2011; Duncan et al., 2010). One survey found that 40 percent of boomers admitted to first abusing drugs while in their 50s and 60s (Molestina, 2012).

According to the Substance Abuse and Mental Health Service Administration (SAMHSA), boomers accounted for almost half (48 percent) of drug-related deaths in 2003. Further, between 2003 and 2005 illicit drug use among people in their fifties increased by 63 percent; SAMHSA estimates that over three million people in their fifties had used marijuana, hashish, cocaine, crack, heroin, hallucinogens, or inhalants (Battaglia, 2009; Capers, 2003).

Much is known about alcohol usage among older adults, but much still needs to be known about other forms of substance abuse (Bacharach et al., 2008; Ligon, 2013). Hasin and colleagues (2008), for example, consider the use of cannabis as the most widely abused illicit drug and what that means for baby boomers who use this drug and have done so over an extended period of time. Dowling, Weiss, and Condon (2008) address the consequences of substance abuse on an aging brain and the challenges it presents for diagnosis and treatment.

Greater rates of lifetime substance use, along with demographic size, combine for greater substance use, abuse, and treatment for this cohort in the next ten years (Colliver, 2006; Trevisan, 2008; Evans, 2008). Wu and Blazer (2011) project that the number of Americans aged fifty years and over with a substance use disorder will more than double from 2.8 million in 2002–2006 to 5.7 million in 2020. Gfroerer and colleagues (2003), based on earlier estimates, have a lower number of older adults in need of substance abuse treatment (4.4 million) in 2020. Nevertheless, they too conclude that this is due to a 50 percent increase in the number of older adults and a 70 percent increase in the rate of treatment needed among older adults.

Baby boomers are the first generation to rely upon medications as a preventive health measure (Edlin, 2010). It is estimated that 75 percent take at least one medication. The net plan cost of medications for this age group is $1,243 per year. Prescription drug abuse among boomers and older adults has been referred to as part of the "invisible epidemic" that consists of alcohol, prescription, and over-the-counter drug abuse (Kalapatapu & Sullivan, 2010). Simoni-Wastila and Yang (2006) address the potential for psychoactive medication abuse and note that these medications are currently used by at least one in four older adults, with a significant potential increase as baby boomers receive these medications.

It is estimated that up to 17 percent of older adults aged sixty-five and older are affected by prescription medication and alcohol misuse (Sullivan et al., 2007). Approximately 30 percent of all medications are consumed by those sixty-five and older, and 40 percent of this group takes five or more medications per week. An increased likelihood of using nonprescription pain relievers further complicates an already complicated scenario (Blazer & Wu, 2009). Consequently, it is not farfetched that the possibilities of abuse increase dramatically with greater access to medications (Kalapatapu & Sullivan, 2010).

Tone and Watkins (2007) note that eight prescription drugs have become an integral part of boomer life: (1) antibiotics, (2) mood stabilizers, (3) hormone replacement drugs, (4) oral contraceptives, (5) stimulants, (6) tranquilizers, (7) statins, (8) and Viagra. Thus one can see the reasons why health officials are so concerned with polydrug use and abuse (Sullivan et al., 2007). Not unexpectedly, there has been an increase in mortality rates due to accidental poisoning among baby boomers, particularly African Americans (Miech, Koester, & Dorsey-Holliman, 2011).

The absence of validated prescription medication screening instruments for uncovering medication abuse severely limits our understanding of the problem (Trevisan, 2008). The lack of clinical trials of medications that can be used to treat substance abuse among boomers, and older adults, further hampers our abilities to successfully help them.

Parker, Wolf, and Kirsch (2008) raise a concern of limited health literacy or English proficiency among boomers entering older adulthood; it raises the potential for overdoses in the case of those who have difficulty reading and following dosage instructions in English.

Alcohol usage is another issue, because a higher percentage of baby boomers drink alcohol, and often do so in larger quantities than previous generations (Stevenson, 2005), with severe health implications (Heuberger, 2009). There is a strong association between alcohol consumption and acculturation among Latino/as and Asians, with those who are more highly acculturated having a greater likelihood of excessive alcohol consumption (Bryant & Kim, 2013). Gender and acculturation exert great influence on alcohol use and the seeking of treatment among Latino/a adults, including baby boomers (Zemore, 2007; Zemore, Mulia, & Greenfield, 2009).

Rosen and colleagues (2011) reviewed the literature on heroin use among boomers and older adults and found research to be scant. Methadone maintenance treatment is entering its fifth decade; many boomers and older adults have long histories of being in treatment (Doukas, 2011), along with the toll of stigma associated with this form of treatment (Connor & Rosen, 2008). Daniel, Smith, and Reynolds (2008) raise attention to the challenge that dually diagnosed methadone baby boomers will face in getting services. They found that over half (57.1 percent) have at least one mental health issue.

Finally, tobacco smoking also generally gets overlooked when discussing boomers (Doolan & Froelicher, 2008). Smoking cessation programs must take into account cultural factors; for example, they must be gender specific (Singleton et al., 2005). Acculturation levels must be taken into account, as shown in interventions involving African Americans (Hooper et al., 2012), Latino/as (Webb, Rodriguez-Esquivel, & Baker, 2010), Filipino immigrant men (Garcia, Romero, & Maxwell, 2010), and Chinese immigrants (Sussman & Truong, 2011). Smoking cessation interventions focused on boomers and acculturation are desperately needed.

Violence: Zink and Fisher summarize the issues and challenges for boomer and older women in intimate partner violence:

> The golden years are not so golden for some older women who experience intimate partner violence. Often the relationship has been abusive for years, for some the abuse began with a physical or mental health status change, for others the relationship may be a new relationship following a divorce or widowhood. Older women were forgotten by both the domestic violence and aging support agencies, until the combined efforts of the American Association of Retired Persons, advocates concerned about the welfare of older domestic violence victims, sociologists and a handful of researchers around the world created awareness and services for older abused women in a number of communities. Providing services for this population requires consistent coordination between the aging and domestic violence agencies. This partnership is not typical but, with nurturing, has occurred. The large number of aging baby boomers will bring about a substantial demand for these services. It is imperative to secure resources so that abuse of older women can be addressed proactively.
>
> (Zink and Fisher, 2007, p. 257)

This increased demand, and the difficulty of increasing awareness of this form of violence, is only further compounded by our lack of knowledge on intimate partner violence among boomer women of color. Cook, Dinnen, and O'Donnell (2011) reviewed the literature and found a dearth of articles and studies that examined boomers and older women of color, limiting our understanding of the subject.

The topics of suicide and homicide are also rarely discussed in association with boomers. Yet, suicide rates were the most significant among men in their fifties (30 per 100,000), representing an increase of almost 50 percent from 1999 to 2010 (Parker-Pope, 2013). The suicide rate for middle-aged men (thirty-five to sixty-four years) was 27.3 per 100,000. Women aged sixty to sixty-four witnessed an almost 60 percent increase to 7.0 per 100,000. In 2009, deaths from suicides surpassed deaths (3,026) from car crashes, and boomers played a significant role in this event (Abad-Santos, 2013). White, non-Latino boomers had a rate of 10 per 100,000. However, Asians had a rate of 4.0 followed by Latino/as with 2.7 (Centers for Disease Control and Prevention, 2010b).

Phillips and colleagues (2010) found that boomer suicide rates increased during the 1999–2005 period and may have been caused by economic stress. If this is the case, then these rates will also reflect a significant increase as the result of the latest recession. Stice and Canetto (2008), in a very specialized suicide study of older adults, also found that physical illness plays a critical role in decisions to commit suicide.

Interpersonal violence, particularly within urban high poverty communities, has a disproportionate impact on people of color. African American boomers had the highest risk of death by firearms, for example, with a rate of 19.0 per 100,000, followed by American Indian/Alaska Natives (16.3) and Latino/as with a rate of 9.6 per 100,000 (Centers for Disease Control and Prevention, 2010c). Addington (2013) argues that a new and more refined definition of elderly or older adult is necessary, as the lifespan has increased and is projected to continue to increase as a result of boomers. A single category cannot adequately capture this heterogeneous population.

Other Health Issues: Due to limited space, a number of other important health care needs cannot be discussed in detail but will be summarized here:

(1) Baby boomer injuries and deaths resulting from traffic accidents are projected to increase dramatically, raising important implications for motor vehicle licensing (Dobbs, 2008).

(2) Women boomers with histories of physical and sexual violence often present serious physical and psychological needs.

(3) Special population groups of boomers of color often present multiple health conditions. Veteran boomers of color, for example, present unique rewards and challenges, which warrant an entire book. Baby boomers in prison or recently released from prison, too, present unique challenges and rewards.

(4) Oral health needs grow more significant with age (McNally et al., 2013). Poor oral health can result in other health conditions.

(5) Homeless baby boomers have significant health needs, requiring specialized strategies to reach for treatment, and have been overlooked in the literature even though this population, which consists of a high percentage of people of color, makes them incredibly vulnerable to a wide range of illnesses and diseases that can be prevented (Kushel, 2012).

All the needs and issues addressed in this section get compounded when the baby boomer is of color, does not speak English as a first language, and/ or is undocumented.

ANTICIPATED MEDICAL WORKFORCE NEEDS

This wide range of anticipated health conditions will require a workforce prepared to meet the diverse medical needs of this cohort. These needs become even more pronounced in the case of boomers with distinctive cultural values and non-English language competencies. The anticipated needed medical workforce with competencies to address this boomer group, such as physical and occupational therapists, medical doctors, nurses, psychologists, psychiatrists, homecare specialists, and social workers, is starting to receive the attention it deserves in recognition of the need for innovation in delivering health care (Dreher, 2008; Rahn & Wartman, 2007; Schwartz, 2012).

Draper and Anderson (2010) raise concerns about psychiatry and the profession's abilities to address the anticipated demands boomers will present in the next twenty years. Laidlaw and Panchana (2009), too, echo similar concerns. In 2103, there were an estimated 1,800 geriatric psychiatrists in the United States and by 2030 there will be approximately 1,650, or less than 1 per 6,000 older adults with mental health and substance use needs, resulting in a severe shortage (Bartels & Naslund, 2013). Wang and Shih (2014) recommend that the field of psychology pay greater attention to boomer retirement and its impact on physical, psychological, and financial well-being.

Social work, fortunately, has a long tradition of preparing practitioners in the field of gerontological health care. Nevertheless, practitioners with cultural competencies to meet the needs of older adults of color are still lacking, and it will take concerted and highly focused initiatives to help close the gap between needs and practitioner availability.

THE UNINSURED

Much of the discourse on Medicare and health costs has focused on those who receive health insurance. However, there are baby boomers, particularly those who are newcomers and undocumented, who do not qualify

(Collins, Doty, & Garber, 2010; Grossman et al., 2009). These boomers, as a result, face particular challenges in obtaining quality and culturally competent health care and may have to rely on folk medicine because of severely limited access to traditional health care.

A Commonwealth Study of uninsured boomers found that 20 percent in working families, and over 50 percent of those in low-income families, had unstable health coverage (Collins et al., 2006). Gould and Hertel-Fernandez (2010) found an erosion of health insurance coverage as the result of the 2007 recession due to decreased labor participation of baby boomers.

Those boomers forced to retire early face economic hardships in general. However, these hardships are compounded by increased health-care costs: "Early retirees without employer coverage can expect to spend an estimated 40 percent of pre-retirement income on their medical expenses. While the new Medicare prescription drug benefit will offset some of those costs for beneficiaries, retirees without retiree health benefits will continue to see a large portion of their income go toward health care costs" (Collins et al., 2006, p. 18). These boomers enter their retirement period with a compromised health status, further increasing the likelihood of declining health as they age.

It is estimated that 17.8 percent of boomers of color aged 45 to 54, and 13.9 percent of those aged 55 to 64.1, are uninsured (Iezzoni, Frakt, & Pizer, 2011). Pol, Mueller, and Adidam (2002) examined racial and ethnic differences in health insurance coverage among boomers and found that African Americans and Latino/as had a higher likelihood of not having coverage, when compared to White, non-Latino/as. Latino/as had almost one-third of boomers (32.9 percent) without health insurance, closely followed by American Indian/Alaskan Natives (32.5 percent), African Americans (18.0 percent), and Asians (16.2 percent). White, non-Latino/a boomers had 17.1 percent who were uninsured (Centers for Disease Control and Prevention, 2010a).

Within ethnic group differences, however, also indicate wide variation, as in the case of Latino/as, for example: Mexicans (35.0 percent) had the highest percentage without health insurance, followed by other Latino/as not Cuban or Puerto Rican (33.4 percent), Cubans (27.8 percent), and Puerto Ricans (17.8 percent). All uninsured boomers with disabilities, as a result, face a tremendous challenge in getting their health-care needs met when compared to those boomers with health insurance (Iezzoni, Frakt, & Pizer, 2011).

Potetz and Cubanski outline the multifaceted challenges facing the nation regarding reforming Medicare:

> Whether changes are part of overall health reform or are unique to Medicare, the level of changes required to sustain the program over the long term will be far-reaching and, as such, contentious. The challenge to policy makers for the coming decades is to find a balance between limiting the growth in Medicare payments to providers, increasing contributions from Medicare beneficiaries, and raising revenue—all the while maintaining, if not improving, beneficiary access to medically necessary services and the quality of care they receive.
>
> (Potetz & Cubanski, 2009, p. 15)

Government health care of any form is bound to elicit a wide range of political responses in this current political climate. However, these responses take on even greater significance when discussing health care and baby boomers. The highly polarized nature of debates focused on Medicare and boomers cannot be escaped. Nevertheless, there are other aspects related to health care that must not be lost in this debate. Health inequities, for example, bring a much needed and important dimension to any discussion of health care costs and culturally competent delivery for boomers of color.

Social work and public health can play and have played important roles in reducing inequities pertaining to health access and health outcomes, and there is no reason to believe these two professions will not do so regarding boomers (Delgado, 2008; Heaphy, Mitra, & Bouldin, 2011). The ability to reach out to boomers of color within a community context further enhances the potential of helping professions to develop a contextual understanding of their lives and options. Further, brokering formal and informal resources to target boomers of color, particularly those who are newcomers and may have English language deficiencies, will help address health inequities (Delgado, 1999).

Low-income and low-wealth boomers have suffered throughout their lifetimes in getting quality health care. As a result, they enter retirement in a compromised health state. The challenges associated with having English as a second language, and the presence of distinctive cultural values, further puts Asians and Latino/as, for example, at a distinct disadvantage in getting quality health care that is culturally competent. Adding documented status, however, further compromises their abilities to seek and obtain quality health care.

6

Financial Indicators

A 2012 NEW YORK TIMES editorial titled "The Road to retirement: The Recession and Its Aftermath Spell Insecurity and Hardship for Millions of Americans" sums up well the status of millions of baby boomers as they face retirement and is the focus of this chapter: "The crux of the problem is that as traditional pensions have disappeared from the private sector replacement plans have proved woefully inadequate. Fewer than half of the nation's private sector workers have 401(k) plans, and more than a third of households have no retirement coverage during their work lives.... Nor do most Americans have significant wealth to fall back on.... Home equity, once thought of as a cushion in retirement, has been especially devastated" (*New York Times* editorial 2012, p. 10).

Wealth and income play an influential role in dictating expectations and quality of life in retirement and are closely associated with health and well-being. Wealth is often thought of as an important indicator of economic well-being because of how well it captures accumulation across generations, and this perspective has particular relevance for older adults and boomers of color (T. Brown, 2012).

Wealth, however, is a topic that is easily as complex as health and must, as a result, be viewed from a multifaceted perspective in order to fully grasp its significance in the life of boomers and their various subgroups (Love, Smith, & McNair, 2008; Wolff, 2007). In 2009, for example, it was estimated that 33 percent of all boomers were unmarried, with 10 percent being widowed (Lin & Brown, 2012). Unmarried boomers, when compared to their married counterparts, face greater economic, health, and social disadvantages as they are about to enter older age. In addition, wealth and income also wield symbolic influence, and baby boomers are not exempt from this symbolism.

Becker (2011) examines the current state of boomers and how their goals for retirement may be compromised:

> As we look at our retirement years, we Baby Boomers are facing a prospect we never would have imagined when we were in our 20s. If we're not careful, we could be the first American generation in a long time to do less well than our parents did in terms of retirement security and enjoyment. Boomers came of age when "30 years and out" with a gold watch and a pension were common. We watched our grandparents retire on Social Security and their own pensions, and even though not many of them lived very long after they retired, those years were pretty free of financial worries. But now we Boomers are facing a potential bust. We've watched our property values go down as fast as our portfolios. Most of us have had several jobs, particularly in the past 20 years—our employers aren't loyal to us, and we certainly can't afford to be loyal to them. Pensions are mostly history, and Social Security may well be before we die.
>
> (Becker, 2011)

Perlman, Kenneally, and Boivi (2011) sum up the precarious state of boomers about to enter retirement: (1) the number of private sector employees with access to conventional pension plans has dwindled from 88 percent (1975) to 33 percent (2005), (2) increases in Social Security retirement age has resulted in lower benefits for lower income boomers who rely heavily on this source of income, (3) in 2009 401(k) accounts had a medium balance of only $59,381, and (4) only 59 percent of American workers have any form of access to employer-sponsored retirement plans and fewer than 50 percent (45) participate in these retirement plans.

Boomers of color, furthermore, are entering this life stage with distinct income and wealth disadvantages, thereby compromising their retirements (Ghilarducci, 2012; Wallace & Villa, 2009). As initially addressed in chapter 1, income and wealth resulting from owning a home and having a high formal level of education were compromised for older adults of color because of systematic racial discrimination for both ex-veterans and nonveterans. Accumulated wealth, as a result, can not be transferred to boomers of color. Consider the following statement by an African American baby boomer:

> All my life I've heard and read about the power, clout and influence that the "baby boomer" generation has had on the culture and direction of American lifestyle and media. I bought into that for the most part but looking back I can see that this was not necessarily the case for a large portion of baby boomers. I'm talking about the African American baby boomer. I mean this generation was supposed to have lived the most charmed life and enjoyed the greatest perks of any group in American history. While I will admit that my generation had it much easier than my parents and grandparents, Black baby boomers haven't exactly had it made. What's worse is that now that we are entering what should be the "golden" years things for a lot of us are bad and may get worse. I know, I know. This economy has had an adverse effect on all of us but having historically been the "last hired/first fired" simply because of our race usually meant that it took us longer to gain any real economic security or job tenure in the first place. Many of us have lost our jobs and had to dip into whatever saving we may have had. Okay, we're used to having to start over from scratch but let's be honest, we're not as young as we used to be. We don't have years to work ourselves up from the bottom. Sure going back to school is an option but then when we graduate we're competing with thousands of younger graduates that'll be more than happy to take a salary less than what we would expect. Besides, although it's supposed to be illegal I KNOW that age discrimination exists when it comes to hiring. I've actually had an interviewer tell me "You're not as young as most applicants I have for this position." Never mind that he could clearly see on my resume that I had done that kind of work for over 10 years at some of America's top companies. Of course I didn't get the job.
>
> (Anonymous, 2010)

Unfortunately, the assessment is not atypical. Boomers of color are generally associated with characteristics of income insecurity, food insecurity, and health disparities (Johnson & Wilson, 2010a). Their "golden years" will be anything but.

This chapter seeks to ground the reader in the financial world and economic circumstances of boomers by examining, to the best of our ability based on available data, their economic status, streams of income, and financial expectations upon retirement. The chapter will end by posing the question whether retirement is even a viable option for many boomers of color.

BABY BOOMER FINANCIAL POWER

Baby boomers are not only the fastest-growing demographic sector in the country, but are also widely considered the wealthiest, healthiest, most vigorous, and best formally educated soon-to–be-older adult group in the history of the United States. However, this generalization is certainly not true for the vast majority of boomers of color. This group faces incredible challenges transitioning to retirement.

Boomers control vast wealth in this country. In 2005 they were estimated to spend $2 trillion annually (*Business Wire,* 2005). They are responsible for approximately 50 percent of all discretionary spending in this country. The United States Census Bureau estimated that in 2009 boomers owned approximately $13 trillion in assets, or 50 percent of all the wealth in the United States, thereby the largest asset-owning age group in the country. Visa estimates that boomers will be responsible for $2.45 trillion in spending by the year 2015 (*Business Wire,* 2007).

Boomer purchasing power gets manifested in a myriad of ways that we normally do not think about. For example, they are responsible for 61 percent of all over-the-counter medications and 77 percent of all prescription drugs, which is not surprising considering the problem with prescription abuse covered in chapter 5. They also account for 80 percent of all leisure travel in the country (*Baby Boomers Generation,* 2009). Mutual funds had $55 billion when boomers started entering the workforce in 1971; at the end of 2010 these funds had grown to $10.7 trillion, with $4.1 trillion in retirement accounts (Waggoner, 2010).

Thus we see that, as a cohort, baby boomer income and wealth are considerable, although upon closer examination not all subgroups have shared in this prosperity (Holden, 2009; Holzer, 2008; Mutchler & Burr, 2009; Penner, 2008b; Wolff, 2007). We will now turn our attention to those boomers that live on the other end of the financial spectrum.

BABY BOOMERS AND POVERTY

The poverty rates for boomers of color are dramatically higher when compared to their White, non-Latino/a counterparts, and this will severely compromise their transition to retirement (Jacobsen et al., 2011).

Asians (11.6 percent) have the lowest poverty rates of the three major boomer groups of color. African Americans (18.6 percent) and Latino/as (15.5 percent) have rates almost double (7.7 percent) that of White, non-Latino/as (Johnson & Wilson, 2010b). Issa and Zedlewski (2011) found that among older adults aged sixty-five to seventy-four years, African Americans (8.4 percent) and Latino/as (7.3 percent) had poverty rates considerably higher than their White, non-Latino (6.6 percent) counterparts, with Asians having the lowest rates (3.5 percent) of any group. These figures are lower by more than half those of boomers of color.

The poverty rate among Latino/a older adults, for example, is 20 percent, and the highest rate in the country for older adults (Richman et al., 2008).

Employment and Income

The quality of life of boomers in, or near, poverty stands to be further compromised by the recent recession because it limits the options for those boomers wishing to supplement their incomes through employment. Unfortunately, U.S. Census data on employment rates among boomers of color are severely limited. Yet we can examine how the recession has impacted employment levels among boomers of color as an example (Gassoumis et al., 2010).

All boomers were hurt by the recession. Unemployment among this cohort doubled from 3.0 percent in 2007 to 7.1 percent in 2009, reflecting the recession's impact (General Accountability Office, 2011). In addition, the report found "that an estimated 25 percent of adults 50 and over had exhausted their savings in response to a layoff or other recession-related event, and half in that age group say they had delayed a medical or dental procedure to make ends meet. Meanwhile, the normal safety net of home equity has been decimated by the housing bubble collapse." Median duration of unemployment almost tripled from eleven to thirteen weeks during the 2007–2010 periods for boomers. Not surprisingly, their median household income dropped by 6 percent during that period.

Johnson and Mommaerts (2010a) studied the impact of the most recent recession on older adults and found that baby boomers on average numbering 1.5 million workers were unemployed each month in 2009, which was more than double the number in 2007. This translates into an unemployment rate of 7.2 percent for baby boomer men and 6.0 percent for women.

Boomers and older adults in the construction, manufacturing, and leisure and hospitality industries were particularly hard hit and are expected to take longer to recover too (Johnson & Mommaerts, 2009; Johnson, Mommaerts, & Park, 2011). These sectors traditionally employ a large number of boomers of color.

The 2009 unemployment rates were much higher among older African Americans and Latino/as. For men, approximately 11 percent of Latinos and 10 percent of African American workers were unemployed, compared with 6 percent of White, non-Latinos. Losing employment has significant ramifications for the health of Latino/a baby boomers, for example, with over one-third reporting having to reduce their medications because of costs and 20 percent of those unemployed having lost their health insurance (New American Media, 2010).

The socioeconomic-political context in which boomers of color grew up as they entered the labor force, as a result, continues to shape their entrance into retirement:

> A typical adult approaching retirement in 2010 was born around 1945 and may have entered the workforce in mid 1960s at a time of racial segregation in schools and communities, little access to college for people of color and employment opportunities with no pension or retirement savings benefits, or even Social Security for African-American and Latino workers. Despite having witnessed much progress, people of color face great barriers to economic opportunities which shaped their life trajectories and continue to shape their economic realities. Past discriminations and current economic realities have long-term economic implications for people of color that are entering retirement today in a more unstable position than their white counterparts.
>
> (Meschede et al., 2011, p. 3)

Similarly, Hughes and Rand comment on the distinct disadvantage that African American/Black boomers find themselves in as they enter retirement age: "Diversity has not led to equality: Baby boomers are the first generation to come of age after the Civil Rights era. . . . Differences of income according to race, ethnicity and country of birth are so entrenched that, in effect, they are ethnic classes. Blacks in the boomer generation, for example, are no better off relative to whites than their parents and grandparents. And educational levels also are unequal across the baby boom generation, which is often described as the best-educated generation in history" (Hughes & Rand, 2004, p. 1).

African American baby boomers, for example, earn two-thirds of what their White, non-Latino/a counterparts earn (Fears, 2004). They are the first generation to come of age after the passage of the Civil Rights Act, yet income and wealth disparities still have not closed since that historic legislation. Further, the Center for Economic and Policy Research (Fremstad, 2011) estimated that approximately 40 percent of African Americans aged fifty-eight years or older work in physically demanding jobs, and 33 percent do so under difficult work circumstances. This has profound outcomes for health as well as wealth. Finally, we have a very limited understanding of boomers of color and the informal economy, which may supplement their formal earnings (Delgado, 2011) and help mitigate their dire economic circumstances.

Median Income: According to the Social Security Administration (2012), the median income of White, non-Latino/as sixty-five and over is almost double that of Latino/as ($27,214 versus $14,400) and 60 percent greater than that of African Americans ($16,463), and 66 percent of Asian and Pacific Islanders ($17,977). Not surprisingly, low median income for boomers of color represents the sum total of inequality across the life span:

> Inequality across the life course will be compounded in old age. For seniors of color, who faced labor market discriminations and restricted access to asset-building opportunities through formal and informal means during their working years, the retirement years are likely to be characterized by economic insecurity and significant challenges to making ends meet. . . . While today's people of color do not face the same levels of overt discrimination as their parents did, segregation and discrimination remain barriers to economic equality across the life course.
>
> (Meschede et al., 2011, p. 3)

This disparity impacts the ability of boomers of color to achieve economic security and well-being in retirement, just as it has throughout earlier stages in their lives. It further impacts their ability to financially assist their relatives and support local businesses in the community. In essence, income disparities cannot be measured or understood solely from an individualistic perspective.

Baby boomer assets fall into three general categories: (1) Social Security; (2) private wealth, such as bank accounts, real estate investments, homes, inheritances; and (3) private retirement accounts, such as 401(k) funds (Skinner, 2009). Each of these will be analyzed in turn over the course of this chapter.

Reliance on Social Security

The importance of Social Security as a key source of income for boomers varies across racial and ethnic groups. The debates about Social Security solvency and the proposed reforms, as a result, take on varying degrees of urgency depending on a host of factors.

Figure 6.1 shows how the major racial and ethnic groups compare in getting their income from sources other than Social Security. It should not

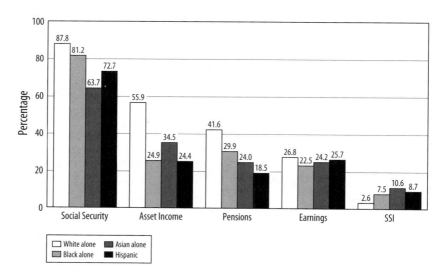

FIGURE 6.1. Percentage receiving income from major sources by race and Hispanic origin, 2010.

Source: U.S. Social Security Administration, Office of Retirement and Disability Policy, Income of the Aged Chartbook, 2010.

come as any great surprise that Social Security constitutes a major portion of retirement income among African Americans (95 percent) and Latino/as (85 percent), as compared to White, non-Latino/as (80 percent) (Rockeymoore & Maitin-Shepard, 2010).

Boomers of color with lifetime low-wage employment are severely limited in obtaining their post-retirement income from sources other than Social Security because of a lack of investments and participation in private pension plans (Gassoumis, Lincoln, & Vega, 2011; Holzer, 2008; Meyer, 2009). Consequently, discussion of Social Security reforms, as covered in chapter 2, will impact them more than those with multiple sources of post-retirement income (Commission to Modernize Social Security, 2011).

A high proportion of baby boomers of color live in poverty and as a result, either currently or eventually, will rely heavily upon Social Security as either their primary or almost exclusive source of income (American Association for Retired Persons, 2004a; Halliwell, Gassoumis, & Wilber, 2007; Kim & Torres-Gil, 2011; Meschede et al., 2011). In 2009, for example, 36 percent of all married older adult Latino couples, and 62 percent of those who were single, depended upon Social Security for 90 percent or more of their income (Social Security Administration, 2011b). Social Security was the only form of income for 40 percent of all Latino/a older adults. In other words, it was their lifeline.

African Americans, too, rely heavily upon Social Security, with 40 percent of households having this as their only source of income, and almost 50 percent relying on it for 90 percent of their incomes (Fleck, 2011). Among Asian and Pacific Islanders, 27 percent of those who were married and 48 percent of those who were single relied on Social Security (Social Security Administration, 2011d). In 2009 45 percent of American Indians receiving Social Security relied on this form of income for 90 percent of their total income (Social Security Administration, 2011e). Finally, 29 percent of married couples and 56 percent of those who were unmarried received 90 percent or more of their income from Social Security (Social Security Administration, 2011c).

The incidence of disabilities, lifetime earnings, and mortality are three factors that are influential in determining how much individuals pay into Social Security and the benefits derived from the system (General Accounting Office, 2003). Low Social Security payments are highly associated with recipients of color, particularly those who are Latino/a and foreign born who have the highest rate of living below the poverty level (52.8 percent), followed by African Americans with 43.2 percent (Favreault, 2010).

Favreault (2009), in a 2009 testimony to the Senate Special Committee on Aging, specifically addressed the needs of low lifetime earners and the oldest of the old, as well as the need to bolster benefits. In addition, she pointed out that addressing the solvency question is not an "arithmetic problem" since tax increases and cuts in benefits impact workers and beneficiaries in dramatically different ways. Introducing minimum benefits is one way of successfully improving the economic status of lifelong low-wage workers and, in the process, helping reduce the poverty rates among older adults and soon-to-be retirees. The impact of such a reform will be profound for the families of these beneficiaries and the neighborhoods they live in too.

The current debates about Social Security, as addressed in chapter 2, cause a great deal of anxiety among current and future boomer beneficiaries who will rely almost totally upon this as a source of income, particularly those who are lifelong low-wage earners (Acs & Nichols, 2007; Yang & Barrett, 2006). Fry and colleagues, for example, show how this debate has specific consequences for Latino/a boomers:

> Latinos have distinct demographic and economic characteristics that give them a unique stake in the debate over the future of Social Security. First, they are younger on average than the remainder of the U.S. population, which means that, as a group, their future as Social Security contributors and beneficiaries will be different from the future of non-Hispanics. Second, Hispanic workers tend to hold lower-paying jobs than the average U.S. worker and are less likely to have an employment-based pension. At all ages of adulthood Hispanics have lower average incomes and have accumulated less wealth than their white counterparts, and Hispanics currently over the age of 65 rely very heavily on Social Security retirement benefits as a source of income. For all these reasons, the nature, extent and timing of any changes to Social Security would have specific and distinct consequences for the Hispanic population.
>
> (Fry et al., 2005, p. i)

The social forces that impinge on Latino/a boomers have deep historical routes that are manifested as Latino/as enter retirement age. Similar and additional social forces, too, are faced by the African American, Asian American, and Native Americans baby boomers who are heavily reliant on Social Security for their economic survival.

Private Wealth

Social Security was never envisioned to be the only source of retirement income. Most retirees would be challenged to live on it as their sole, or principal, source of income. Accumulated wealth and other sources must be present to help baby boomers have economic security in older adulthood. Five primary sources of wealth and income will be addressed in this section: (1) home assets, (2) investment income, (3) employment, (4) savings, and (5) inheritance.

In general, wealth accumulation among boomers of color is low compared to their White, non-Latino/a counterparts, particularly because of histories of low formal educational attainment and relegation to low-wage employment (Johnson, Haaga, & Simms, 2011). Marital history also influences wealth; boomers who are married enjoy stronger economic footing than those who are single. Single women, for example, have received lower pay than men over a lifetime, resulting in lower Social Security benefits and lower pensions (Wheary, 2011). Pre-retirement wealth accumulation of older African American women, for example, is greatly influenced by differences in marriage (never married, divorce, widowhood) over the life course, reenforcing patterns of inequality in older adulthood (Addo & Lichter, 2010).

Private wealth is also greatly impacted by financial literacy and/or access to sound financial guidance, which many boomers may not have. Older adults, in general, are subject to increasing abuses from the financial services industry (Catalano & Lazaro, 2010), such as taking on predatory loans, which can undermine their already precarious economic situation. The targeting of racially segregated neighborhoods where boomers of color most likely live has further exacerbated their precarious economic position. As noted, financial illiteracy is another important factor (Lusardi & Mitchell, 2011; Mitchell, Lusardi, & Curto, 2009). Sadly, it is estimated that financial literacy declines by 2 percent for every year past sixty (Finke, Howe, & Huston, 2011). In addition, a high percentage of African Americans and Latino/as are unbanked (meaning they have no formal accounts or relationships with banks), thus limiting their access to banking services that can assist them in retirement (Delgado, 2011; Lusardi, 2011).

Home Assets: Much of the national attention of the pending wave of boomer retirement has focused on the impact on federal expenditures. However, the housing sector, too, will be transformed in dramatic fashion (Painter & Lee, 2009). Home assets are considered the greatest source of wealth for the average family in this country. Homes often can be tapped for securing loans and lines of credit to meet a wide range of expected and unexpected expenses. Consequently, it is appropriate to start an analysis of wealth with these assets for an in-depth understanding of boomer worth.

In 2006, almost 80 percent of boomers owned their own home and 25 percent owned at least one other form of real estate (Heavens, 2006). Yet the housing crash changed that dramatically. Rosnick and Baker sum up the current state of baby boomer housing assets: "As a result of the plunge in house prices, many baby boomers now have little or no equity in their home. According to our calculations, of those who own their primary residence, nearly 30 percent of households' headed by someone between the ages of 45 to 54 will need to bring money to their closing (to cover their mortgage and transactions costs) if they were to sell their home. More than 15 percent of the early baby boomers, people between the ages of 55 and 64, will need to bring money to a closing when they sell their home" (Rosnick and Baker, 2009, p. 1). Thus for many boomers these assets have evaporated as the result of the housing bubble during this past recession.

The recession of 2008 caused a tremendous loss in home equity across all age groups. It is estimated that approximately $6 trillion in equity was lost overall, resulting in almost 13 million individuals owing over $660 billion more on their homes than their homes were worth (*New York Times,* 2012).

The impact of the housing crash was particularly severe for baby boomers (T. Brown, 2012; Rosnick & Baker, 2009, 2010; Baker & Rosnick, 2009). An estimated 30 percent of boomers were "underwater" in their homes in 2009 (Christie, 2009). Further, 28 percent of those fifty years and older were delinquent in mortgage payments or in the process of foreclosure (Bruin et al., 2011). However, boomers with higher formal education, owning homes that had appreciated significantly, and with higher incomes were most likely to be in a financial position to draw upon housing equity and refinancing (Gist, Figueiredo, & Verma, 2012). The crash was far more devastating among boomers of color (Trawinski, 2012). Latino/a median level of home equity fell by 51 percent ($99,983 to $49,145), followed by Asians with 32 percent ($219,742 to $150,000), and African Americans by 23 percent ($76,910 to $59,000) in 2009. Among White, non-Latino/as, it fell by 18 percent, from $115,364 to $95,000 (Taylor, Fry, & Kochhar, 2011).

The Center for Responsible Lending summed up the impact of the housing crisis on communities of color: "We have estimated that two million families have lost their primary homes and that African-American and Latino/a borrowers have borne and will continue to disproportionately bear the burden of foreclosures. . . . Foreclosures will likely continue to grow substantially while continuing to have a disproportionate impact on communities of color" (Bocian, Li, & Ernst, 2010). Baby boomers of color, by having the majority of their wealth tied into their homes, have been put at further economic risk in their retirement. These boomers often live in segregated areas where home assets are significantly lower than those in White, non-Latino/a sectors. Not surprisingly, their homes have not appreciated at the rate as those of their more affluent counterparts, making the impact of any loss in home value that much more devastating.

Becker (2010) addresses a disturbing trend among boomers who are desperate to hold on to their financial security: the reverse mortgage industry. Reverse mortgages have become popular among seniors who receive payments from the bank against the equity in their homes. Essentially, what they are doing is pawning their homes. The value of the house, which might have been passed on to the next generation, instead is paid to a bank or mortgage company. "Twenty years ago, they predicted that the 'great wealth transfer' would take place when the Boomers passed their homes and estates on to their children. Now it is going to the mortgage companies, not to the families" (Becker, 2011).

It is also important to note the percentage of baby boomers who are homeless. Life in the streets is harsh regardless of age. However, homelessness in older adulthood brings with it dire health consequences, particularly for those residing in neighborhoods that provoke distress (Rudolph et al., 2013). In a New York City study of the homeless, baby boomers represented a significant portion of the adult population, and they bring needs that are both similar to and different from those of other age groups (Culhane et al., 2013).

Investments: Investment income can be an important source of income and security in retirement. As with housing, however, the 2008 economic recession has impacted baby boomers in general and boomers of color in particular. It is estimated that individual investors lost—at minimum—$113 billion during the recent financial market collapse, with boomers and older adults suffering significant losses (Wasik, 2011).

Employment: For some baby boomers, retirement is a time to reinvent themselves through higher education (Cruce & Hillman, 2012; Fabrikant, 2013), starting new careers and even new businesses (Kelly, 2013; Olson, 2013; Pethokoukis & Brandon, 2006; Zipkin, 2013). Part-time employment is also an option: Prynoos and Liebig (2009) argue that an increased availability of part-time work has made it easier for boomers and older adults to continue working and thus supplementing their income. Another option, however, is to simply postpone retirement and continue employment in their current position (Toossi, 2009).

Raising the retirement age has been suggested as a way of relieving the immediate burden on Social Security, as addressed in chapter 2. However, a number of scholars have argued against this potential solution (Aaron, 2011; Coile & Gruber, 2007; Kurtzleben, 2011; Steuerle, 2011). Such actions serve only to increase the benefits retirees eventually receive because of later retirement (Tanner, 2001). However, lower-income workers would benefit from staying in the labor pool past retirement age (Butrica, Smith, & Steuerle, 2006). Moreover, the Social Security crisis cannot be solved by cutting benefits and raising taxes either because such actions will have a disproportionate impact on the most vulnerable of boomers and older adults (Estes et al., 2009a; Howard, 2010).

Nevertheless, even if baby boomers want, or need, to work past their retirement age, it does not mean they will be given the option to do so by their employers (Maestas & Zissimopoulos, 2010). Boomers with high formal education levels, and corresponding skill sets, may have that option. However, those whose jobs are physical in nature and do not require high educational attainment or skill sets may not (Mermin, Johnson, & Toder, 2008). This, unfortunately, is the case for many lifetime low-wage boomers of color in this country (Acs & Nichols, 2007). Approximately 12 percent of all boomers have no high school diploma: 17.6 of African Americans fall into this category, 19 percent of Asian Americans and Pacific Islanders, and 40.9 percent of Latino/as (Wallace & Villa, 2009). (Those with low formal education are at an increased earnings disadvantage throughout the lifespan (Butrica, Smith, & Iams, 2012). According to the United States Census Bureau, the lack of formal educational attainment translates into a significant lifetime income gap (DeNavas-Walt, Proctor, & Smith, 2012). The difference between the annual earnings of someone with an eighth grade formal education and someone with a professional degree is almost $72,000 a year (Hispanic PR Blog, 2011).

Further, the Age Discrimination in Employment Act is predicted to face increased challenges as employers wishing to cut costs increasingly turn to younger workers instead of the older workers who wish to hold onto their jobs (McCann & Ventrell-Monsees, 2010; Neumark, 2009; Poytheway, 2012). Neumark and Song (2011) researched age discrimination and found that states with strong age discrimination laws benefited workers "caught" in the increases of Social Security Full Employment Age this past decade.

Finally, as already noted, boomers of color are often concentrated in jobs that are physically demanding and possibly unsafe as well. The health issues that typically arise with age may mean that boomers cannot hold these jobs as long as they might like.

Savings: Many individuals and families like the comfort of being able to draw upon savings during times of crisis. However, baby boomers have a low savings rate. Their savings rate went from 10 percent in the mid-1980s to approximately 2 percent in 2008 (Beinhocker, Farrell, & Greenberg, 2008). Savings averaged $18,000 in 2010 or a decrease of over 50 percent from 2004 (Ecker, 2012). Consequently, drawing upon this source of money, including interest, cannot be considered a steady revenue stream for a majority of baby boomers.

Access to interest income often represents an essential component of wealth and a retirement portfolio. Approximately half (52 percent) of all households receive interest income (Meschede et al., 2011). However, it, too, is not evenly distributed across race and ethnicity, with White, Non-Latino/as over the age of sixty-five (52 percent) having the greatest access, followed by 22 percent among African Americans. Savings among Asian and Latino/a boomers and older adults are considerably lower than those of their White, non-Latino/a counterparts (Burr et al., 2008–2009). Access to dividend income is even more rare among older adults, with 22.5 of all older adults receiving this form of income, but more so among African

Americans, with only 5.2 percent receiving this form of income (Meschede et al., 2011).

Inheritance: Inherited wealth is another potential source of wealth disparity (Strand, 2010). The potential of intergenerational transfer of money (inheritance) to assist baby boomers in their retirement, however, has taken a serious decline because of the economic recession, increased lifespan of their parents, increased medical costs, and a severe decline in housing values (Munnell et al., 2011). Low-income boomers of color, unfortunately, are not in a position to inherit wealth, nor are they in a position to leave wealth to their families upon their death, thereby perpetuating inheritance inequality over generations (Angel, 2008; Angel & Mudrazija, 2010). Histories of racial discrimination in housing, education, and employment has compromised older adults of color transferring wealth to their children, further putting boomers of color in a difficult financial state (Ross & Levine, 2012).

Private Pension Plans

Retirement accounts and private pension plans, in the case of those who are in institutions that offer them, often represent important parts of a retiree's wealth. In 2010, retirement savings averaged $42,000, a decrease from $45,000 in 2004 (Ecker, 2012). Participation in defined benefit pension plans (those that pay a lifelong annuity based on employment longevity and final salary) declined steadily from 38 percent in 1980 to 20 percent in 2008. However, participation in defined contribution pension plans (worker contribution) increased from 8 percent in 1980 to 31 percent in 2008 (Butrica et al., 2009). This shift from employer to employee contributions increases the likelihood of these plans being severely underfunded.

There are significant differences in retirement plan usage across racial and ethnic groups (Butrica & Johnson, 2010). For one thing, many baby boomers of color have not attained the same level of formal education as their white non-Latino/a counterparts and have thereby been relegated to manufacturing and service professions. Their jobs (as opposed to careers) rarely offer pension plans. In 2006 it was estimated that 50 percent of all boomers had a company-sponsored pension plan (Moore, 2006). For

African American workers, their participation decreased from 45.8 percent in 1979 to 37.5 percent in 2006 (Meschede et al., 2011). Among Latino/as, only 40 percent participated in pension plans (Fry et al., 2005). In 2011 the level of access and participation in company pension programs diminished.

Overall, it is currently estimated that 59 percent of all full-time employees have access to a company retirement plan. However, only 54.4 percent of those aged twenty-five to forty-three do so, representing a disturbing trend on the part of companies not to offer retirement plans. This is even more pronounced among workers in the lowest quartile with 38.4 percent having access to such plans (Hiltonsmith, 2010). In addition, they do not have access to expertise to help them navigate the world of finances, which more privileged boomers often have (Prudential, 2011).

And as with all other forms of wealth discussed in this chapter, the 2008 economic recession has caused a considerable loss of investment in most boomers' pension plans. The values of IRA and Keogh accounts among African Americans dropped by 13 percent from $17,319 in 2005 to $15,000 in 2009, along with corresponding drops in thrift accounts from $15,382 to $11,000 or 28 percent (Taylor, Fry, & Kochhar, 2011). The extent of this drop to the current day is unknown because of a lack of data. However, it is safe to assume that it has not fully recovered. Latino/as and White, non-Latino/as, however, did not experience such a precipitous drop. IRA and Keogh accounts increased slightly during this period and median value of 401(k) decreased slightly for both groups. Asian households experienced an increase of 19 percent in the median value of their stocks and mutual funds, from $25,270 in 2005 to $30,000 in 2009, but lost 12 percent of the value of their 401(k) and thrift accounts during this period (Taylor, Fry, & Kochhar, 2011). It is important to note that boomers with low incomes receive relatively little tax benefits from participating in 401(k) plans, unlike high income workers who can forgo the earnings in favor of tax benefits (Toder & Smith, 2011).

Finally, access to retirement funds represents an immediate source of income in emergency situations for those who have no other safety net. Thus, in the case of African-Americans, even when they participate in 401(k) programs they are three times more likely to withdraw funds than White, non-Latino/as (Prudential, 2011), which compromises their tax status and retirement goals.

IS RETIREMENT A VIABLE OPTION?

This is the critical question facing boomers of color. Is retirement an option? And, if so, what sacrifices will be required in order to live on a greatly reduced income? Obviously, the answer to this question goes beyond finances, although there is no denying the influence of economics (Tang, Choi, & Goode, 2013). The concept of "cumulative disadvantage" captures the impact of various factors, such as ethnicity/race, marital status, formal educational attainment, health, wealth/debt, and participation in pension plans. They interact with each other to create a favorable or unfavorable foundation from which to decide on retirement. In the case of boomers of color, this cumulative disadvantage has been inherited from their parents because of their lack of access to the same opportunities as their White, non-Latino/a counterparts, as addressed in the accumulation of wealth.

Grandich identifies three key reasons why baby boomers will continue to face financial hardships unless there are dramatic changes in the country:

> First, is their ability to live off their investments. Baby Boomers were raised to believe that if they saved enough during their working years, when they retired they could live off the interest of their savings. Obviously, with interest rates on CDs at 3 percent or less, that's no longer true. To make matters worse, they "chased yield"—trying to make up some of their losses on riskier investments like real estate, which tanked even harder. The second thing that has clobbered the Baby Boomers financially is the decline of their two most important investments: their stock portfolios and their homes. Everybody knows what happened there. Boomers planned on cashing in when they liquidated homes and stocks, which are now worth a fraction of just a few years ago . . . and they do not have the years to wait for a rebound. Finally, they always knew that no matter what, they'd have good, affordable health care, thanks to government-sponsored programs like Medicare and Medicaid. Yet, the only conceivable way forward from here is a dramatic change in the way medical coverage is provided, which will impact seniors financially and physically.
>
> (Grandich, 2010)

Grandich's conclusions about boomer financial prospects are sobering. However, the financial picture is far more disastrous for lifelong low-wage boomers of color when compared to their middle-class and upper-middle-class counterparts.

Financial security is a vital part of a quality-of-life equation for boomers (Johnson, 2008). The National Council on Aging summarizes the economic challenges they face: "The current economic downturn has had an impact on older adults nearing retirement. Employment and unemployment, pension changes, housing assets and debt, and health insurance and health care costs all play a part in how financially secure older adults are as they move into their retirement years" (Johnson & Wilson, 2010b, p. 7). Recent estimates have boomers retiring at least five years past their expected retirement age (Hicks, 2011).

Those closest to retirement age have less time to recover from any recent financial losses. Older women and people of color are particularly vulnerable, with higher poverty rates and lower levels of home equity than their white, male counterparts. When using the Senior Financial Stability Index to measure financial well-being, 76 percent of African Americans and 85 percent of Latino/as do not have sufficient financial resources to cover projected lifetime expenses. This compares unfavorably with White, non-Latino/as with 27 percent (Wheary & Meschede, 2010).

Anxiety about being able to afford retirement is prevalent among baby boomers. A November 2011 poll found that 53 percent did not feel confident that they would be able to afford retirement; this represents an increase from 44 percent in a similar poll in March 2011 (CBS, 2011). Seventy-three percent plan to work past the retirement age, an increase from 67 percent in the March poll. The March 2011 poll found that 55 percent were either somewhat or very certain about being able to retire with financial security, but 44 percent stated that they had little or no faith that they would have enough money upon retirement (Fram, 2011). In fact, one in four expects great difficulty in paying their bills upon retirement.

Another 2011 survey conducted by the ING Retirement Research Institute (Hannon, 2012) found similar results. In this poll, Latino/as were most likely to say that they were not prepared for retirement (54 percent), with African Americans (50 percent), White, non-Latino/as (48 percent), and Asians (44 percent) following. These feelings serve as an indicator of potential future difficulties in managing the difficult transition to retirement.

A 2008 analysis found that 69 percent of boomers cannot maintain 80 percent of their peak pre-retirement spending and are thereby unprepared to retire (Beinhocker, Farrell, & Greenberg, 2008). Munnell, Webb, and Golub-Sass (2009) found that 50 percent of households in 2009 would not be able to maintain their pre-retirement standard of living upon retirement, when and if they continued to work to age sixty-five. Postponing retirement, as a result, not only increases their worth and income but also continues to fuel the overall economy through their spending.

A 2011 Prudential study of African American boomers found that 60 percent had less than $50,000 in company pensions. Not surprisingly, only 20 percent said that they believed they were "on track" to achieve savings for retirement.

Flynn concluded that the "truism [is] that the older workforce is a wide range of workers whose experience in work impacts on their attitudes toward and planning for retirement. Policy makers cannot, therefore, take a 'one size fits all' approach to designing incentives for delaying retirement. This diversity could be of advantage to policy makers" (Flynn, 2010, p. 322). The call for a nuanced approach to policy resonates even further when examining boomers of color.

Hodge (2006) examines gender and concludes that "baby boomer women are in trouble." As noted earlier in this book, women have a longer life expectancy than men, have histories of being underpaid when compared to men, and as a result are in a very vulnerable economic position upon retirement (Wheary, 2011). Their status necessitates gender-specific services.

> Unlike any other time in our nation's history, unless there are dramatic policy shifts, in terms of absolute numbers, baby boomer women, most particularly minority women, will find their elder years to be a "never ending" struggle. After selflessly caring for their children and aging parents, a significant number of our country's 40 million plus boomer women will not be able to afford to retire, will fall below the poverty line and experience financial insecurity and poorer health in their later years with limited aid from traditional safety nets.
>
> (McCourt, 2008)

Unfortunately, old age and retirement will clearly not constitute "golden years" for countless numbers of baby boomers of color. Their economic situation places them in an at-risk category for severe economic hardships and the social and health consequences associated with a low income level.

After this grim assessment, part 2 provides a positive and hopeful view of baby boomers of color and their potential contribution to their communities and society. The three chapters that comprise part 2 examine a variety of ways that these boomers can continue to play active and meaningful roles in their immediate family and community. The following chapter provides a conceptual foundation for identifying assets and the rewards and challenges social workers will encounter in tapping these important resources in service to boomers of color and their respective families and communities.

PART | 2

Cultural Assets

Baby Boomer Assets

A CONCEPTUAL FOUNDATION

PART 1 OF THIS BOOK provided a plethora of government data and research on boomers that can be classified as deficit oriented. It provided a statistical portrait of boomers, including those of color, with a particular focus on health and finances and the multi-faceted sociopolitical-economic challenges they face as they transition to retirement and beyond. All of part 1 stressed a "deficit perspective." This viewpoint casts boomers of color as helpless and/or dependent, as albatrosses around their necks of families, communities, and society. The silver tsunami metaphor conveys images of destruction, upheaval, and calamity. Clearly, the central message is negative and meant to convey a state of crisis for the nation, for which an entire generation is the scapegoat. A new narrative is much needed, and social workers are in a position to help create one because of our history of embracing assets or strengths.

It is hard to assess boomer assets that are nonfinancial for a variety of reasons. Social workers and other helping professionals working with boomers first must overcome any biases they may have about this age group. This shift in mind-set represents one of the greatest challenges in identifying, assessing, and mobilizing boomer assets. This chapter will lay the groundwork for utilizing an assets perspective when working with baby boomers.

AGING AND A DEFICIT PERSPECTIVE

Ageism, as defined in chapter 1, can be pernicious. Johnson argues that individuals who are "nonold" embrace ideas about older adults as "others" by constructing their own future selves as being different from that of older people and thus rationalizing practice and views that are ageist (Johnson, 2013, p. 198). In other words, "I will not be like them when I get to be their age."

Knechtel points out the dilemma that older adults face in an ageist society that seeks to disempower them:

> In a commercial culture aimed at the young, the beautiful and the nimble we do not like to think about aging. Although aging is as inescapable as phases of the moon, negative stereotypes about older adults proliferate. Unfortunately they still find their loudest expression in the workplace. We cheer roundly when older people demonstrate creativity, can do attitudes and athletic agility. An 88 year old skier or tennis buff is looked on with admiration and respect and may well be saluted in the media. Older celebrities are revered. But for the most part, esteem for seniors paradoxically ceases abruptly at the hiring gate. What changes is not older peoples' capacity to be vigorous, productive and creative. Rather, society is unwilling to see seniors as vital and active contributors far beyond traditional retirement age. It's assumed that people of a certain age suddenly turn senile and accept being seen as useless and dispatched to decades on the golf course, playing bingo or just plain idleness as a way of life. You're expected to embrace inconsequence and oblivion.
>
> (Knechtel, 2007)

When ageism is added to other forms of oppression, such as racism and classism, it wields an even greater negative influence on lifetime low-wage-earning boomers of color. Female boomers may also be prey to sexist views, LGBT boomers may face homophobia, and disabled older adults may have to challenge discrimination (or "ableism"). How these oppressive forces are identified and disentangled plays an important role in shaping assessments and interventions that embrace socially just values and principles.

Judd addresses the deleterious consequences of a deficit perspective on older adults: "Pervasive stereotypes about psychological decline in later life may also be self-perpetuating. Focusing on deficits also does not take into account the importance of subjective well-being and qualitative shifts in world perspective that often accompany the later years. An increased interest in the strengths of older adults will help to counteract ageism and enables older adults to live meaningful and valued lives" (Judd, 2007, p. 1).

Scholars are in a position to help counter the consequences of a deficit perspective, although there is not a critical mass of scholars currently doing this form of scholarship. Funding accounts for the popularity of a deficit perspective in research and scholarship. Problems, needs, and issues get public attention (and thus research money), while strengths and assets often do not.

It is important to point out that a focus on assets does not diminish the importance of understanding problems. An assets focus provides a balanced perspective on those with problems; broadening our understanding of them to include assets as well as needs provides a comprehensive picture.

The need for social work and other helping professions to counter the conventional "deficit" perspective and emphasize assets or strengths has resulted in exciting developments in participatory and empowering social interventions that incorporate social justice values and principles (Delgado & Humm-Delgado, 2013; Donaldson & Daughtery, 2011; Hardcastle, Powers, & Wenocur, 2011). These interventions resonate with social work's historical mission of working with undervalued groups.

There are tremendous benefits to having boomers actively engaged and contributing to their communities (Goldsmith, 2008; Healy, 2004; Lewis, 2008). Such activity enhances the capacity of communities by tapping indigenous resources and increasing the commitment of community members toward working for the well-being of the entire community (Chaskin, 2013). This takes on added significance in communities that have suffered from disenfranchisement, stigma, marginalization, and/or devaluation. Such communities can ill afford to disregard any group that can make a substantial contribution. The assets that boomers of color possess, as a result, can be tapped in service to their communities and society in general.

THE ASSETS PERSPECTIVE

An assets or strengths perspective finds saliency in practice and scholarship that specifically embraces empowerment of marginalized groups. It seeks to identify and mobilize what is "right" about a group, regardless of how negatively society views that group.

Some critics argue that an assets perspective has more to do with language and how we label a social condition or phenomenon, rather than having any real significance in how we practice ("Is the glass half-full or half-empty?") To be sure, language plays a highly influential role in how we view social circumstances and behaviors. However, an assets perspective is much more because it influences our worldviews and the actions (practice) that follow as a result. Consequently, assets practice is a philosophy, a process, a method, and a set of goals.

Eng and colleagues highlight the way in which an assets paradigm builds upon a community's foundations: "Although identifying community needs and gaps is important . . . identifying assets that the community can build on or further develop is equally important. Building on social structures and existing networks, decision-making processes, and local resources and strengths can yield intervention strategies that are rooted in the community, develop local critical-thinking and problem-solving skills, and ensure sustained efforts" (Eng et al., 2005, p. 97).

It is very easy to take a deficit perspective on lifelong low-income/low-wealth boomers of color and highlight all their problems and challenges. However, in doing so, we ignore the fact that boomers and their communities have survived, and even thrived, to this age against very impressive odds. Survival is never to be minimized! An understanding of how lifelong low-income/low-wealth boomers of color have successfully reached older age cannot be possible without an embrace of an assets paradigm. Many of these boomers have lasted through high rates of violence in their neighborhoods, substance abuse, inferior schools and formal systems of care, high rates of imprisonment, poor nutrition, participation in wars, employment in dangerous occupations, and more economic recessions than any other previous generation. How did they manage to make it to this life stage? It certainly was not by accident. There were individual and social forces operating to help them succeed and enter older adulthood. An assets perspective helps us put this puzzle together.

Langer highlights why a resiliency or strength perspective is needed: "Old age is characterized as a period of resiliency and how the older person uses internal and external resources to overcome the challenges presented by this stage of life. By acknowledging older adults' resiliency and spiritual resources in light of past and present risk factors, care providers can focus on capabilities, assets, and positive attributes rather than problems and pathologies" (Langer, 2004, p. 611). Similarly, Gilroy (2006) proposes the use of a "capabilities" approach to evaluating supportive environments rather than a deficit approach that stresses needs and problems.

A number of scholars have advocated for a viewpoint based on strengths, resiliency, and assets. Carr (2005) argues for a shift in thinking about older adults and boomers from a "problem" to a "social value" perspective. Wagnild and Collins (2009), too, stress the importance of understanding and assessing resilience in baby boomers. Black, Dobbs, and Young (2012) advance a social paradigm that highlights the unique assets/strengths of baby boomers and older adults, which can be conceptualized as a "core social resource" that can be mobilized for service to community. Wild, Wiles, and Allen (2013) integrate the concept of resilience within a critical gerontologist perspective as a means of broadening its influence beyond conventional usage.

Avery brings forth a risk-resilience ecological perspective and applies it to boomers: "Many baby boomers envision themselves as active, independent elders. . . . Fortunately, baby boomers have amassed personal, social, experiential, economic, and even spiritual assets to call upon as they reach later life. Each person organizes these assets into highly idiosyncratic ecosystems of people, places, institutions, and technologies to support them as they manage risk and create resilience" (Avery, 2010, p. 16). The concept of resiliency, when discussed in scholarship or the popular media, is often discussed in connection with youth; however, it has applicability across the lifespan and can also be applied to communities (Delgado & Humm-Delgado, 2013).

Social work has played an instrumental role in providing a counterpoint to the deficit perspective. The popularity of the strengths perspective has a long history within social work, and was popularized by Saleebey in the 1990s (1992, 1996). Perkins and Tire (1995) published an article applying the strengths perspective to older adults almost thirty years ago. Since then, this perspective has increased in popularity (see, for example, Gray & Kakadaki, 2005). However, baby boomers are often not identified directly in the strengths literature, which typically focuses on "middle age" or "older adult" categories. Scholars of resilience should view boomers as occupying a unique stage in the life cycle.

The strengths perspective has been broadened to an assets paradigm that encompasses individual as well as ecological resources (Delgado, 1999; Delgado & Humm-Delgado, 2013). Such a perspective attempts to humanize those in need, give them voice and self-determination, and encourage empowerment.

A word of caution is in order as the profession seeks to embrace an assets perspective on baby boomers of color. This perspective is not meant to relieve government and other official entities from their responsibilities to support boomers and older adults.

This may seem obvious to the reader. However, there is a long history of efforts to curtail services to older adults by suggesting that they have their own resources and do not need governmental assistance. An assets paradigm emphasizes the positive, but does not ignore needs and concerns.

Defining Assets

On the surface, defining "assets" may appear to be a straightforward task: anything that helps boomers of color enjoy a healthy existence could be thought of as an asset. Yet defining assets is far more complex, and efforts to do so are ever evolving (Delgado & Humm-Delgado, 2013). For the purposes of this book, assets will be broadly defined to facilitate the inclusion of various manifestations. Assets are resources that can be identified and mobilized in service to a particular group or community. Assets can be human or physical in form and encompass formal and informal manifestations.

Each discipline or profession can emphasize and operationalize assets from its particular vantage point, drawing upon its own key values. Economists may think in terms of financial assets and human capital; political scientists will embrace political capital; urban planners may emphasize physical assets such as buildings and structures. Social workers, not surprisingly, may emphasize the virtues of social and cultural capital. A comprehensive viewpoint necessitates an embrace of multiple forms of capital, as addressed in the following section.

Assets can draw upon a host of sociocultural-ecological factors and be operationalized accordingly. Gibson provides a broad definition of assets (with an emphasis on cultural assets):

> In every community that manages to sustain or revive itself over time, there are cultural factors that contribute to the vitality and robustness of the people living there. These factors are shared and creative, which is to say they are cultural and they are assets that make life valuable, that make life worth living. These cultural assets can be material, immaterial, emotional, or even spiritual. They can be "solid" things like concert halls, galleries, gardens,

parklands and stadiums. They can be special tracts of the natural environment which encourage particular types of cultural activities. Or the climate itself might be a cultural asset if it encourages special kinds of creative and communal activities that bind people together in a place over time. Stories too might be cultural assets if they are attached to particular peoples and places, if they are powerful enough to encourage people to care about and care for their place. In these stories, values can circulate, and special memories often reside in particular locations mentioned in the tales. Thus the places mentioned in the stories can be regarded as cultural assets if people tell of these places and visit them regularly and develop regular practices or rituals or ceremonies to care for them.

(Gibson, 2007)

Rabb, although referring to entrepreneurial opportunities, provides a definition of invisible capital that incorporates the various assets used in this book regarding boomers of color: "Invisible capital is the toolkit of our skills, knowledge, language, networks, and experiences, along with the set of assets we were born with: our race and gender, our family's wealth and status, the type of community in which we were raised, and the education we had as children. Some of these assets are fixed—we cannot change who our parents are. Others are in our power to modify. What makes them "invisible" is that our society does not acknowledge [them]" (Rabb, 2010, p. 6).

Rabb's definition incorporates many different types of assets that the scholarly literature identifies, particularly social, human, cultural, political, and economic. It is essential that these assets be identified and examined individually in order to understand the properties they bring to an intervention.

Types of Assets

Delgado and Humm-Delgado (2013) found seven types of assets or capital: (A) social; (B) human; (C) economic; (D) political; (E) physical; (F) intangible; and (G) cultural. Each of these assets can be evaluated individually, although there certainly is considerable overlap between different forms. Each will be briefly defined over the following pages.

Social Assets: Social capital is arguably the most popular form of asset or capital in the literature and also the most recognized by social workers.

Some critics would argue that social capital is the vaguest asset and the hardest to define. Not surprisingly, there is no universal definition of social capital. However, the Asian Development Bank provides a definition that lends itself to social work research and practice: "The term encompasses those relationships that help people to get along with each other and act more effectively than they could as isolated individuals. In this way, patterns of social organization, especially, trust, mutuality, and reciprocity, are seen as important resources, which can result in benefits to individuals, groups, and society" (Asian Developmental Bank, 2001, p. 1).

The role and importance of social capital to baby boomers of color makes it central to any intervention. It is possible to enhance and alter social capital by introducing potential new members to a client's social network. It also may be desirable to decrease reliance upon social contacts if they are negative and introduce those that are potentially positive in response.

Waite and Das (2010) note that as people age, so does the social network with whom they are connected. Phillipson and colleagues (2001), for example, studied the social networks of older adult groups in three English cities and found a shift in reliance from family groups to friendship networks.

Baby boomers and older adults, contrary to some conventional thinking, can be quite socially resilient and able to adapt to changes in their social ties, thereby having the potential of increasing engagement with kin and nonkin networks (Unger, 2010). There is no "social law" that says that as we age our social network must decrease. If provided with opportunities and supports, this network can expand and bring new growth experiences in the process.

Human Assets: In this book, the term human capital refers to the ability, desire, and willingness of the baby boomer generation to "give back" to community and society (Spira, 2006). Boomers can enhance their human capital through civic engagement within their communities.

A more conventional definition of human capital, however, usually has a strong economic basis: "The concept of human capital is rooted in economic theory and refers to the education, job experience, acquired skills, and the health of individuals" (Beckley et al., 2008, p. 63). The knowledge and competencies possessed by individuals, in those case boomers of color, can be acquired through formal and informal education and experiences in the formal or informal economy.

Economic Assets: Economic capital is sometimes referred to as financial capital. Economic capital, not surprisingly, is commonly narrowly defined as possession of fixed and liquid assets (Beckley et al., 2008). Economic capital is dependent upon a wide range of factors, including occupation and level of formal education. Chapter 6 provided the reader with various sources of economic capital. However, economic capital generally has been viewed from a formal perspective; the informal economy, which can play a large role in the lives of baby boomers of color, is usually ignored.

Political Assets: Political capital, simply defined, is the ability to exert political influence. It is often associated with boomers and older adults through their ability to vote in elections and lobby on behalf of issues of importance to them.

Ginieniewicz (2010) conceptualized political capital as consisting of two types: (1) civic and (2) political. Civic capital refers to an ability to influence one's quality of life, for example, through participation in community and voluntary organizations. Political capital refers to individual power relations. This form of asset is often applied to electoral politics and elections.

Physical Assets: Often overlooked in social work circles, physical capital "comprises the roads, buildings, infrastructure and natural resources" (Haines, 2009, p. 41) Physical capital plays an instrumental role in helping to create a "sense of place" or belonging. Physical assets can play a tremendous role in shaping quality of life, particularly for older adults. Communities with an abundance of public transportation, parks, exercise areas, and community resources can facilitate social interaction between residents.

Community gardens, for example, are a form of physical capital that can promote exercise and proper nutrition, increase property values, and provide opportunities for intergenerational programs. They are a place where older adults can share their wisdom and experiences with gardening to new generations (Delgado, 1999). Gardens also facilitate social capital development when boomers who may not have English as their first language, and may have come from different parts of the world, have gardening or farming in their histories, thereby having this experience serve as a bridge between different ethnic and racial groups.

Intangible Assets: This encompasses assets that are difficult to capture, yet wield considerable influence on individuals and communities, and is sometimes referred to as "invisible" capital or social science's version of "dark matter." Intangible capital refers to factors and circumstances that help shape daily life and help communities acquire an identity, and it is often taken for granted (Delgado, 2013).

Intangible capital has been applied to communication within communities (Bronn, 2008), and communities having a long history of innovation and generosity (Denton & Robertson, 2010). Yoon (2005) found communities with sizable numbers of older adults as a form of intangible assets. Delgado and Humm-Delgado (2013) identified four types of intangible assets: (1) historical (possession of an understanding of a community's history that is not recorded by formal authorities), (2) temporal (optimal time for events or interventions), (3) momentum (key factors and considerations have come together in a manner that seems improbable), and (4) hopes and dreams (aspirations).

Cultural Assets: This book's embrace of cultural capital as a central asset for baby boomers of color necessitates that it receive extra attention in this section. Social work embraces cultural capital in a way that few other helping professions do, which bodes well for its use in reaching out to baby boomers of color.

Cultural assets, for our purposes, can be defined as "the beliefs, traditions, principles, knowledge, and skills that effectively help people, particularly those who have been marginalized economically and socially, to persevere and succeed in spite of immense odds against them. The collectivity of these elements forms a groups' or community's cultural assets" (Delgado, 2007, p. 20). Thus cultural assets represent inherent strengths derived from beliefs, values, attitudes, and traditions that reinforce pride and identity. This broad definition far exceeds what we typically think of when discussing culture.

Bourdieu (1986) conceptualized cultural capital as falling into three categories or "states": (1) objectified state: poetry, writing, sculpturing, painting, music composition, tools and machinery; (2) institutionalized state: certificates and degrees granted by institutions of higher learning; and (3) embodied state: personal knowledge and know-how. McLaren's description of cultural capital places heavy emphasis on personal and group qualities and material objects or cultural artifacts: "Cultural capital can exist in the embodied state, as long-lasting dispositions of the mind and body; in the objectified state as cultural artifacts such as pictures, books, diplomas, and other material objects" (McLaren, 1998, p. 130).

Pollmann (2013) highlights the importance of intercultural capital and an ability to socially/culturally navigate across groups as a natural extension of Bourdieu's embodied state of capital.

In the case of baby boomers of color, cultural assets are contained within a generational set of experiences, attitudes, and expectations.

> Each generation occupies a unique position in the course of history, a position that endows its members with a particular perspective and set of experiences. . . . As a result of this shared location in history, there are things one generation of elders can understand and communicate with each other that are inaccessible to other cohorts. Only people who entered the stream of history together can share their view of the same moment in time. Thus, people of the same age need each other in a unique way, and where we find cohorts gathered we find resourceful people helping each other to grapple with the physical and social conditions that characterize old age.
>
> (Kirshenblatt-Gimblett et al., 2006, p. 34)

Social workers know the importance of culture to individuals, families, organizations, and communities. Culture, according to Yosso and Garcia (2007), is a source of strength that facilitates an oppressed group's survival and nurtures community resistance.

Cultural capital also can include other important dimensions, such as spiritual and/or religious assets. Hodge reports on the emergence of a new form of assessment focused on spiritual community assets: "Increasingly, social workers are being called on to conduct spiritual assessments, yet few assessment methods have appeared in academic literature. . . . Five complementary assessment approaches that have recently been developed to highlight different facets of clients' spiritual lives" (Hodge, 2005, p. 314). Hodge opens up an exciting new arena for identifying and mobilizing boomer assets. Spiritual/religious capital has served many boomers of color by helping them navigate difficult periods or challenges in their lives (Langer, 2004). This form of capital, when applicable, must be captured or assessed.

Cultural assets are dynamic and can be strengthened or weakened, appear or disappear, and be replaced. Viewing baby boomers of color from an assets perspective fits well within the tradition of the social work profession tapping strengths and community assets in assessment and interventions (Delgado & Humm-Delgado, 2013; Saleebey, 1992, 1996).

A cultural assets paradigm analyzes the level and nature of culture-of-origin involvement (Smokowski, Rose, & Bacallao, 2008). Biculturality (being able to socially navigate two cultures and draw upon cultural capital in both worlds) is an asset that is starting to be applied to boomers and older adults, no longer the exclusive domain of youth (Rodriguez, 2011). Bilingual ability is another form of human capital.

One of the many exciting aspects of a cultural assets paradigm is that it opens up vast new arenas for social work practice with baby boomers of color. A cultural assets paradigm provides social workers and other helping professionals with a conceptual frame through which to assess baby boomer strengths in order to understand their needs, expectations, and potential contributions to their community and society in general. Efforts to identify, support, and enhance these assets must take on significance in any concerted community effort to reach out to, and serve, boomers of color in a culturally competent manner.

Needs Addressed by Assets

Assets can be used to address instrumental, expressive, and informational needs of boomers and their communities. Instrumental needs refers to concrete needs related to well-being, such as health, transportation, interpretation/translation (non-English-speaking boomers), immigration (boomers who are undocumented), assistance with daily living activities, repairs and maintenance on dwellings, and errands. These needs may appear mundane to the uninitiated. However, as every social worker knows, instrumental needs must be met before others are addressed.

Expressive needs refers to psychological/social aspects of well-being, such as companionship, friendship, cultural affirmation, religion/spirituality, advice, and feelings of being valued, for example, that influence boomer self-confidence and sense of belonging. Finally, informational needs refers to aspects of daily life that necessitate data or information. In essence, information can refer to news of family back in the country of origin for boomers who are newcomers, politics, or events and activities occurring within the country that are of particular importance. The sources for meeting instrumental, expressive, and informational needs can cover multiple types of assets depending upon how these are defined within their respective communities.

Meeting these needs can play a crucial role in helping boomers of color live as well as contribute to their ability to remain embedded within their respective families and communities. Each of them is dynamic, increasing and decreasing in importance depending upon a host of personal and environmental circumstances. The presence and absence of assets will dictate whether needs go fulfilled or unmet.

Challenges in Using Assets

The use of an assets paradigm when working with boomers of color raises formidable, but not insurmountable, challenges. Some of these challenges are related to the newness of the assets perspective. Wheras the deficits approach has been in place, and highly subscribed to, for over a century, the assets perspective is still in its infancy. Other challenges, however, are definitional, conceptual, and financial. Five challenges will be addressed in this section, and they have been selected because they represent, to this author, the most immediate and significant barriers for impeding progress in this field.

Need for evidence-based research: The need for evidence informed social work practice has grown over the past decade and become prominent within the profession. However it has also raised considerable debate and controversy: For example, the question of what qualifies as "evidence" and the generalizability of research results across and within groups of color.

The importance of group-specific evidence cannot be underestimated. The danger of taking research findings from one ethnic or racial group and generalizing those findings across multiple groups raises serious questions about the efficiency and ethics of practice influenced by this research. When studying or using asset-based approaches, the diversity within and between boomers of color requires the development of interventions that are nuanced and highly contextualized.

Labor intensity: Practice involving assets is unconventional and labor intensive (Delgado & Humm-Delgado, 2013). Engaging members of a community who do not have a history of involvement with social workers and social service organizations (or, worse, with negative histories) is a complicated and lengthy process. For example, some boomers of color may not speak English or have cultural values and experiences that make them suspicious of organizations and governmental entities. The absence of trust is a major barrier for effectively engaging boomers and older adults in these communities. Consequently, typical methods of contact (e-mails, telephone calls, or formal letters) may be viewed as alien and ineffective, necessitating personal contacts and reliance on intermediaries or cultural brokers.

One effective strategy in this instance is to identify and involve formal and informal community leaders at the outset. They, in turn, are able to enlist the support of the community. The "old-fashioned" methods of establishing relationships are time consuming but ultimately the most rewarding and effective. The effort is best thought of as an investment that will pay off in future returns.

Finding ways of enlisting boomers of color in these efforts is one way of achieving multiple immediate and long range goals: (1) identifying and supporting community leaders, (2) tapping insider/informal knowledge of particular subgroups, (3) establishing a cadre of potential experts, and (4) enhancing the reputation of sponsoring organizations that can lead to other community engagement projects.

Language and cultural barriers: These can be an issue when working with boomers that do not have English as their primary language or have low levels of acculturation.

One way of conceptualizing is to think of acculturation as consisting of three developmental levels (Three Degrees of Acculturation, 2005): (1) largely unacculturated: newcomers born outside the United States who have been in the United States fewer than ten years; (2) partially acculturated: newcomers who have lived in the United States more than eleven years and speak their native language at home and English at work or in school; and (3) highly acculturated: these individuals are generally born in the United States and are either bilingual or English dominant in their language of preference. Each of these levels of acculturation influences how newcomers view their environment or surroundings, as well as their abilities to socially navigate in their daily life. Efforts to engage clients must be tailored to match their degree of acculturation.

Acculturation, however, has rarely been applied to boomers or older adults (Delgado, 2006). Miyawaki's (2013) study of Japanese American baby boomers and seniors, for example, found that despite being acculturated they preferred participating in mixed organizational environments that offered both Japanese-specific and nonspecific services and activities, raising implications for the importance of cultural factors in shaping organizational context and services.

Funding and documentation: The role and importance of funding for asset-based social work practice with boomers of color is, and will continue to be, a major challenge since most funding targets problems or deficits, as mentioned earlier in this chapter. Funding for asset-focused practice, as a result, often depends upon nongovernmental sources. Lack of funding, however, should not serve as an excuse to avoid being creative in providing needed support for these types of programs and services.

Documentation is a related issue, since funders often dictate the types of documentation required in order to approve funds. Since funders still emphasize deficits, intake forms and other mechanisms for gathering data typically emphasize problems, needs, and issues. This is not to say that this information is not important. However, information related to competencies, interests, levels of acculturation, aspirations, for example, rarely get captured and reported, limiting the picture that can be developed about boomer assets and a more well-rounded narrative of their existence.

Any attempt to gather data on assets necessitates the introduction of new categories of questions. Open-ended questions will take on greater prominence, and this type of information must be recorded in a manner that facilitates retrieval for reporting and evaluation purposes. It will also necessitate the training of social workers to purposefully seek and utilize this newfound information in the development of services.

Individual versus organizational relationships: This refers to the value many baby boomers of color place on relationships between individuals as opposed to relationships between individuals and organizations. Some boomers of color may relate to individual staff members rather than the organizations where they are employed.

An emphasis on individual relationships highlights the importance of personal engagement strategies and the role that trust will play in whether an intervention is or is not successful. It also stresses the need for social workers to be able to communicate in the language that boomers feel most comfortable conversing in.

OPERATIONALIZING AN ASSETS PERSPECTIVE

The following section will analyze three aspects of how to operationalize an asset-based approach with baby boomers of color: values and guiding principles, arenas, and practice methods.

Values and guiding principles: Assets come alive by operationalization of values through guiding principles. Delgado and Humm-Delgado (2013) identified seven values that lend themselves to helping practitioners and scholars operationalize the concept of assets: (1) empowerment, (2) self-knowledge/informal knowledge, (3) cultural competence, (4) community involvement, (5) social justice, (6) leadership development, and (7) community investment.

Social interventions are predicated upon values and principles that either explicitly or implicitly uphold a particular worldview regarding the origins of the client's problems and the necessary solutions. Interventions that stress greater transparency of values, however, facilitate an understanding as to why certain goals are emphasized over others, including why social justice is or is not a central feature of an intervention.

Arenas: Arenas, or settings, are places within a community where practice can transpire involving assets. These arenas can be formal or informal (nontraditional settings) in character and can consist of open spaces such as playgrounds, parks, and other natural settings; formal settings such as social service and educational settings; and places such as houses of worship, beauty parlors/barbershops, food establishments (restaurants and grocery stores), social clubs, gyms, and theaters. In essence, there is a need to embrace an expansive view of community settings that goes beyond conventional places often associated with human service delivery (Delgado, 1999), increasing the likelihood that engagement transpires where boomers of color feel comfortable.

Broadening practice arenas, however, brings a corresponding set of challenges for social workers, who either are not accustomed to working in "unusual" settings or prohibited from doing so by social agencies. Practicing in unconventional settings or arenas pushes the boundaries of social work practice, making administrators in conventional human service settings uncomfortable. However, it is my belief that the rewards far outpace the limitations or challenges in reaching boomers of color.

Practice Methods: Interventions bring theory to life and are the cornerstone of the social work profession. Theory, in addition, gives expression to values and principles that a profession holds and helps define its role and purpose in society. These values and principles must be explicit and, at minimum, stress the importance of dignity, respect, self-determination, social justice, and the embrace of participatory democratic ideals. In addition, practice methods must reflect a creative element that is sociocultural-ecological contextualized, as evidenced in the following examples.

Coffman (2002) explored the role of music in enhancing the quality of life for older adults. Brown, Novak, and Kitchener (2008) found music and storytelling to be important vehicles for engaging older adults of color.

Cultural traditions fulfill critical functions in the life of boomers of color: "Continuity in our life course is predicated on keeping a sense of who we are, who we have become, and what we value as we age" (Whaley & Paul-Ward, 2011, p. 25). Cultural traditions help people reinforce their identities in a world that often does not understand their traditions and values. Music, storytelling, and games, for example, are mechanisms for maintaining and transmitting culture and can be incorporated into successful interventions with clients for whom these cultural aspects are important.

Utilization of assets or capital provides a window through which we can see, and appreciate, the world of boomers of color, and their potential contributions to their communities and society, through a different light. Just as important, this perspective counters the prevailing deficit views of this population.

Social work has a long history of meeting a community's needs without losing sight of its attributes and indigenous resources. Other helping professions have started to see the value of this comprehensive view, which brings to the fore community strengths as well as needs. This view can be tremendously powerful when working with baby boomers of color.

The next chapter addresses the family and its potential to be a major asset or strength in the lives of boomers of color and their communities. Any concerted effort to understand the lives of baby boomers of color cannot be accomplished without also analyzing their families.

8

Family-Focused Assets

ASSETS, AS NOTED IN CHAPTER 7, can be found in all spheres of life. Cultural and other assets take a wide variety of forms, allowing for community needs and resources, or individual circumstances, to dictate which approaches have saliency for a particular client, community, or boomer cohort.

The family can be a particularly powerful asset in the lives of baby boomers of color. The crucial role of the family in communities of color, as well as an expectation that family members will play major caregiver roles in the lives of older adults, is well documented in the literature. The family is the most basic and arguably most important unit of organization in society. The family unit is often the foundation upon which social relations are learned, values inculcated, and human needs met. The role and importance of family must be viewed and appreciated within a lifespan perspective in order to understand its significance to baby boomers of color. Although much work has been done in the area of family relationships and aging, gaps do exist, particularly among families of color (Silverstein & Giarusso, 2010).

The family's importance increases as boomers enter later life (Fingerman et al., 2012). When a family is disenfranchised, economically constrained, or under severe stress, the consequences are far reaching for all age groups, but most particularly for boomers and older adults of color from economically marginalized backgrounds.

This chapter focuses on the importance of the family and four specific aspects: (1) grandparents raising grandchildren, (2) family support,

(3) transmission of cultural history and values, and (4) financial support. These four dimensions are not mutually exclusive and not equally represented in strength across all boomer families. Further, each of these aspects is dynamic in character. It is important not to romanticize or underappreciate families, and that is why attention will be paid to the rewards and challenges associated with viewing family as a boomer asset.

The aging process brings with it losses and gains as family members die and new members are added through marriages, births, and adoptions. There are challenges in thinking about families and boomers, and particularly those of color, from an asset perspective, however. These challenges will also be covered in this chapter in order to prepare social workers for this form of practice.

THE IMPORTANCE OF FAMILY

Waite and Das point out the importance of family in the lives of older adults:

> Families provide an important—perhaps the most important—context for aging. Although many older adults do not live in families, very few have no family members. Families bring resources like time, money, goods, and services to their members. Families also bring demands, such as claims on time, money, goods, and services. Family members offer instrumental and emotional support, information, and connections, but also introduce conflict, criticism, demands, and occasionally unhealthy or unhelpful advice or examples. Families offer connections to others in a web of supports and demands, . . . The experience of aging is quite different for women than it is for men for a number of reasons. Racial and ethnic groups also tend to follow divergent paths during later adulthood.
>
> (Waite & Das, 2010, p. S87)

When discussing family relationships, it is important to note that boomers should not be viewed solely as care receivers, because they are also potentially caregivers (Barrett & Blackburn, 2010). According to one estimate, roughly 13 million baby boomers are actively involved in caring for their parents (Greenblatt, 2007). The percentage of baby boomers of color caring for their parents is likely even higher because of the lack of viable formal alternatives that are acceptable from a cultural and economic point of view. Latino/a boomers are more likely (33 percent) to take responsibility for caring for their parents when compared to their African American and Asian counterparts (Belden, Russonello & Stewart, 2001). Asian boomers, however, have a higher likelihood of caring for both their parents and children. Those with such dual responsibilities have been called the "Sandwich Generation" (Cravey & Mitra, 2011). As will be discussed later in this chapter, it is also increasingly common to find boomer grandparents acting as surrogate parents to their grandchildren in low-income/low-wealth urban communities of color.

The demand for formal and informal caregiving is projected to increase as a result of longer longevity for the parents of boomers (Agree & Glaser, 2009; Rubin & White-Means, 2009). The increased physical, emotional, and financial stresses of caregiving that boomers face, however, can be taxing; the result is that boomers enter their retirement years in compromised health and economic positions when compared to previous generations (Anngela-Cole & Hilton, 2009).

Hoffman, Lee, and Mendez-Luck (2012), for example, found that baby boomer caregivers were at risk for certain behavioral factors associated with disabilities and chronic illnesses. Finkelstein and colleagues (2012) found that baby boomers that care for their older parents often do not plan for their own future long-term care needs.

Boomers can and do have a profound influence on the basic fabric and function of their families. Over the following pages we will examine four critical family roles often taken on by baby boomers, particularly those of color.

GRANDPARENTS RAISING GRANDCHILDREN

The importance of parents' nurturing children is well understood and cannot be underestimated (Silverstein, 2007). When parents are unable to handle the responsibility of child rearing (whether for financial, health, emotional, or other reasons), their children may be raised by the state or by other family members (known as kinship care). Neither solution is ideal. State care is often of poor quality and may undermine the basic fabric of the family and the community; kinship care often stresses families that are already hard-pressed to meet their own basic needs and may further compromise their well-being.

Weaver (2013) argues that grandparent caregivers have had a profound impact on the evolution of the family, which has gone largely unnoticed from a legal perspective. The average age of becoming a grandparent is forty-seven years, and, with increased longevity, it is not out of the question that grandparenting can cover a forty-year span (Orel & Fruhauf, 2013). This role becomes even more challenging when a child has a disability or chronic mental or physical illness. It is estimated that 50 percent of all adults aged forty and older in the United States now have an adult child with a serious illness, resulting in financial challenges throughout their lifespan (White & Beach, 2012). There is little question that there are rewards and drawbacks for both grandparent caregivers and their families (Bailey, Letiecq, & Porterfield, 2009; Pinazo-Hernandis & Tompkins, 2009).

Bengtson (2001) suggests that the conception of the American family is gradually expanding to include multiple generations and moving away from the more narrow image of the traditional nuclear family (parents and children). This transformation highlights the importance of grandparents and other family members who are fulfilling critical roles that traditionally were reserved solely for parents. Grandfathers, too, have started to receive increased attention in their own right (Achenbaum, 2011).

The role and importance of grandparenting within communities of color has historical significance and can be viewed from an assets perspective (Stelle et al., 2010). One study found that African American and Latino/a grandparents were more likely than their White, non-Latino/a, counterparts to have initiated and maintained a multigenerational household or be in what is referred to as a "skipped-generation" home (a household with absent parents) (*Huffington Post*, 2012).

Ince studied the importance of kinship care in African American families: "Kinship care is a survival strategy that has historical significance for people of African descent, because it is linked to a tradition of help and a broad base of support" (Ince, 2010, p. 1). Kinship care is a source of resilience that can greatly increase family preservation.

In general, of those children living with their grandparents, 41 percent are being raised primarily by their grandparents, and this translates into 2.9 million children. All ethnic and racial groups have been affected by this trend: White, non-Latino/as (3 percent), African American/Black (8 percent), Latino/as (4 percent), and Asians (2 percent) (Livingston & Parker, 2010).

High incarceration rates found in Latino/a and African American communities have often resulted in fathers (and increasingly mothers) who have been separated from their children for extended periods of time serving prison sentences (Delgado, 2012). This disruption can have a severe impact on children's social development. Boomer grandparents are often thrust into parental roles to maintain children of incarcerated parents within the family.

Mui and Shibusawa (2008) highlight the multifaceted roles boomers and older adults are expected to play within Asian American families and communities and how that benefits all parties. Models that tap grandparent knowledge and skills are currently being used to help bridge relationship and communication gaps between patients and helping professionals (Garson, 2009) and have the potential to be expanded into other arenas.

There is a tremendous need for policies, professional support, and community services to help grandparents minimize the negative impact of child rearing on their own well-being (Cox, 2009; Gerard, Landry-Meyer, & Roe, 2006; Hayslip & Goodman, 2008; Williams, 2011). Greater understanding of the diversity of this caregiver group is essential in helping grandparents assume the parenting role (Kropf & Kolomer, 2004; Park, 2009). Cox (2008) advocates for empowerment training for grandparent caregivers. Unfortunately, grandparenting is generally underrecognized and appreciated in this society (Kim & Antonopoulos, 2011).

Instrumental and Expressive Support

The support provided by the family can be extremely significant in the lives of boomers who face significant financial and social challenges in meeting their daily living requirements. Such support can be classified in two ways: instrumental support consists of housing, food, advocacy, and assistance with daily living in the case of boomers facing physical and psychological challenges. Expressive support generally entails actions that improve psychological well-being and provide a sense of belonging and caring, love and respect. Different cultures have terms for family caregiving. Among

Latino/as, for example, the concept of *familismo* is often used to convey a sense of mutual obligations and rewards (Delgado, 2006).

Lowman, Hunter, and Reddy describe the importance of family in the lives of older immigrants in North Carolina: "Older immigrants also demonstrate notable strengths, including spiritual conviction, a sense of community that is linked to their involvement in religion, and remarkable resilience in the face of continuing life challenges. Many maintain close relationships with family and engage family members in decision making" (Lowman, Hunter, & Reddy, 2008, p. 390).

Family support can be especially important when a family member has an illness. For example, Edgerly and Sullivan address the manner in which culture manifests itself in relation to dementia and family caregiving:

> Culture plays a role in the coping strategies used by diverse caregivers as well as the caregivers' perceptions of the situation. Cultural values, beliefs, and norms about caregiving as well as a sense of obligations to take care of one's elders appears to foster a more positive view of caregiving and the role of the caregiver in diverse communities. The sense of pride and fulfillment of an obligation, not surprisingly, could serve to decrease diverse caregivers' sense of need for help. A clear understanding of and respect for this would potentially alter how we promote certain formal services.
>
> (Edgerly and Sullivan, 2006, pp. 363–363)

Ruiz and Ransford, in their study of Latino/a elders' perceptions of familismo and health support, found shifting expectations: "Latinos have traditionally been portrayed as adhering to a familistic orientation with the presumption of duty and obligation to care for aging parents. Latino elders . . . shared ways they are reframing the familismo construct. Despite a greater need for support, elders reported infrequent contact with family. In the absence of family, family boundaries have been extended, so that others become 'like family to me'" (Ruiz & Ransford, 2012, p. 51). Similarly, in a study of older adults with HIV, Poindexter and Shippy (2008) found that their respondents defined "family" differently, incorporating individuals who were not biological or legal family members.

Gelman (2010) found that although the value of familismo is present among Latino/a families caring for older adults with Alzheimer's disease (AD), the physical and emotional stressors involved were overwhelming to some family members, many of whom had numerous economic and social stressors of their own. Gelman (2014), in a more recent publication, found familismo to be a complex concept when studying Latino/a Alzheimer's disease caregivers.

Financial Support

Given the harsh economic futures faced by many baby boomers of color, as described earlier in this volume, it may be difficult to envision boomers as providers of financial support for their families. Nevertheless, financial support can take various forms, such as the exchange of money, buying of groceries, and paying of utility bills, and often accomplished at great financial sacrifice for those who are low income.

The increased longevity reported in earlier chapters brings with it significant social and financial consequences. Nevertheless, social workers cannot assume that financial assistance cannot be provided by boomers and older adults of color.

Transmission of Cultural History and Values

Baby boomers can be a key source of cultural history and tradition for their children and extended families. Through vehicles such as photos, storytelling, music, and songs, for example, baby boomers can ensure that cultural values and stories are shared and remembered by the rest of the family. This is especially crucial in an age when many cultural traditions are not taught in the nation's school curricula.

Cultural knowledge can be transmitted in a variety of ways. Reminiscence (Lai, 2007), for example, is one common form of transmitting culture. McCoy (2011) brings to the fore the cultural transmission role of African American older adults and how this role gets carried out in family reunions, as well as the potential of these gatherings to serve as a forum for health promotion and development of other forms of interventions. Armstrong (2012) sees tremendous benefits for intergenerational efforts that bring history to life for younger generations. Boomers and older adults are able to share history of their communities and cultural backgrounds that is not available in textbooks. Oral history projects are one vehicle for younger generations to learn about their cultural and community history. Who better than boomers and older adults to provide this knowledge?

The popularity of dominos among Latino/as is one example of how culturally based traditions of games, for example, can be a mechanism for creating intergenerational relations that convey history, transmission of cultural traditions, and the teaching of math-related skills: "Spend some time in [Latino] neighborhoods and you will understand this leisure pursuit is not only a way to pass time, but it is also a link to people's culture. For some immigrants, the game is a link to their homeland" (Whaley & Paul-Ward, 2011, p. 22).

Challenges Facing Boomers and Their Families

Although the role and importance of family in the lives of boomers of color is recognized among practitioners and scholars, and boomers can play a supportive and culturally enriching role within this unit, there are challenges that must be acknowledged. While many families are sources of strength and resilience, some families can be the source of significant trauma and disappointment in the lives of boomers.

Five specific challenges will be addressed in this section: (1) changes in family composition, (2) sharing physical space, (3) health issues, (4) stressors specific to immigration issues, and (5) financial stressors. These challenges are not mutually exclusive, but will be considered individually.

1. Changes in family composition: Although boomer cultural values can serve as important sources of strength within their families, they can also cause tension and stress in families who are facing dramatic changes in the social environment. Today's families are dealing with tremendous geographical mobility, changing values, declining family size, increasing childlessness, increasing divorce rates, and increasing female employment rates. All of these factors lead to a lower likelihood of baby boomers having a spouse or adult child living in close proximity, thus lessening the availability of informal caregivers in their lives (Johnson, Toohey & Weiner, 2007; Ryan et al., 2012).

Kinney and Kart (2012) argue for the advancement of a family gerontological perspective that helps ensure that baby boomers and older adults be viewed within the context of their family to increase the effectiveness of interventions. The definition of family may vary considerably. Having friends or neighbors who are "just like family" is a good example. Consequently, social workers must never assume that there is but one definition of family. Effort must be made to have boomers define what constitutes family for them and note how this definition may have changed over a lifespan.

2. Sharing physical space: The 2010 US Census found that after fifty years of steady decline, household size has been increasing in recent years. This increase is the result of a variety of social forces, such as the recession and "boomerang kids" of boomers who left home and now are returning (El Nazzar & Overberg, 2011).

Postigo and Honrubia (2010) found that grandparenting brings with it a range of rewards for both caregiver and children, but it can also result in increasing tensions because of limited physical space within the home. Tensions resulting from increased proximity are exacerbated in the case of families of color because these are families that have more children than their White, non-Latino/a counterparts.

3. Health issues: This society's emphasis on individualism as a value results in a boomer's health being viewed from a narrow individualistic viewpoint. This perspective, however, fails to take into account how boomers of color often live within a family unit. Social supports within families affect chronic illness outcomes (Roseland, Heisley & Piette, 2012).

Waite and Das place the health of boomers and older adults within a familial context: "Families provide a key context in which health is produced and challenges to health are met. The health and well-being of each member depends on the health and well-being of the others, since the resources that family members command and the demands they make both depend on their health and functioning" (Waite & Das, 2010, p. S87). Consequently, health status is best viewed within a broader familial and cultural context.

Casado and Sacco's (2012) study of caregiver burden among family caregivers of older Korean Americans found caregivers to be more effective if interventions specifically seek to build family support and improve family agreement concerning treatment. Cultural values cannot be ignored; neither can patients be separated from their families in the decision-making process.

Health-seeking patterns of the family, such as how often they seek medical assistance, their expectations of what constitutes effective medical help, and where they go for this care, will have an impact on all members of the family. Families with proper health insurance and traditions of prevention will be in a much better position to address a boomer's illness than families with histories of poor health care, experiences with discrimination, and help-seeking patterns that emphasize emergency room care. Older adults are generally accompanied by family members during a medical visit. Wolff and Roter (2011), in a unique study of family presence during routine medical visits, found families to play an important role helping their relatives (boomers and older adults), with medical personnel providing more information while a relative was present.

Eggenberger and colleagues reflect on the role of the family in managing for a member with chronic illness: "Illness has been described as a family affair triggering families to shift their individual and family patterns as they attempt to manage ongoing life with a chronic illness. Family processes are central to the tasks and goals of a family living with a chronic illness. One in two families will experience a chronic illness in the next decade, hence it is important that research focus on understanding family processes that can influence health of the member with an illness and family health" (Eggenberger et al., 2011, p. 283).

Individual and family managed theory has shown the role and importance of the family unit regarding health and illness (Ryan & Sawin, 2009). As boomers of color continue to age and encounter an increasing number of illnesses associated with aging, the demands they make upon their families will increase, resulting in stressors that can compromise the health of family members as they struggle to have their own health needs met.

4. Stressors specific to immigration issues: As noted in earlier chapters, documented status wields considerable influence over a baby boomer's financial status, wealth accumulation, and health. A life of underground employment severely limits wealth accumulation and also results in limited access to health care and other services. Consequently, these individuals and their families are at an even greater disadvantage within their communities. The undocumented are at the lowest level, followed by those who are noncitizen immigrants, and followed by those who are citizens.

5. Financial Stressors: Burr, Mutchler, and Gerst (2010, p. 176) highlight the importance of solutions to the challenges of older adults of color (also applied to boomers) being tied to their family well-being: "One of the long-term policy solutions for improving the well-being of older adult members

of diverse racial and ethnic groups may be improving the well-being of children and young families" (Burr, Mutchler, & Gerst, 2010, p. 176). Long term can be conceptualized as a personal responsibility that requires planning for the future and reliance on family in the instance of those who did not plan (Edlund, Lufkin, & Franklin, 2003).

There is little wonder as to why the family has been identified as an influential asset in the life of boomers of color. The family is both a refuge and a source of inspiration and support for boomers. Boomers, however, are vital contributing members as well as recipients of family support. The dynamic nature of this reciprocal relationship taps into long-held cultural traditions and values that have evolved over centuries. Families, however, are not static units that are immune to social-environmental stressors. Consequently, these stressors threaten internal relationships, including the potential shifting of boomer influence and ability to provide aid during these stressful periods.

The following chapter focuses on the importance of neighborhoods and communities and further contextualizes the potential of boomers of color to be an asset, as well as draw upon assets found where they reside. In addition, this next chapter opens up new and potentially rewarding arenas for social work practice in reaching out to boomers and older adults of color, including the development of highly innovative programs and services that seek to build upon cultural assets and strengths.

9

Neighborhood/ Community-Focused Assets

CONTEXT HAS PLAYED A PROMINENT role in shaping social work practice and research. Hardcastle, Powers, and Wenocur (2011) compare the importance of context to the importance of location in the selling of real estate: "Location, location, location," is to real estate what "context, context, context," is to social work practice.

Neighborhoods and communities represent key elements of the way in which context is conceptualized in social work. The profession has a long and distinguished history of embracing neighborhoods and communities as the focus of interventions, the context from which to understand behaviors of individuals, particularly those who are undervalued by society. In essence, communities are an integral part of social work's history and future (Chaskin, 2013). This, however, is not meant to minimize the incredible conceptual and practical challenges that practitioners of community-based interventions face in reaching marginalized population groups (Hardcastle, Powers, & Wenocur, 2011; Reisch, Ife, & Weil, 2013). Fortunately, the rewards associated with community practice far outweigh the challenges.

This chapter builds upon the discussion of assets in the preceding chapters by examining the potential of baby boomers of color to make significant contributions to their communities and society through various forms of community service, referred to here collectively as civic engagement (Delgado, 2008; Kaskie et al., 2008; Perry, 2007; Saint Paul Foundation, 2007). Historically, civic engagement has been primarily associated with White, non-Latino/a, and middle-class and upper-middle-class groups who formally participate in organized programs (Delaney, 2012). This chapter will aim to broaden the discussion of civic engagement. As the reader will see, boomers of color can provide services to their communities either formally or informally, in traditional and nontraditional settings, and across the entire lifespan into later older adulthood (Delgado, 1999).

Even though there is widespread agreement concerning the potential benefits of civic engagement for boomers of color, their opportunities for formal volunteering may be limited, especially given their lifelong histories of low-wage employment. In essence, a subgroup of boomers cannot "afford" to volunteer because of financial needs or familial responsibilities. Monetary compensation, such as money for gasoline/transportation or meals, increases the likelihood of volunteering (Hong & Morrow-Howell, 2013).

Low-income and low-wealth boomers and older adults of color do not represent a sizable portion of volunteer corps, but arguably this has more to do with the lack of sustained efforts at reaching them, rather than unwillingness on their part to engage. African American/Black older adults are less likely than their White, non-Latino/a, and counterparts to volunteer. However, one study found that, once engaged, they can be expected to commit more time and enjoy perceived greater psychosocial benefits from volunteering (Tang, Copeland, & Wexler, 2012).

COMMUNITY AS CONTEXT

The use of community as a context for interventions of any kind is well understood in social work. Ammann and Heckenroth (2012) argue for the importance of intergenerational neighborhoods and the role that government can play in fostering connectedness between generations, with all generations and society as a whole benefiting from these relationships.

Similarly to family, community represents a lens through which we can better understand boomers of color and the significance of their contributions. However, unlike family, the concept of "community" as a unit of analysis is quite broad and consists of flexible boundaries and settings. This conceptualization, as a result, brings with it a host of rewards and challenges. Austin, Des Camp, and Flux, for example, advocate for a broader conceptualization of social work practice that encompasses an assets paradigm and community development: "Gerontological social work practice has been shaped in the context of health care, where workers attend to psycho-social concerns within the dominant medical model. A broader framework for gerontological social work practice is emerging, one that includes community development and new approaches to volunteerism. Older adults can be engaged in a variety of activities that build on their diverse backgrounds and experiences, creating community capacity and social capital" (Austin, Des Camp, & Flux, 2005, p. 1).

As a result of this broader conceptualization of practice, this chapter presents the reader with some of the latest examples of exemplary efforts to reach baby boomers within an urban community context, with special attention paid to baby boomers of color. Culp (2009) argues that baby boomers are unlike any other generation of volunteers, with different experiences and views pertaining to retirement and volunteering, necessitating different approaches toward civic engagement. This argument can also be applied to boomer subgroups without histories of formally volunteering.

Viewing boomers of color as assets within a community brings numerous rewards and challenges for the social work profession. Community practice is often very labor intensive and demands that social workers be prepared to find themselves in the middle of such arenas as community politics.

Social work's embrace of a socioecological framework and social justice values means that the profession must include community within any discussion of interventions, regardless of their focus (micro, mezzo, or macro). In essence, the profession cannot afford not to venture into communities, particularly when it seeks to reach out to marginalized groups, as in the case of low-income/low-wealth boomers of color.

CIVIC ENGAGEMENT: DEFINITION AND DIMENSIONS

The subject of civic engagement has received considerable national attention, even among baby boomers and older adults (Cole & MacDonald, 2010; Harvard School of Public Health, 2004; Morrow-Howell & Greenfield, 2010). Civic engagement is viewed as a way of spurring civic forms of participation:

> With a record-setting wave of older Americans now reaching retirement age, the demand for community services is growing at an unprecedented rate. But do communities across the country have the capacity to keep up with it? In fact, they do—although they may not yet realize it. While it's true that

some "young" older adults require support services, a large number remain vital, active, and socially engaged, constituting a rich pool of available talent. Many are highly skilled, and a significant percentage has managerial or professional experience. For nonprofit community-service organizations, they represent an abundant, burgeoning, and untapped resource.

(National Council on Aging, 2010, p. 3)

The professional literature on volunteering has been conceptualized as falling into two categories: (1) antecedents to volunteering and (2) the actual experience of volunteering. Wilson (2012) argues that the former has received the bulk of the attention. (One could argue that a third category, postvolunteering, could be added to address what happens to those individuals who stop volunteering.) Eisner and colleagues (2009), for example, estimate that one-third of those who formally volunteer in nonprofits do not return for the second year, resulting in an estimated $38 billion in lost labor for these institutions. Examining retention rates is an important topic on par with understanding how to recruit volunteers in the first place.

Not surprisingly, most volunteering is accomplished at the community level. Brown (1999) found that religious organizations, education, youth development, and human service organizations ("church, children and charity") accounted for 75 percent of all voluntary activity in the United States. It is estimated that 66 percent of boomer volunteers fifty-five and older got involved through their houses of worship, because they were asked, or as a result of children's activities (Culp, 2009).

The topic of civic contributions has expanded to take into account a growing older adult sector, particularly those entering the baby boomer phase (Elnolf, 2008; Freedman, 1999, 2006–2007; Rozario, 2006–2007; Wilson & Harlow-Rosentraub, 2009; Wilson & Simson, 2006). Van Den Bogaard, Henkens, and Kalmijn (2013) note that with a transition to retirement comes decisions and opportunities for civic engagement: "Retirement is an event that often brings about great changes in a person's personal and social life. For many people, work is not only a way to fill time and earn money, but also important for their identity and meaning in life. After retirement, these benefits of work are lost, and it is expected that people will seek substitutes for this loss."

Dr. Edwin Tan (director of the Senior Corps program at the Corporation for National and Community Service) raises an important question regarding boomers: "What we have with the transition of the boomers across the traditional age of retirement is a great opportunity. . . . The question for us is how we as a country cannot afford to mobilize this huge source of human capital to meet the vital needs of our communities" (Kerr & Biese, 2012).

Hales (2012) notes how older adults wanted to volunteer during the Mississippi Gulf disaster but could not due to a host of factors related to lack of opportunities, not being asked, and lack of accessibility to these efforts. A tremendous potential community resource was simply unable to help or simply overlooked. Morrow-Howell (2010) reviewed the research literature on volunteering in later life and concluded that it does not decline significantly until the mid seventies, with older adults volunteering more hours than their younger counterparts.

Friedman and colleagues, in a rare multiracial/ethnic study of boomers and older adults, found community and civic engagement to be perceived as beneficial by all the multiethnic and racial groups in the study: "Examples of community engagement included: joining discussion groups; volunteering; going to a senior center; shopping; singing at banquets; going to church; participating in Bible study; participating in school board meetings, golf, or bingo; and going out for dinner or coffee with friends. All participants stressed the importance of being proactive and getting involved in the community" (Friedman et al., 2011, p. 42). This list illustrates the wide range of activities that are community centered and can accommodate a variety of cultural traditions, interests, and opportunities.

Civic engagement activities can transpire in a variety of community settings. Anderson and Dabelko-Schoeny (2011) advocate for the use of civic engagement activities among residents of nursing homes, noting that there is no sector involving older adults that cannot benefit from civic engagement. Nevertheless, offering civic engagement opportunities does not necessarily result in getting and keeping volunteers.

Principles of Civic Engagement

The popularity of civic engagement has benefited from the development of practice principles. These principles, as noted in the work done by the National Council on Aging that follows, helps both define the dimensions of civic engagement and identify the most common goals associated with it.

Principles serve as a bridge between theory, research, and practice, as well as a guide, and possibly a moral compass, that can help practitioners in reaching and serving communities, such as baby boomers of color. For this reason, the author wishes to include ten principles for civic engagement among adults aged fifty-five and older, as identified by the National Council on Aging (Endres & Holmes, 2006):

(1) Integration and alignment of participant and organizational interests
(2) Valuing the assets of aging
(3) Building intentional relationships
(4) Creating empowered participation
(5) Learning as a pathway to engagement
(6) Developing capacity by actualizing leadership
(7) Embracing cultural competency
(8) Putting meaning into partnership
(9) Producing evidence and accountability
(10) Reestablishing the foundation of community

Each of these principles addresses key sociocultural dimensions of civic engagement. Enacting these principles helps ensure that organizations reach out to all sectors of the boomer community in the spirit of cooperation, mutual benefits, and affirming of cultural values.

Rewards of Civic Engagement

Civic engagement brings with it numerous benefits to the individual and community, which will be discussed over the following pages.

Individual benefits: As already noted, the concept of "productive aging" has stressed the importance of boomers and older adults remaining active in their retirement years, and continuing to occupy an important role in their community and society (Achenbaum, 2009). Productively engaging baby boomers of color brings with it a host of positive outcomes, such as increased functional status and self-rated health (Brown, Consedine, & Magai, 2005; Hinterlong, 2006) and even delayed mortality (Harris & Thoresen, 2005).

Psychological/social benefits: Boomer and older adult volunteers derive a great number of psychological and social benefits from civic engagement (Piercy, Cheek, & Teemant, 2011). In their study of older adults, Black,

Dobbs, and Young found that meaningful involvement in volunteering enhanced volunteer sense of self-worth: "The importance of 'making a difference' and 'giving back' are part of what matters most and enhances dignity and independence according to the community participants" (Black, Dobbs, & Young, 2012, p. 13).

Flatt and Hughes (2013) note that although research has shown that regular engagement in social activities is critical to maintaining cognitive health, researchers are not sure why this is the case. The role of enjoyment, or happiness, achieved through participation plays a prominent part in cognitive health. A better understanding of the elements associated with enjoyment and activities, including a cultural dimension, can have a significant impact in other spheres, too, including civic engagement.

The importance of psychological/social benefits, and more specifically cognitive functioning, is well understood. We do know, however, that informal helping, altruistic attitudes, and volunteering make unique contributions to life satisfaction and positive affect in later life (Kahana et al., 2013).

Physical/health benefits: The physical benefits of civic engagement can be significant, regardless of age, and wide-ranging (Rozario, 2006–2007). Ristau points out how social interaction increases brain health among older adults: "Research shows that people with regular social ties demonstrate significantly less cognitive decline when compared to those who are lonely or isolated. Some researchers believe that socialization boots brain reserve, and is an essential component of a brain-healthy lifestyle" (Ristau, 2011, p. 70).

Friedman and colleagues (2011) researched the views of boomers and older adults (African Americans, American Indians, Chinese Americans, Latino/as, Vietnamese Americans, and White, non-Latino/as) on how to stay "mentally sharp." They found that all groups, regardless of their language abilities and ethnic and racial backgrounds, agreed that social interactions and mental stimulation (particularly involving reading) were critical to maintaining mental sharpness. All groups also mentioned that community engagement resulted in benefits. However, Chinese and African Americans found this form of engagement particularly beneficial. Fuller and colleagues (2012) illustrate how a community-level demonstration project on awareness of cognitive function can be successful in reaching African Americans boomers and older adults.

Not surprisingly, there is reciprocity in volunteering with both the volunteers and those they help benefiting from this relationship. Tan and colleagues (2009, p. 304) studied older African American women volunteers and found that they had a higher likelihood of achieving increased sustained levels of physical activity, with important implications for civic engagement and health promotion. Swinson (2006) goes so far as to highlight the health benefits of volunteering as part of a recruitment strategy targeting boomers.

Community benefits: It is important to point out that civic engagement in communities of color can transpire in both formal and informal ways. The literature on civic engagement tends to emphasize formal efforts, such as volunteering with businesses or nonprofits, at the expense of informal efforts, such as community celebratory events (e.g., festivals, parades, heritage weeks) or neighbors helping neighbors, thereby providing a very limited understanding and appreciation on civic engagement. A comprehensive understanding of boomer civic engagement needs to examine all forms of boomer and older adult contributions to their community, formal as well as informal.

Four aspects of community benefits have been selected for special attention in this section: (a) mentoring, (b) owners of community businesses, (c) financial, and (d) religious institutions. Each emphasizes different rewards (monetary and nonmonetary), institutions, and activities and has great potential for innovative initiatives.

Mentoring: Taylor (2007) suggests ways that baby boomers and older adults can engage in mentoring. Chaudhuri and Ghosh (2012) advance the concept of "reverse mentoring" as a way of having boomers mentor younger generations.

Boomers can be role models. Denmark and Williams (2012) suggest that mentoring among boomer and older adult women can be a means of empowerment, as well as a way of giving back to their community. Bergmann (2008) advocates for mentoring by boomers in the legal profession. Stewart (2006) recommends that mentoring opportunities be made available for boomer nurses.

Clearly we are not at a loss for finding mentoring opportunities for those in the skilled professions. But what happens in the case of those boomers who did not work in white-collar jobs? Postretirement mentoring should not be relegated to professionals.

Owners of community businesses: Small businesses do not generally receive much attention from the social work profession, even though they often represent critical elements of communities (Delgado, 2011). Nevertheless, baby boomer owners of small businesses often can play influential roles in the life of the community beyond that of selling a product or a service. To successfully run a small business, owners should be actively involved in the life of their community. These individuals must be well respected and deeply rooted. They can be tapped for roles on community boards, advisory committees, and task forces.

Local businesses serving communities of color can play important roles in helping baby boomers. Carlton-LaNey and Washington (2009) address the influential role these small businesses play in the lives of African American older adults. Delgado (2011) addresses the role that Latino/a small businesses have played in their communities (including those that are owned and run by baby boomers) from the perspective of the range of services they often provide.

Small businesses often play a central role in the life of the communities they serve by sponsoring community cultural events such as fairs, parades, sports teams/leagues, donating food in natural disasters, and serving as a focal point for distributing important information to the community. Small business owners often contribute goods, services, and money to community organizations. It is not unusual to find them serving as a social broker for residents. Asian- and African American–owned small businesses have received considerable attention in the scholarly literature (Delgado, 2011). Their businesses, like those of their Latino/a counterparts, often give owners an opportunity to provide important social support, which can cast them as spokespersons and leaders in their search for social justice.

Financial: Contrary to popular opinion, there is a history and willingness for boomers of color to provide financial assistance that often goes unrecognized. African American charitable giving among baby boomers, for example, has yet to receive the attention it deserves (Carter & Marx, 2007). One Prudential study (2011) found that African American boomers have a greater likelihood (68 percent versus 55 percent) than the general population to cite charitable donations as an important element in achieving financial retirement goals. Unfortunately, similar studies regarding Asians/Pacific Islanders, Latino/as, and Native Americans have not yet been conducted. However, Banks's (2013) study of later-life decision making among Latinos in Southern California found that philanthropy was considered important in their lives.

Ho (2008) described Asian American giving circles, which pool together funds from various individuals and make donations to Asian American community organizations. Boomers play an important role in the decision-making process of these ventures. These efforts are predicated upon the embrace of cultural values that stress intergenerational and interdependent obligations. These types of organized efforts, however, generally go unrecognized by mainstream organizations and scholars and, as a result, are not factored in discussion of the financial contributions of baby boomers of color to their communities.

Religious institutions: Religious institutions often are expected to play influential roles within their communities. They are not restricted to serving spiritual or religious needs, however. Baby boomers may often be involved in volunteer opportunities through their religious organizations, which demonstrate the breadth of their civic engagement, and the potential for future involvement (Marler & Hadaway, 2002). Landau and colleagues (2013), for example, describe a long-term care model program for provision of sustainable spiritual care that relies upon leadership from a professional chaplain and taps into a pool of potential volunteers within respective houses of worship.

It is important to pause and note a distinction between spirituality and religion since not all baby boomers may be religious or spiritual, and this distinction has important service delivery consequences:

> The baby boomer generation or the "senior boomers" is a group that is as diverse spiritually as they are politically and socially. This poses a problem for many seniors and senior community directors. For the past several decades, one of the most common benefits listed for activities has been church services. Now, activities directors must consider a broader spectrum of spiritual options. They have to consider the spiritual but not religious baby boomers, baby boomers who converted to Buddhism, Hinduism, Sikhism and other non-Abrahamic religions during the 60s and 70s as well as secular boomers. So, what options should communities consider for this variety of spiritual beliefs since "church services" may not apply?
>
> (LivingSenior, 2012)

Consequently, an approach involving using spirituality or religion must be tailored to be most effective in reaching boomers and boomer subgroups. Carter-Edwards and colleagues (2011) argue that innovative models are needed regarding African American boomers and older adult health, and the Black church and Black clergy can play important roles in this area.

Houses of worship represent a promising community venue for reaching boomer and older adult women of color. Quinn and Guion (2010) advocate the use of faith-based and culturally competent approaches to promoting self-efficacy and regular exercise among boomer and older adult women. Religious settings have space, are nonstigmatizing, and often are geographically accessible to residents, facilitating their use for a variety of nonreligious activities.

Boomers can be providers as well as recipients of services, assuming leadership roles, for example. An assessment of their formal and informal needs and assets provides a comprehensive picture of this age cohort, including their current and potential contributions to their communities and society.

Organizational benefits: The budgetary restraints faced by many human service organizations will increase their reliance on volunteers in the immediate future as a way of maintaining staffing patterns and services (Piercy, Cheek, & Teemant, 2011). Organizations serving boomers of color will likely feel these budgetary constraints even more severely because of the wide range of health and human services they are required to provide, making volunteers that much more indispensable. Nevertheless, it is important not to view these volunteers as mere supplements to budgets, but rather as bringing innovation, energy, and purpose to the organization. Boomers bring a wide range of talents in addition to their time. Organizational benefits will be addressed through a focus on three types: (a) financial, (b) bold initiatives, and (c) empowerment.

Financial: A National Council on Aging (2010) study found that older adult volunteers provide an 800 percent return on investment for nonprofits. While this financial impact is considerable, one should also include the nonmonetary aspects of how they can influence community well-being. There is a propensity to measure the contributions of boomer and older adult volunteers from a financial perspective, particularly since that is relatively easy to calculate. There is a tendency to assign a minimum wage amount to volunteer services (although that may be significantly underestimating their financial worth). This wage perspective, although attractive to organizations wishing to quantify and promote their contributions to communities and society, and funders wishing to impress with how their dollars are being stretched, represents a very narrow interpretation of "worth."

Bold initiatives: Bold initiatives generate organizational excitement, energy, and high expectations, which can carry over to other organizational services. The need for bold new initiatives for program development that take an asset perspective toward baby boomers in general, and boomers of color in particular, is urgent (Delgado, 2008; Martin & Pardini, 2009; National Council on Aging, 2010).

Nonprofit institutions must facilitate the inclusion of boomers of color in a manner that is empowering and culturally competent (Tang, Morrow-Howell, & Hong, 2008), through leadership positions whenever possible. Organizations and older adult volunteers mutually benefit from their participation, and this mutuality must be exploited in the development of outreach and programming (Tang, Choi, & Morrow-Howell, 2010).

Empowerment: The concept of empowerment is one that has been around for several decades (Gutierrez, 1990; Lee, 1994; Solomon, 1976), and its appeal for groups that are marginalized is certainly well understood by the social work profession. However, I do not believe it has fully taken hold among boomers and older adults (Haber, 2009). (There are exceptions; McHugh (2012) specifically addresses the role and importance of empowerment for older adult women, for example.) Nevertheless, this "oversight" on marginalized boomers and older adults will no doubt be corrected as they, and particularly those with multiple forms of oppression, confront their marginalization (Mulbauer & Christer, 2012).

The benefits of empowerment, although widely applauded, are not easily measured. Nevertheless, empowerment can be a goal, process, philosophy, or outcome. The value of an empowerment stance, particularly among boomers and older adults of color, is critical to interventions. Tang, Copeland, and Wexler proved this to be the case when studying African American older adults, finding "that black older adults have more to gain from volunteer engagement and feel empowered through meaningful involvement in the community and improved physical and emotional quality of life" (Tang, Copeland, & Wexler, 2012, p. 89).

Challenges

The rewards associated with civic engagement must be tempered with an understanding of the varied challenges organizations will face in engaging boomers of color. These challenges are not insurmountable, but do wield significant influence in the implementation of innovative programs targeting boomers of color. Five challenges will be addressed: (a) caution, (b) finances, (c) healthy aging, (d) reaching and engaging, and (e) new models needed.

Caution: A word of caution is in order as we embrace civic engagement and boomers. Several scholars (Martinson & Minkler, 2006; Minkler & Holstein, 2008; Netting, 2011) raise cautions and concerns about how civic engagement and older adults is conceptualized and the importance of providing options for engagement on the part of those who cannot afford to volunteer because of their economic status. An inability to volunteer must not be equated with a lack of desire to do so, nor does it make boomers and older adults less "worthy."

Scholars have also raised serious questions about why older adults must be active in order to feel valued by society. Further, they argue for a broader interpretation of civic engagement to include social activism, citing the work of the Gray Panthers as an example (Sanjek, 2009). Delgado (2008) raises concerns about how nonprofits need to consider creative ways of engaging older adults of color with limited financial means and familial obligations. Walker (2005) also cautions us not to view older adults as free labor or a surplus labor pool that can be tapped at will without regard to their social and economic circumstances.

Finances: The prospects of encouraging boomers of color with lifetime low-income histories to volunteer raises a financial challenge that cannot be ignored. Efforts such as Title V of the Older Americans Act's Senior Community Service Employment Program has been successful in training unemployed boomers and older adults of color and is worthy of expansion to make it even more inclusive for engaging boomers of color:

> Title V of the Older Americans Act, the Senior Community Service Employment Program (SCSEP), is a 40+-year-old federal program providing subsidized community service and employment training to low-income,

unemployed individuals aged 55 and older. It is the only nationally man-
dated workforce training program for seniors. Because of SCSEP's dual
mission, participants added 48 million hours of community service (valued
at almost $1 billion) to the U.S. economy in 2008. Almost half (48.9%) of
the participants are racial or ethnic minorities, which makes it crucial to
understand the program experience of these individuals.

(Washko et al., 2011, p. 182)

Offering to pay boomer volunteers offers great promise for engaging boomers who cannot afford to volunteer but still wish to help their communities.
Healthy aging: Aging is a natural process that has physical, cognitive, social,
political, and cultural dimensions and is not a linear process (Barondess,
2008). One significant challenge for social workers will be to develop a
definition of healthy aging that is grounded within local circumstances,
culture, and takes into account a nuanced view of boomers of color and
their environmental surroundings. Further, practitioners must be prepared
in their definition to take into account the vast distinctions among boomers based on racial, ethnic, sexual orientation, and other factors.
Reaching and engaging: The importance of effective outreach and engagement cannot be underestimated. Reaching and actively engaging boomers
of color and older adults as volunteers is a challenge that is well recognized
in the field of gerontology. This challenge goes beyond identifying them
and bringing them into activities. It also involves engaging them in culturally based activities that are meaningful, lead to growth (educational, social, and psychological), and taps their talents and needs for meaningful
contributions to their communities.

Sundeen, Raskoff, and Garcia (2007) found that three key factors influence formal volunteering, all of which have implications for boomers in
general: (1) lack of time, (2) lack of interest, and (3) ill health. Sander and
Putnam (2006, p. 35) note that even if a small percentage of this age-group
volunteers, their significance can be great: "Given their large numbers,
even modest changes in the boomers' trajectory could have dramatic consequences. . . . All parents and grandparents should hope that these efforts
succeed as they will directly shape how civically nutritious a culture and
legacy our children and grandchildren will inherent."

Not being asked to volunteer is an important factor not touched upon
by many scholars focused on formal volunteering. One AARP study

(Bridgeland, Putnam, & Wofford, 2008), for example, found that 58 percent of the respondents have never been asked to volunteer.

McNamara and Gonzales (2011) examined volunteer transitions among older adults, including baby boomers, and specifically focused on the use of a capital concept, with specific attention on human, social, and cultural capital, as a way to better understand how these forms of capital facilitated volunteering. They found that increasing capital, particularly among those with lower socioeconomic status can result in an increase in volunteering activities and intensity. McNamara and Gonzalez concluded that "with regard to human capital, policies and programs that enhance older adults' educational levels, assets, and health are critical as these factors are positively associated with volunteering engagement and intensity and negatively associated with cessation. Enhancing human capital may also reduce volunteer turn-over and the costs associated with volunteer termination and training" (McNamara & Gonzalez, 2011, p. 499).

New models needed: Having boomers of color playing active and decision-making roles in community organizations necessitates the creation of bold initiatives that have participatory democratic principles guiding their focus. That, however, is much easier said than done. New models for initiatives are often reliant on an ability to "think outside of the box," with the requisite funding and time. Consequently, even though these types of initiatives are exciting and generate a great deal of energy and hope, as noted earlier, they also pose incredible challenges for the field.

Funding, of course, plays a critical role in launching and sustaining initiatives. However, the challenges in dictating restrictions and demands upon organizations go beyond funding and entail at least three significant types that help ground these initiatives in a comprehensive manner: (1) administrative support, (2) documentation to determine impact, and (3) requisite training/education of all participants, staff as well as boomers themselves.

Boomers of color have a prominent place within their communities and families. The existence of concepts and mechanisms for tapping volunteers offers much promise for the field. However, the field must be prepared to expand its definition of "community contributions" beyond the narrow confines of civic engagement and formal human service organizations.

Such a narrow lens does a disservice to boomers and older adults of color and their communities by ignoring the active and meaningful role they occupy. Their involvement in incidentally assisting within nontraditional settings goes beyond houses of worship and can include those that are deeply steeped in cultural history and traditions.

This chapter has highlighted the rewards associated with identifying, mobilizing, and incorporating community assets into interventions focused on boomers of color. The reader's appreciation of these assets, however, must not go without an understanding of the myriad challenges associated with this form of practice. The final chapters that follow in part 3 of this volume highlight policy and practice and research implications.

Implications for Policy, Practice, and Research

10

Classification of Asset-Driven Interventions

THIS CHAPTER'S PRIMARY FOCUS IS on helping practitioners classify examples of innovative efforts at the outreach, engagement, and assisting of baby boomers of color, with an emphasis on utilization of cultural assets. The previous chapters on family and community assets provided the reader with an appreciation of the range that can be found within these two arenas. Determining when and where to undertake these types of initiatives requires a community assessment.

Asset-driven interventions stress the role of empowerment and participatory democratic principles through partnerships between baby boomers of color and human service organizations. Further, asset-driven efforts also undertake community capacity enhancement in the process of engaging boomers of color in service to their communities (Delgado, 1999). They build upon community assets to significantly alter community environment to better serve and enlist the support of boomers of color.

Categorizing interventions in a manner that facilitates their understanding and use by practitioners represents an important step in shaping practice. There is a call for increased research specific to boomers of color because of the unique set of demographics and circumstances they bring to human services. Washington and Moxley (2008), for example, speak to the need for using innovative initiatives and programming, such as the arts and humanities, for developing a better understanding of homeless boomer and older African American women and why their perspective must guide service delivery to this vulnerable group. These types of initiatives have an increased chance of success when they are grounded within cultural values and actively seek the input of these boomers in shaping them.

Gilroy offers a simple but profound recommendation: "the starting point is listening to older people . . . the considerable potential of elders as a creative and active resource for the community can be released through innovative methodologies. . . . Policy makers, service providers and researchers need to be more imaginative in promoting methods that fuse product and process: in working with older people in these creative ways these methods can also make a contribution to quality of life. Older people are increasingly looking for voice in their communities" (Gilroy, 2006, p. 354).

CLASSIFYING AND EVALUATING PRACTICE

Categorizing asset-focused boomer initiatives plays a critical role in facilitating the introduction and support of this paradigm for social work. Fortunately, an increasing number of ways to classify these types of initiatives is available. Lehning (2012), for example, based on a meta-analysis, developed a typology that assigns older-adult initiatives into five categories that can then be used for evaluation and sustainability efforts: (1) communitywide planning, (2) consumer-driven support networks (peer groups), (3) cross-sector systems change initiatives (interagency collaborations), (4) residence-based support services, and (5) single-sector services. Their typology, with certain modifications, can be used for conceptualizing and implementing a range of asset-focused boomer of color initiatives.

There are other classification typologies that can be tapped to assist practitioners in developing boomer-focused initiatives. Delgado and Humm-Delgado (2013), in their book titled *Asset Assessments and Community Social Work Practice,* for example, have laid out a conceptual foundation for classifying assets and identified the assessment methods that lend themselves to gathering this form of data, also empowering and increasing community participation in the process.

CLASSIFICATION TYPOLOGY

The following three-part classification and seven-point criteria for evaluating practice holds much promise for the field. As the reader will see, they bring rewards and inherent challenges, as any framework would. Practices can be categorized into three classes: (1) best practices, (2) promising practices, and (3) emerging practices. Determining into which of these three categories to put a particular practice is not simple, as the decision often requires a judgment call. Nevertheless, these three categories can assist practitioners in better serving boomers of color by identifying challenges and gaps in evidence.

Best practices: Most social workers and other helping professionals are well versed in the concept of evidenced-based practice and the importance of using evidence to shape interventions. The concept of evidence-based practice is an integral part of our lexicon, although not without controversy. The Council on Social Work Education has stressed the importance of evidence in determining social work content covered in social work departments and schools (Franklin & Hopson, 2007). Social workers, however, may not be familiar with the following concepts of promising and emerging practices.

Promising practices: Promising practices refers to interventions that have all the elements associated with effective practice but have not benefited from research validation and extensive scrutiny by impartial reviewers. When these programs are reviewed, if the evidence warrants, they will be classified as evidenced based. There is still work to be done, using research to substantiate these practices, but their promise makes this investment worthwhile.

Emerging practices: Finally, emerging practices represents innovative interventions that are new and capture excitement, reflecting the best principles and values associated with practice. These interventions, however, have not been subject to independent research and review but still show signs of effectiveness and resonate with communities. With closer attention and research, emerging practices may eventually fall into the promising or even best practices category. Nevertheless, they are not there at this point in time.

EVALUATION CRITERIA

Cummings and colleagues (2011) identified seven criteria that can be applied to best, promising, and emerging practices: (1) culturally appropriate, (2) effectiveness, (3) impact, (4) replicability, (5) scalabilty, (6) sustainability, and (7) innovativeness. These criteria are of equal importance; however, practitioners and organizations may emphasize some over others. Ideally, interventions can be assessed using all seven.

Culturally appropriate: Social workers are familiar with a cultural criterion. Interventions that are guided and incorporate key elements related to culture and assets, such as language, values, symbols, acculturation, and legal status, meet this requirement. All of the examples discussed in the following chapter integrate various cultural elements to reach and engage boomers of color. Interventions that are culturally appropriate are sufficiently nuanced to take into account local circumstances and are sufficiently dynamic to also incorporate changes in culture over time.

Effectiveness: This criterion relies upon research findings substantiating the goals and objectives of an intervention. Effectiveness is associated with evidence-based data; the role and importance of data cannot be underestimated in an age where measurable results are so critical in program funding and program development. Further, these findings must have been published in scholarly outlets to add an additional measure of "worthiness" or legitimacy.

Impact: Interventions often are measured based upon how successfully they alter the lives of the population group they target. A weight-loss nutrition and exercise regimen, for example, should actually result in the loss of weight. It isn't enough to measure participant's attendance in a program or how well participants enjoy a program; the program must actually deliver results.

Reliability: The ability of an intervention and its results to be duplicated or reproduced among new clients and/or populations is very important, particularly when discussing interventions that are funded as demonstration projects. Achieving this measure is predicated upon a sufficient number of projects being studied to facilitate translation of findings. Unfortunately, the examples of asset-focused projects with boomers of color have not advanced sufficiently to achieve the goal of replicability. The challenge associated with a nuanced approach that is specifically tailored to account for unique aspects of boomer ethnicity and race stands out as to why replication is so arduous and necessary.

Scalability: Flexibility in program design size becomes an important consideration in order to allow local circumstances (e.g., agency history, budget, characteristics of community) to dictate the nature and scope of an intervention. All the interventions covered in the next chapter should be sufficiently flexible to be implemented in a variety of locales.

Sustainability: Social interventions must be sensitive to the need for communities to rely upon them over a period of time. It takes a considerable amount of time to create positive organization-community relations. Consequently, organizations must endeavor to develop programs that will be in existence over an extended period. These interventions, as a result, should not be capital intensive, but should instead be structured in a manner that encourages collaboration, local contributions, enlistment of volunteers, and a minimum reliance on extensive financing.

Sustainable efforts to reach and engage boomers of color requires social workers and their organizations to venture out into communities and develop collaborative relationships with a wide range of formal and informal, or nontraditional, settings. The role and importance of collaboration is well understood in human service sectors, but so are the challenges of getting two or more institutions to work together in pursuit of a common goal. Nontraditional settings are starting to get attention in relation to boomers, both as settings for boomers to obtain needed information and as possible places where they can be recruited for civic engagement in the formal sector.

Current efforts have attempted to offer social and health services through houses of worship in African American and Latino/a communities. Delgado (2008) advocates for boomers and older adults of color to be enlisted in planning and leading health promotion efforts within houses of worship. These institutions are accessible (geographically, psychologically, culturally, and operationally), making them very attractive. Robbins (2012) recommends that service providers not overlook libraries as settings for reaching out to baby boomers carrying out caregiver roles because these are places they patronize and feel comfortable with. Barbershops and beauty parlors have been nontraditional urban settings that have pioneered highly innovative services that are gender specific (Delgado, 1998). These efforts have illustrated the immense potential that nontraditional settings bring to reaching and engaging at-risk population cohorts in manners that are nonstigmatizing. Collaboration serves many different purposes and facilitates the sharing of resources and experiences as well as the reduction of costs.

There are a variety of ways of thinking about consumer-driven initiatives. The concept of older-adult led is without question the most empowering and participatory manner in which to bring these types of asset-focused initiatives to life (Delgado, 2008). The vast majority of baby boomer asset-focused interventions in this chapter can be considered sustainable.

Innovative: Asset-based interventions are by their very nature innovative and will probably continue to be considered as such. A "business as usual" approach will not be successful with this cohort.

The use of a classification typology and development of criteria for assessing programs provides a handle for practitioners and academics in helping to determine the rewards and challenges associated with various forms of intervention. Initiatives that can lend themselves to evaluation and replication will survive and prosper; those that cannot survive will face hurdles and may eventually not survive.

The introduction of an assets perspective on boomers of color brings great potential for innovation and the excitement that often accompanies bold new approaches. Unfortunately, bold new approaches also bring resistance to change and cause anxiety, and this can be coupled with the presence of racism, classism, and ageism to make these changes in thinking and service delivery that much more arduous to accomplish. This chapter has provided a broad overview, furnishing brief examples, of a way to classify innovative initiatives that tap boomer of color assets.

As covered in this chapter as well as previous ones, embrace of an assets perspective toward boomers of color serves to strengthen the social work professions' abilities to make significant contribution to this group and their community. All population groups benefit from an assets perspective. However, boomers of color that are marginalized by society stand to make the greater gains and even greater contributions. The following chapter provides the reader with policy for, practice in, and research implications of embracing an assets paradigm.

11

Policy, Practice, and Research Implications

EMBRACING A VIEW OF BOOMERS of color as possessing assets and strengths that can be incorporated into practice opens up a new world for social workers, along with numerous corresponding challenges. The future relevance of the social work profession lies in responding to emerging issues and opportunities, such as how the field addresses a "graying and browning" population.

The field will be ill prepared for the multitude of challenges in reaching and engaging boomer subgroups if it views the entire generation as a monolithic cohort. The profession's ability to position itself strategically, including its willingness to take an open-minded and collaborative approach to boomers of color, opens up countless opportunities for innovative practice. This chapter outlines the implications and challenges for social work in meeting the projected needs of baby boomers of color over the next decade, and doing so while tapping their strengths and assets through an embrace of democratic participatory principles associated with social justice.

Gillick (2007) identifies the potential contributions that boomers can make to society, and themselves, if they enter retirement with the right frame of mind and requisite competencies/resources. If retirement is viewed as an end-stage without concrete plans for life beyond, the potential outcomes are negative. However, if soon-to-retire boomers embrace a paradigm that views this stage as an opportunity to reinvent themselves and embark on a new personal mission, then they are much more likely to realize positive outcomes. Boomers of color with lifelong low-wage jobs that provided an income, but minimal or no job satisfaction, are provided with an opportunity to engage in a new mission that is self-satisfying and rewarding for others.

The following recommendations for policy, practice, and research are an attempt to identify and support the potential key contributions of baby boomers of color. Finally, a special section on nursing homes will address the potential role they can play in being ready for future residents of color. These recommendations must be addressed and viewed with the classification and criteria covered in chapter 10.

COMMUNITY AS A FOCUS

The role and importance of community must be recognized and supported when attempting to tap boomer assets and increase their well-being (Kroff, 2012). The initiatives covered in this chapter all have community as a central context in mobilizing boomer assets. However, this centrality does not diminish the conceptual and practical challenges associated with incorporating community into initiatives (Delanty, 2003).

McDonough and Davitt (2011) emphasize the important role community can take in reaching boomers and older adults and advocate for the use of a "takes a village" model of community:

> Not all aspects of aging in place can be addressed via volunteer services or at the community-level. Likewise, not all older adults will choose to remain in a particular community and thus a continuum of options is needed. We are not proposing a devolutionary response to long-term care services, whereby the community becomes the focal point and main provider of service. Rather, we are suggesting that Village initiatives have a role to play in supporting aging in place by expanding access to critical resources within communities and raising awareness of the need for long-term care. The rapidly-growing Village movement has presented a new community-based service medium for older adults who choose to age in their communities.
>
> (McDonough & Davitt, 2011, 539)

Killett and colleagues (2010) identify the need and challenge of providing cost-effective community-based long-term care systems for boomers and older adults with mental illness, for example. These community-based services help minimize the social isolation associated with the stigma of having a mental illness diagnosis. Bartley and Bartley (2011), in a Canadian study of quality-of-life outcomes among Alzheimer's disease family caregivers, found community-based interventions to be promising in meeting the multifaceted needs of caregivers.

Kerz, Teufel, and Dinman (2013) describe the impact of OASIS, a national nonprofit organization that stresses community-based programs focused on successful aging for boomers and older adults. Community is not only a context for services (Rowan, Faul, & Birkenmeier, 2011), it is also a context for research informing services. Valle, Garrett, and Velasquez (2013), for example, address dementia and the need for locally derived data on Latino/as for development of community-centered programming and services. Regardless of the need being addressed, community must take a prominent role whenever possible because it increases the likelihood of assets being mobilized in service to boomers—and for having boomers play important roles in these initiatives.

PREVENTION

There is a national and international call to increase prevention programs for baby boomers (Buckley et al., 2013). While prevention programs typically center around health issues (such as preventing obesity and thus hopefully avoiding the diseases that it can cause, for example), for the purposes of this discussion prevention will go beyond a narrow definition of health. Prevention can also apply to maintaining adequate housing, income, and companionship, for example. These areas wield considerable influence in shaping boomer well-being. Prevention programs can help address future boomer health care costs, as evidenced by the initiatives launched by the Administration on Aging (Tilly, 2010). However, a focus on financial costs should not come at the expense of humanitarian costs, for boomers, their families, and their communities.

Waidmann, Ormond, and Bovbjerg identified five prevention strategies that have a potential impact on boomers (as well as younger populations): (1) diabetes prevention, (2) smoking cessation, (3) HIV prevention, (4) multifactorial community initiatives (nutrition and physical activity), and (5) targeting health disparities. The authors, however, go on to issue a caution that bears noting: "It is important to note that we do not purport to reduce disease prevalence from current levels, but rather to simply slow the current rate of growth largely by preventing some fraction of new cases. Even with reductions . . . by 2030 each disease will have increased in prevalence, albeit by less than would have been the case without modeled reduction" (Waidmann, Ormond, & Bovbjerg, 2011, p. 3).

Prevention programs can tackle a vast number of quality of life issues. Buckley and colleagues (2013) stress the importance of prevention in reducing obesity and sedentary behavior. Kim, Szabo, and Marder (2012) highlight the importance of prevention of fractures, a common occurrence in aging groups. Hebert et al. (2013) focus on the importance of early detection of Alzheimer's disease. McCullion, Ferretti, and Park (2013) draw attention to preventing financial abuse and exploitation of boomers and older adults. Finally, prevention of prescription medication and alcohol abuse is an important issue for many boomers (Benza, Calvert, & McQuown, 2010). Prevention takes on great prominence in the lives of boomers of color with health disparities.

FINANCIAL LITERACY AND RETIREMENT COUNSELING

Many boomers require assistance with the economic aspects associated with retirement, including financial guidance. This assistance takes on even greater importance in the case of boomers of color with lifetime low wages who, unlike their middle-class and upper-middle-class counterparts, have never had the benefit of financial counseling. The broadening of social work practice to encompass financial guidance represents a new dimension to practice.

This is not to say that social workers must become financial advisers. However, they must possess a working knowledge of this field and have access to financial adviswrs who can provide in-depth advice. Financial-related services can encompass one or more of the following: (1) development of user-friendly software to explore retirement planning, (2) improvement of financial literacy education to increase understanding and motivation, and (3) creation of programs to encourage greater savings (Brucker & Leppel, 2013). Other helping professions are assisting boomers with their retirement decisions. Adams and Rau (2011), for example, address the role that psychologists can play in helping boomers better prepare for transition to retirement.

Wilson and colleagues (2009) argue for social workers to play important broker and advocate roles in helping boomers navigate financial spheres.

Social workers are in an excellent position to aid in this retirement transition because of our knowledge of community, and community resources, which can be marshaled to aid boomers. Birkenmaier, Sherraden, and Curley (2013) stress the importance of social workers being financially literate, with implications for work with marginalized groups such as boomers of color.

SUPPORTING CIVIC ENGAGEMENT

Social workers and human service organizations would be irresponsible if they did not actively provide boomers of color with meaningful options for further serving their communities and society. Supporting civic engagement also means supporting lifelong learning because of the training, consultation, and other supports associated with services.

The encouragement of new models of civic engagement is needed since this generation is unlike any previous generation and the country has changed so dramatically socially, economically, and culturally. These models must take into account sexual identity, racial and ethnic backgrounds, cultural values and acculturation, and the financial needs of boomers of color. There also is a call for civic engagement opportunities to be tailored to the needs and expectations of boomer men and women, considering the influence of gender (Moon & Flood, 2013). As has been previously mentioned, these new models for civic engagement must have some form of financial supports for boomers who retired but have done so from jobs which were low wage.

Providing assistance to low-income/low-wealth boomers and older adults in securing employment and volunteer positions that pay a stipend or wages is a role that ties into social work's historical mission of working with the economically disadvantaged: "By reducing barriers to employment, people may discover an underutilized path to well-being for low-income older adults and the communities in which they live. This is especially important for those living closest to the cusp of poverty and at greatest risk of disparities in health and well-being. By increasing the understanding of employment for low-income older adults, moving aging to the forefront, forming strong coalitions, and finding champions to advance the issue, social workers have an opportunity to be a leading force in this worthy national effort" (Anderson et al., 2013, p. 332).

Another critical way to support boomers is to have curriculum on civic engagement and boomers/older adults in schools of social work and other helping professions. Welleford and Netting (2012), for example, advocate for the integration of aging and civic engagement into curricula as a means of better preparing helping professions face the growing challenge of meeting the needs of baby boomers and older adults.

ROLE OF HUMAN SERVICE ORGANIZATIONS

Human and social service organizations represent the cornerstone of any formal service delivery system (Furman & Gibelman, 2013). These institutions often represent the focal point of policies directed at specific population groups. These organizations, in turn, must resist the forces that emphasize the status quo and instead represent a willingness to entertain new ways of conceptualizing and delivering services to reach undervalued groups, such as low-income and low-wealth boomers of color.

The Corporation for National and Community Service challenges organizations to think creatively about engaging baby boomers: "To attract Baby Boomers to volunteering, experts on aging agree that nonprofit groups and others must boldly rethink the types of opportunities they offer—to 're-imagine' roles for older American volunteers that cater to Boomers' skills and desire to make their mark in their own way. This is vitally important to ensuring that the potential of this vast resource is tapped to its fullest" (quoted in Eccleston & Priestman, 2007, p. 4).

Increasing responsiveness and effectiveness in reaching marginalized subgroups within the boomer population remains a goal that all human service organizations must strive to achieve. The development and support of a service infrastructure that is prepared to meet the diverse cultural and linguistic needs of boomers is probably the biggest current challenge facing the field of gerontology (Beach & Langeland, 2010; Culp, 2009; Cummings et al., 2011; Williamson, 2008b; Weaver, 2011).

Effectively serving boomers requires new models for outreach and engagement that are responsive to the social, economic, and political realities of the early part of the millennium. Creation of a supportive organizational environment requires a comprehensive and ecologically sensitive examination of how transition to retirement for a subgroup of a generation that has, with notable exceptions, faced incredible challenges to survive to the age of retirement.

Cultural competence from a multifaceted perspective will play an influential role in this transition:

> As both the workforce caring for aging Americans and the aging population itself grow more diverse along multiple dimensions, the need for increased awareness and understanding of cultural factors also increases. In fact, the care demands for the aging—often extending beyond brief encounters into extended episodes of home or nursing care—heighten the need for cultural competence. Interventions to enhance cultural competence can and should be embedded in broader efforts to enhance communication skills both within the workforce and with aging clients.
>
> (Parker, 2010–2011, p. 97)

Although the importance of cultural competence is well recognized in social work, its importance will increase in significance as boomers of color seek services: "Our 'one size fits all' service model is outdated and becoming increasingly irrelevant. Yet, current challenges such as downturns in the economy and backlash against immigrant communities make it even more difficult to uphold the social contract and continue to provide services to all members of our society" (Stanford, Yee, & Rivas, 2009, p. 187).

Senior centers need to make dramatic changes in order to be more attractive to boomers and those of color if they are to remain viable for this new generation of older adults. Racial and ethnic diversity factors, for example, wield significant influence on types of activities and composition of participants (Giunta et al., 2012). "Significant concerns exist that current senior center programs will not appeal to baby boomers, making it difficult to recruit them as either volunteers or participants" (Jensen & Little, 2008, p. 4).

There is a need for research to increase our understanding of the influence of diversity within senior centers (Giunta et al., 2012). How will senior centers respond to an ever increasing membership with preferences for languages other than English or food that appeals to a wide variety of ethnic groups? The answer will have profound social ramifications for senior centers across the country.

Cultural competence is about human service organizations meeting the unique cultural values and preferences of boomers of color in the interest of providing relevant and effective services. Cultural competence, in addition, is a dynamic concept that needs to respond to an ever changing context and environment and take into account the role of oppression in all aspects of assessment and intervention development. In this sense, cultural competence cannot be separate from social justice.

Participatory democracy is also an essential element of organizational empowerment and cultural competence. The degree to which boomers want to play an active role in the decision-making process related to health care, for example, highlights significant differences based upon cultural values (Levinson et al., 2005). The extent to which health-related organizations incorporate boomers into their decision making goes a long way toward making these institutions effective.

The role of alternative and complementary medicine also enters into boomer health-seeking patterns and this, too, must be understood by health providers, particularly those serving boomers of color who are newcomers (Senzon, 2010). Consequently, service delivery models that can incorporate alternative and complementary medicine hold much promise for reaching boomers and older adults with low levels of acculturation, and these must be supported from an organizational perspective.

Social work and other helping professions will be called upon to successfully help baby boomers of color transition into older adulthood and access the services that are often needed in this life stage. Jacobsen and colleagues, as addressed in chapter 3, make an important observation about the importance of demographic characteristics shaping the baby boomer experience as they enter retirement: "Baby boomers transformed U.S. age structure and society as they moved through each life cycle stage, and they will do so again as they enter retirement. It is not only their sheer numbers that will determine their economic and social impact, but also their characteristics" (Jacobsen et al., 2011, p. 14).

The need for innovative thinking with regard to serving and engaging boomers in general and those of color in particular will determine the success or failure of older adult serving organizations in engaging this cohort (National Council on Aging, 2010). Institutions that serve older adults need to be creative in how they structure and deliver services that are attuned to boomers' cultural values (Gonyea, 2009). This book represents one effort at helping to bridge the gap between current older adult services and the needs and assets of a new generation.

RESEARCH

Research will play an influential role in shaping programs, initiatives, and services targeting boomers of color, as specifically addressed in chapter 10. More attention must be paid to racial and/or ethnic factors, for example. We can also change how social workers undertake research to inform our practice. Crewe (2004), for example, challenges social workers to undertake ethnogerontological research as a way of informing practice that is culturally competent and responsive to social-ecological forces. Cultural competence, however, must go beyond ethnicity and race and address sexual identity, abilities, and factors such as acculturation (Muracz & Akinsulure-Smith, 2013). Research sensitive to community context is particularly relevant in helping social workers understand and address the needs of boomers of color within a comprehensive context that does not ignore assets.

The use of participatory action research (active and meaningful participation and decision making of residents) offers much progress for use with boomers and older adults, as it has with other marginalized groups (Blair & Minkler, 2009). Moxley and Washington (2013), for example, describe the use of a highly innovative community participatory research approach toward homeless boomer and older adult African American women, stressing personal support and social action. Just as important, research that furthers our understanding of strengths and assets brings an added and much needed perspective.

Scharlach and Sanchez (2010) present an innovative model that bridges the divide often found between research and practice involving Latino/a older adults, but has applicability for boomers and other seniors of color. Their project commenced as a community-participatory needs assessment and evolved into a collaborative model for engaging this undervalued population.

The use of photovoice (an arts-based research method that relies on images and narratives on the part of the individual taking the photographs) with baby boomers has great potential, but has generally been overlooked, with a few exceptions (see for example Rosen, Goodkind & Smith, 2011;

Yankeslov et al., 2013). Photovoice has enjoyed a tremendous amount of popularity across multiple undervalued or marginalized groups (Delgado & Humm-Delgado, 2013). This form of research can be used to assess needs, and is founded upon empowering and participatory principles. Digital storytelling, too, offers much promise to capture the voices of boomers whose lives have been overlooked but have much to share about their experiences (Lambert, 2012).

SOCIAL WORK EDUCATION

Social work education must assume an active role, if not one of leadership, in shaping how helping professions meet the current and projected needs of boomers of color. There are no facets that are exempt; in this section, however, I will highlight some of key importance.

Building the capacity of the profession to address issues of finances (Birkenmaier et al., 2013), for example, is of critical importance, as addressed earlier in this chapter and book. Their transition to retirement requires careful attention to their financial needs (Jokela, Hendrickson, & Haynes, 2013). These needs, incidentally, have profound impact on their families and communities (Delgado, 2011). In essence, helping professions need to embrace a socioecological view of these boomers.

Boomers, it should be reemphasized, may be both caregivers as well as care receivers. Toseland, Hagler, and Monahan (2011) stress the importance of caregivers and the role that education can play in helping providers as well as caregivers themselves. This attention, however, must be tailored to the sociodemographic characteristics of caregivers because they are not monolithic. It must also take into account the types of illnesses they are helping with. The heavy emotional and physical toll taken on cancer caregivers, for example, can manifest itself in health issues (Goodheart, 2012), calling for interventions to support these caregivers. Alzheimer's disease caregivers, too, face risks for health consequences (Mausbach et al., 2013). Many caregivers face stressors unique to the illnesses they are caring for.

The role and importance of nontraditional settings in the lives of boomers and older adults of color set the stage of social work education initiatives involving these institutions (Delgado, 1999). Development of field placements in social agencies that are currently in a position to engage nontraditional settings as part of outreach, education, and service provision helps prepare social workers for practice with boomers. These efforts at establishing innovative education and service models can be modified for reaching other groups that are marginalized and invisible.

Social work–focused initiatives targeting boomers of color, in similar fashion to the Hartford Geriatric Social Work Institute (Hooyman, 2009), can serve to produce practitioners and scholars with specific competencies to reach this population group. International and cross-cultural opportunities in gerontology open up opportunities for scholars and students to broaden their perspective of boomers (Martin et al., 2012).

Ferguson and Shriver issue a challenge to social work gerontologists to narrow the structural lag that exists in this field of practice, and this certainly has implications for how the profession addresses boomers of color: "To best prepare for the future needs of the older population and for gerontological social work, social work leadership must be more involved in dialogue at the national level about policies that effect the growing older population. . . . To be engaged at the policy level, social workers must be informed about the issues that contribute to the lag including issues of supply and demand, professional turf, skimpy evidence base, and role definition" (Fergusan & Shriver, 2012, p. 318).

Provision of scholarships and stipends targeted specifically to prepare a cadre of social workers for practice in the twenty-first century are urgently needed. Providing opportunities at key social work practice, research, and education conferences, too, will highlight the importance of micro, mezzo, and macro practice and scholarship focused on boomers of color. Having social work faculty interested in the boomer cohort will influence student interests in this group (Wang et al., 2013). These and other special educational initiatives will help the profession assume a leadership role in service to this age cohort.

THE DIGITAL DIVIDE

The increased prominence of technology and social media will continue to wield influence in the lives of boomers as they age: "Computers and the Internet offer older adults resources for improving health. For many older adults, the 'Digital Divide' (the social, economic, and demographic factors that exist between individuals who use computers and those who do not) is a barrier to taking advantage of these resources. Bridging the Digital

Divide by making computers and the Internet more accessible and making online health information more usable for older adults have the potential to improve health of older adults" (Cresci & Jarosz, 2010, p. 455).

The digital divide is particularly pronounced when examining lifetime low-income boomers of color, even though technology and social media can play a positive role in keeping them in contact with distant relatives, giving them access to health and social services, and providing them with an opportunity to achieve lifelong learning (Cresci, Yarandi & Morrell, 2010a, b; Gilmour, 2007).

Older adults (65+) have the lowest rate of using the Internet for health information. Those that do go online are typically White, non-Latino/a, have postgraduate education, medium to high income, and possess a computer with a broadband connection (Campbell, 2004, 2009; Campbell, Nolfi, & Bowen, 2005; Fox, 2006; Losh, 2009). Yet Campbell's study found that the Internet could have multiple benefits for boomers of color: (1) it assists them in understanding better their particular health needs, (2) this information does result in self-care, (3) health information results in behavior changes related to eating and exercise patterns, and (4) the information aids in the treatment they are receiving (Campbell, 2009, p. 195).

Use of assistive technology in health care and in the home, for example, is severely limited in the case of those who are of color (Lemke & Medonca, 2013; Pavel, Jimison, Wactlar & Hayes, 2013; Wickramasinghe & Goldberg, 2013). Healthcare technologies will play an increasingly more important role in the future, but bring with them increased challenges for subgroups (Choi, 2013; Czaja et al., 2013). The information age is here and will continue to increase in importance in the future. Getting boomers of color connected will help them in multifaceted ways that include their health.

HEALTHY AGING INITIATIVES

Paradigms that emphasize health and aging will see an upsurge in practice and academic popularity. A national thrust toward healthier living applies across the lifespan, and helping professions have been quick to mount initiatives stressing these goals. The public health profession, for example, has specifically addressed the needs of baby boomers (Williamson, 2008a). Talley and Crews (2007), in turn, view caregiving as an emerging public health issue and acknowledge the complexity of this construct when applied to baby boomers.

Healthy aging initiatives can be conceptualized as falling under a health promotion rubric. They stress activities that can assist baby boomers in successfully transitioning to older adulthood in an optimized healthy shape. Healthy behaviors and thought patterns at age fifty can impact how boomers feel, and act, at age eighty (Hartman-Stein & Polkanowicz, 2003). Seven arenas for initiatives have been identified that have particular significance for baby boomers: (1) not smoking, (2) adaptive coping style, (3) not abusing alcohol, (4) maintenance of a healthy weight, (5) stability of marriage or relationship, (6) exercising, and (7) education to prevent cognitive decline. How these initiatives get translated to reach boomers of color remains to be determined, and the success of these types of efforts will rest in the way in which they take cultural and environmental factors into account.

Many of these behaviors can be traced back to adolescence or even earlier, making the starting of new and more healthy behaviors that much more difficult to achieve. Environmental forces, too, will be important. Access to healthy foods, for example, is not universal; many marginalized urban communities are considered food deserts (Delgado, 2013).

LONG-TERM CARE, NURSING HOMES, AND HOSPICE CARE

It is appropriate to end this chapter with an emphasis on long-term care, nursing homes, and hospice care. Taking an asset perspective on services for boomers of color introduces the potential of these services being culturally transformed to incorporate these older adults in shaping how they are planned and implemented. Medicare was not designed to meet long-term care needs, increasing the importance of tapping boomer assets (Edlund, Lufkin, & Franklin, 2003).

The introduction of a cultural competence/cultural humility perspective makes their participation more relevant and helps increase the likelihood that human services reflect the priorities of these individuals and are integral to their lives and the communities in which they reside. The cultural context associated with race and ethnicity brings a dimension that makes it much more challenging to meet the health needs of boomers when health systems are predicated upon individualistic values (Herrera et al., 2012). Reliance on individualistic values as addressed in the discussion of individualistic and interdependence perspectives on older adults, effectively renders the cultural values of boomers of color a significant barrier to quality health care.

The need for long-term care will increase dramatically in the next forty years, with an estimated 27 million needing this service, up from 15 million in 2000 (Johnson, Toohey & Wiener, 2007; Katz, 2011; Knickman & Snell, 2002). However, a growing long-term care workforce crisis is occurring whereby there are significant shortages of skilled direct service workers to care for a growing older adult population (Cangelosi, 2011; Harahan, 2010–2011), particularly one that is monolingual in languages other than English. Liu and Zhang (2013) examined disability trends among boomers and older adults and found growth of disabilities and growth of unmarried older adults, projecting an increase in national long-term care system needs, particularly among African Americans.

Konetzka and Werner's (2009) study of racial disparities in long-term care found that use of this service has increased, but the quality of care has not. Ng (2010), too, found disparities based on gender, race/ethnicity, and socioeconomic status. Guzzardo and Sheehan's (2012) study of Puerto Rican elders found that as reliance on informal care provided by family decreases, there is a corresponding increase in the need for formal long-term care.

Growing demographic representation and unequal access to home and community alternatives, for example, play an influential role in increasing the number of baby boomers of color, particularly Asian and Latino/a, who will enter nursing homes in the next decade (Feng et al., 2011; Portner, 2011). Herrera and colleagues (2012) raise concerns about how Mexican boomers and older adults can have their needs met within a cultural context as Mexican families decrease in size and women find work outside the home, necessitating greater reliance on long-term care options.

The period of 1999 to 2008 witnessed the number of Latino/as (54.9 percent) and Asians (54.1 percent) in nursing homes increasing dramatically (Feng et al., 2011). African Americans, however, are still less likely, when compared to White, non-Latino/as, to enter nursing homes (Akamigbo & Wollensky, 2007). Latino/as with lower income and fewer assets when compared to White, non-Latino/as are still reluctant to utilize nursing homes, however (Kim & Chiriboga, 2009). The baby boomer influx brings an increased need to make nursing home activities culturally competent (Boyd-Seale, 2008), as well as making nursing homes that much more attractive for those who cannot stay at home.

The importance of nursing homes in institutionalized care further heightens the urgency (Eskildsen & Price, 2009). Parker and Geron raise concerns about the field being able to meet the needs of boomers of color in nursing homes as they age: "The influx of the baby boomer generation will reform the long-term care industry, and the needs of ethnically/racially diverse baby boomers will play a significant role in the reformation. In as much as nursing homes are the primary provider of institutionalized eldercare, examining their ability to serve diverse populations is warranted in light of the changing elder demographics" (Parker & Geron, 2007, p. 37).

For those boomers of color who may elect to use nursing homes within their communities, this has become an even greater challenge. Closures of nursing homes have been particularly dramatic within low-income urban communities (Katz, 2011). Further, the quality of care in these institutions is inferior to those outside of these communities (Fennell et al., 2012; Smith & Feng, 2010). If boomers of color must leave their neighborhoods to enter a nursing home, which is not an attractive option from a cultural-familial point of view, it will make it more difficult for their families to visit them and deprive the neighborhood of the opportunity of interacting with older adults.

The subject of sexual identity and boomers of color will increase in significance as this group enters assisted living, for those who can afford it, and nursing homes, for the majority. Their lived experiences in these institutions, including negotiating family dynamics in situations where support for their sexual identity is less than optimal, will challenge how these institutions engage in culturally competent services.

One study of midlife and older lesbian, gay, bisexual, and transgendered adults found that they are less likely to have a legal caregiver and more likely to be a caregiver to someone that is not a legal caregiver, too, than those who are heterosexual in orientation (Crogan, Moone, & Olson, 2014). These caregiving arrangements represent an important element in their lives and will be severely compromised as they enter alternative institutional living arrangements.

There is a recognition that gay, lesbian, bisexual, and transgendered boomers will face incredible social pressures if they are moved into older adult facilities that are either not prepared to meet their needs or are unwilling to do so because of homophobia. Consequently, retirement communities targeting gays and lesbians, for example, are starting to be developed to meet their specific needs (James, 2012). These establishments are relatively expensive, limiting those who can afford these settings as alternative living arrangements. How many boomers of color will find these settings attractive and welcoming remains to be determined.

Development of alternatives to nursing homes will prove challenging for all helping professions involved in this industry. There is virtually no sector of the human service field that will not be confronted with these challenges (Harahan & Stone, 2009). Pharmacy, for example, faces a crisis because only 1 percent of this nation's pharmacologists are certified in geriatrics (Gray, Elliott, & Semla, 2009). In addition, since a high percentage of boomers of color live in urban areas, such settings will experience these challenges to a greater degree than other geographical areas.

Use of hospice care among older adults of color has been very limited, raising questions about how boomers of color perceptions will influence future utilization of this service. Asian Americans and Pacific Islanders with cancer, for example, have a lower likelihood of using hospice care when compared to White, non-Latino/as, even though cancer is the leading cause of death in these groups (Ngo-Metzger, Phillips, & McCarthy, 2008). This underutilization has also been found among Latino/as (Bullock, 2011; Carrion, 2010; Carrion & Bullock, 2012) and African Americans (Dillon, Roscoe, & Jenkins, 2012). More specifically, underutilization among Mexicans is particularly troubling as this is the largest group of Latino/as starting to enter the boomer years (Gelfaud et al., 2004). It is estimated that they numbered 33.7 million in 2012 (Pew Hispanic Center, 2013).

Ko and colleagues (2013) identified five categories that address concepts of good and bad death among Mexican American older adults, casting death within a cultural context. These categories address the importance of no suffering, living life with faith, having time for closure with family, dying at home, and experiencing a natural death. Death must be viewed within a cultural context as a way of integrating cultural sensitivity for families and those in end-of-life care. Although their sample consisted of individuals in their mid-seventies, a comparable study of boomers is needed to see how their views of good and bad deaths evolve or remain the same as they enter older adulthood, with implications for hospice care utilization. The subject of death and its cultural meaning needs to be explored in other ethnic and racial groups.

As the reader must now realize, the profession of social work can position itself strategically to play an influential role in helping baby boomers of color transition into retirement, although what this new stage of life looks like is certainly open to new interpretations and debates. However, regardless of how this life phase is conceptualized, boomers of color will be unlike any of their predecessors, offering a unique set of rewards and challenges for their families, communities, and society.

Although it is essential to view boomers of color within a humanistic perspective, there is no denying how economic factors are shaping discourse on their current state. However, current and projected economic aspects are dominating political discourse and corresponding policy decisions. The need for a nuanced understanding of these boomers, while requiring considerable effort, must be grounded in a socioecological context that may be drowned out by an economic-political and deficit perspective that overlooks the needs of this group. Nothing short of such a concerted effort will suffice in helping the profession carry out its historic mission of reaching and serving this nation's marginalized groups.

AN EPILOGUE PROVIDES AUTHORS WITH opportunities to raise issues that remain either unresolved or are particularly controversial for the profession as we embrace an assets paradigm toward boomers of color. Some of these issues emerged through the process of writing the book. However, others were predictable and, based on daily events in the country, painfully obvious.

The field of gerontology must make a concerted effort to recruit, train, and support social workers that reflect the racial and ethnic composition of baby boomers of color. This necessitates development of special initiatives that recruit a cadre of social workers interested in this group into graduate school and the field of gerontology, preparing those who are not of color to undertake culturally competent practice with this growing cohort. However, this charge must be viewed against a backdrop that is increasingly antithetical to older adults and national concerns about budget deficits and debt.

Older adult-serving institutions, too, must undertake special efforts to develop outreach and service provisions that consider the cultural values, traditions, and language preferences of baby boomers of color (Cummings et al., 2011). These efforts, it should be emphasized, must take into account the unique talents and needs that boomers bring, and organizational leaders should not automatically think that this new group will just mix into the fold of existing services. The literature is quite clear that this age cohort is different than any of those that preceded it.

Fiscal constraints combined with concerns about the "excessive demands" of baby boomers in general, and those of color in particular, will make funding these initiatives controversial. Nevertheless, the sheer size of the boomer generation of color cannot be ignored from a policy, research, and practice perspective. The increase in boomers of color with language preferences other than English necessitates a workforce better able to meet their service needs in their language of preference. A total of eleven issues have been highlighted, although the reader can no doubt debate these issues and substitute others not covered.

1. Racial disparities, racism, and boomers: The primary focus of this book is to highlight boomers of color from an assets/strengths perspective. The reader, I sincerely hope, has gained new insights into and appreciation for this topic. The backdrop to this focus will find the ugly head of racism and other forms of oppression for boomers of color, with multiple jeopardies operating to shape the social, wealth, and health status of this group.

As social workers, we are well versed on the pernicious nature of racism and how it compromises the daily existence of people of color of all ages. Addressing racism is part of the National Social Work Association's Code of Ethics. A socioecological perspective on this subject serves to illustrate how discrimination in one sphere or arena translates into deleterious consequences in other areas, as in the case of discrimination in housing, for example.

The dismal socioeconomic circumstances that the vast majority of boomers of color face necessitates that we as social workers, practitioners and academics, never have the luxury of dismissing these forces in our assessment of and recommendations for working with boomers of color as they transition into retirement, for those fortunate enough to have this as an option.

2. Aging as a social-cultural construct: Age is in the eye of the beholder. Ours is a society that views age from a chronological standpoint and attaches profound social meaning to it as well. Aging, however, is a natural developmental process that must be viewed through a social-cultural lens. The social work profession understands this viewpoint and why social interventions must be predicated upon the perspectives (values, beliefs, attitudes) of those we wish to reach. Nevertheless, this perspective must play out against a backdrop that often equates aging with sickness and death.

As emphasized throughout this book, current popular definitions over-whelmingly stress that to age successfully we must continue to remain active, preferably through continued employment or civic engagement. However, tying aging to economic productivity is such a narrow, and I and many others would argue, capitalistic viewpoint and limits our understand-ing of the myriad ways that civic engagement can be realized. Aging, in addition, is not a disease that we can medicalize and in the process make considerable profits on; this view limits the role the profession can play in helping boomers transition into older adulthood and retirement. Boomers, regardless of their ethnic and racial backgrounds, are an expanding market for all kinds of rejuvenation products and surgical procedures that seek to keep them feeling and looking young. Aging is no longer associated with wisdom, but increasingly looked at from a deficit perspective.

The commercialization of aging that goes hand in hand with defining successful aging as looking and feeling younger further stigmatizes those boomers who cannot afford the products and medical treatments necessary to make them look and feel younger. These older adults, it must be noted, have suffered the consequences of poor medical treatment and employment in sectors that take their toll on their physical appearances. Some critics of this viewpoint would go so far as to argue that we must continue to work in order to afford the products and medical procedures associated with pos-sessing a "youthful appearance."

3. The financial future of the nation is at stake: It is a sad state of affairs to put the entire burden of the financial future of this nation on one genera-tion, as in the case of boomers, and blame them for a future economic crisis that will forever alter the nation. The term *greedy geezers* seems to capture this state of mind. A false argument has been made that the boomer gen-eration got the nation into this trouble (debt) and it is only right to have boomers get us out of it through acceptance of blame and personal sacri-fice. This false argument has been addressed in numerous sections among the chapters of this book. The current debate about the nation's debt ceil-ing, and the need to control current and future costs, must be a shared gen-erational responsibility that does not single out a particular age group.

Nevertheless, an emphasis on individualism and self-sacrifice for the good of the nation will have a disproportionate impact on boomer sub-groups that can ill afford to make economic sacrifices through lower Social Security payments and limiting access to quality health care. The argument that an expanding economy will result in increased payments into the Trust Fund, along with adjustments to eligibility and payments, can help ensure that current and future beneficiaries benefit.

4. Making the invisible visible: As social workers, we have confronted the insidiousness in the way in which society makes marginalized groups disappear from public discourse on policies and then makes them reappear when it is advantageous for making a point about policy. Invariably this rediscovery results in a blaming-the-victim consequence. The concept of blaming the victim is etched in every social worker's vocabulary and captures this perspective very well. A focus on baby boomers of color makes this age group appear as if out of the blue, but in the process opens them up for possible targeting. However, empowerment and the resulting social change that can transpire when groups become visible are, in and of themselves, empowering.

Social justice values and principles, as a result, aid social workers in crafting interventions and launching advocacy and system change efforts that highlight the unique strengths and challenges facing boomers of color in a changing society. These values and principles help the profession navigate socially and politically through heated debates about Social Security and Medicare, for example, because, as already noted in chapters 2, 5, and 6, these boomers share unprecedented challenges in having their economic and health security needs met in the forthcoming years.

Making baby boomers of color visible, however, must not focus on or highlight their needs. This is not to say that we cannot give voice to these needs. However, we must also focus on their contributions and assets—a central message of this book. Do we have a definitive understanding of these assets? No. However, no marginalized group, regardless of its marginalization, consists of nothing but needs and problems. The fact that it has survived and, in some cases, preserved its cultural heritage, must not be lost on the social work profession and society.

5. Diversity and the challenge of reaching boomers: The quest and need for health and social services to be culturally competent is one that we as social workers are well versed in. This goal, however, will in all likelihood be undertaken against a highly charged political background that finds it increasingly easier to create different types of warfare between groups, be they racial/ethnic, age, socioeconomic class, sexual identity, or gender. The increasing diversity among the ranks of boomers necessitates that the

profession and organizations wishing to serve them be cognizant of how increasingly diverse this group has become and avoid painting a picture of boomers that is simplistic and monolithic in composition.

We cannot group African Americans, Asians, Latinos/as, and Native Americans into broad categories without concerted efforts to examine how gender identity, immigration status, acculturation, and place of residence (urban, suburban, rural) impact on their well-being, how they define themselves, and how their communities view them. Further, communities of color are not monolithic in composition, thereby requiring serious efforts at considering "place" as a key factor to go along with other sociodemographic factors in developing a picture of boomers of color.

Social work has understood the meaning and importance of sociocultural context (space and place) in helping the profession respond to current and projected needs. This nuanced approach toward boomers of color is a necessity for social work and other helping professions to understand the situation many boomers of color find themselves in and what is needed to help them achieve the multifaceted aspects associated with well-being. Diversity is increasing in our society, and the importance of "keeping up" with new and varied ways of understanding groups of people will also increase in significance in the future as the nation continues graying and browning and new groups enter the country.

6. The future of social insurance: What does the future hold in store for advocates of social insurance and social contracts in the United States? Hopefully, our future will be different from that of Europe, where efforts to limit social insurance in scale and scope are gaining traction (Walker, 2009) in attempts to address fiscal deficits and debt.

There is no question that baby boomers, Social Security, and Medicare, will be part of the debate in post-2012 presidential elections and congressional campaigns and may be part of the political landscape in even more distant elections because so much is at stake for the nation. *Entitlement reform* is very much in our vocabulary as social entitlements get debated in political arenas. Who "loses" and "wins" must not be lost to view, because there surely are winners and losers.

Any effort to significantly alter expectations of boomers will have profound social, economic, and political consequences that will reverberate throughout all sectors of this country. These efforts must be sufficiently nuanced to take into account their impact on all sections of the population rather than paint a population group with a broad stroke. Further, boomers of color do not exist in isolation from their families and communities. The impact of these changes cannot be viewed from a narrow scope.

7. Social work values and boomers of color: The current debate about the future of Social Security and Medicare strikes at a basic set of social work values pertaining to social justice that guides us and serves as a moral compass to where we stand as a profession. It is of critical importance that the profession not lose sight of how social justice values serve to ground interventions and advocacy efforts. Unfortunately, as noted throughout this book, proponents of drastic changes to social insurance programs have eschewed any reference to values, although their arguments do embrace implicit ones.

Our abilities to help broaden the discourse on boomers or color, and those most vulnerable within the boomer generation, will help silence or counter the chores of naysayers associated with the "graying" and "browning" of this country. Aging is a natural progression that must not be stigmatized and politicized in national discourses. Our work with this group will help put voices and faces to the numbers that are often bandied about without regard to the stories of population groups that are often invisible, or scapegoated, in our society. Baby boomers of color that are low income and low wealth are such an example. Debates on changing the retirement age or reducing benefits will have a disproportionate impact on boomers of color.

8. A nation of immigrants will again be a saving grace for the United States: This country's demographic composition evolved over many decades and has been a strength rather than a weakness for the nation. European countries that have systematically worked to exclude immigrants are now struggling with replenishing their ranks because of low birth rates as their societies continue to gray in record numbers, resulting in great concerns about the future of these countries (Daley & Kulish, 2013). The United States is in the enviable position of not having to struggle to replace its aging and dying population because of the role immigration has played in the distant, and not so distant, past.

However, the politicization and criminalization of immigrants has profound short- and long-term consequences for boomers and older adults, with certain sectors of the country where they reside in significant numbers being more adversely affected than other regions. Criminalizing groups of individuals who are law abiding when the only "crime" they have committed is to be in this country unauthorized raises important social justice issues for the profession.

The ability of Congress to develop an immigration policy that is non-punitive will go a long way toward helping these newcomers, boomers and nonboomers, to enter the American mainstream and play an even more active role in contributing and shaping this country in the twenty-first century. The outcome of the debates on immigration, as this book goes to press, will impact current and future generations of newcomers and the communities they live in, not to mention society overall.

9. Evidence-based practice and boomers of color: The unique position that boomers occupy in the life cycle presents a challenge for researchers since they can be considered "middle-age" as well as older adults. The increase in longevity also calls into question those age stages that historically were also closely tied to retirement age. The unique position of boomers, in turn, has been made that much more challenging because this cohort, as countless number of scholars have argued, is unlike any generation that preceded them and has a sizable portion that is of color. Consequently, any effort at developing interventions founded on evidence-based results must take into account the unique cultural and linguistic background of this population, as covered in chapter 10.

The cultural viewpoint of boomer and older adult is rarely taken into account in examining the role of age in self- and community perceptions. How does the cultural heritage of the boomer influence how they, and others, view them, particularly their potential contributions to the well-being of families and communities? In essence, entering "boomerhood" cannot be solely based upon chronological age, although in this society it is.

Evidenced-based practice, as a consequence, necessitates assuming a more nuanced approach, and sensitivity, in order to capture the role that culturally-based values play in shaping help-seeking patterns and reactions to social interventions. Such an approach, although widely acknowledged, necessitates having the funding and time to carry out a carefully planned evaluation. A broad-stroke approach, so to speak, cannot provide the findings that are necessary to make intervention meaningful.

10. Age warfare, class warfare, race warfare: There is little disputing that we live in a nation accustomed to all kinds of warfare. However, bringing age, class, and race to the battlefield, so to speak, is a new form of warfare. Unfortunately, that is where we are headed as a nation. The intersection of

these three demographic factors presents what is arguably one of the biggest challenges this country is facing, with terrorism taking a distinct second in the next decade.

Tankersley's (2012) article, titled "Generational Warfare: The Case Against Parasitic Baby Boomers," in the *National Journal* highlights why a warfare metaphor is not hyperbole. Berger (2010), too, issues a call out to baby boomer haters: "Self-loathing is a Boomer characteristic, and Boomer bashing a sport for all the other generations. Boomers, in fact, are both scapegoat and piñata, the cause of all misery which is relieved only by swarming them with blows using a very big stick."

The popularity of metaphors, particularly the use of the silver tsunami, crystalizes the role of language in shaping opinions and perspectives. Barusch provides an important insight into the use of the silver tsunami metaphor: "In the Pacific we have experience with tsunamis: great walls of water that destroy or displace everything in their path and then recede, leaving nothing behind but rubble, salty mud, and broken lives. There's nothing human about a tsunami. It's a nasty metaphor for older adults" (Barusch, 2013, p. 181). Andrea Charise (2012) points out that "'it testifies to the barely conscious figurative language that serves to construct perceptions of an aging population'—inaccurate, damaging perceptions, at that."

It becomes critical for helping professions to weigh in on the debate and not allow economics and politicians to control the discourse. We are in a propitious position to put faces and stories to those boomers who are most vulnerable and faceless in this debate. This country has historically viewed older adults with a degree of respect. However, allowing boomers to be relegated to a catchphrase, slogan, or a line on a bumper sticker does a serious injustice to the lives of millions of individuals who have sacrificed over their lifetimes. Our effectiveness as helping professions, as individuals, or through our national organizations must be mobilized to act. Scapegoating one generation undermines our democratic principles and, as a result, weakens the nation.

11. What role is there for social work education? It would be irresponsible not to turn attention to the role that departments and schools of social work can play in advancing social justice and boomers of color. Content related to boomers of color, however, should not be relegated to courses on gerontology. This cohort must be addressed across the curriculum to help ensure that we as a profession can play a leadership role in shaping services

and policies that are culturally competent and social justice inspired. Quite frankly, this charge must be viewed as an opportunity to help other professions form partnerships and join in collaborative efforts at reaching and engaging boomers and building upon boomer assets.

A failure of social work education to prepare the next generation of social workers in the field of gerontology will effectively marginalize the profession and its potential influence in this ever growing field of practice. It has, however, disastrous consequences for this nation's most marginalized groups, and we can certainly include low-income boomers of color in this category. These boomers are part of existing families and communities. Consequently, a socioecological perspective will uncover numerous intended and unintended consequences from these two spheres of influence.

The next decade promises to be a highly tumultuous time in this country as the ranks of older adults and retirees gather momentum and their increased presence becomes an even hotter economic and political issue. The influence of demographics is well understood and wields great significance from an economic, political, social, and cultural perspective. Although many can argue that demography is not destiny, it surely is arduous to argue that demography has nothing to do with the future of a country.

Social work and other helping professions will not have the "luxury" to sit on the sidelines. We will have to enter the political arena to advocate for social justice for marginalized older adults as national debt and deficits are debated and elected officials stake their position in either a deficit or asset perspective. The fate of the country hangs in the balance, and we as a profession must weigh in on the outcome.

REFERENCES

Aaron, H. J. (2011). Social Security reconsidered. *National Tax Journal* 64 (2, part 1): 385–414.

Abad-Santos, A. (2013, May 2). 3,026 more people die from suicide in America each year than in car crashes. www.theatlanticwire.com/national/2013/05/suicide-vs-car-crashes-cdc-study/64827. Accessed July 15, 2013.

Abraido-Lanza, A. F., White, K., and Vasques, E. (2004). Immigrant populations and health. In N. Anderson (ed.), *Encyclopedia of Health and Behavior* (pp. 533–537). Thousand Oaks, CA: Sage.

Achenbaum, W. A. (2011). On becoming a grandfather. *Generations* 35 (3): 11–15.

Achenbaum, W. A. (2009). A history of productive aging and the boomers. In R. B. Hudson (ed.), *Boomer Bust? Perspectives on the Boomers* (pp. 47–60). Westport, CT: Praeger.

Acs, G. & Nichols, A. (2007). *Low-Income Workers and Their Employers: Characteristics and Challenges.* Washington, DC: Urban Institute.

Adams, D. (2011, April 11). GOP Senators: Raise retirement age, "means test" Social Security. New York: NBC.

Adams, G. A. & Rau, B. L. (2011). Putting off tomorrow to do what you want to do today: Planning for retirement. *American Psychologist* 66 (3): 180–192.

Addington, L. A. (2013). Who are you calling old? Making "elderly" and what it means for homicide research. *Homicide Studies* 17 (2): 134–153.

Addo, F. & Lichter, D. T. (2010). Marital stock and wealth accumulation of older Black women. Ithaca, NY: Cornell University.

Administration on Aging. (2010a). A statistical profile of Asian older Americans aged 65+. Washington, DC: U.S. Department of Health & Human Services.

Administration on Aging. (2010b). A statistical profile of Black older Americans aged 65+. Washington, DC: U.S. Department of Health & Human Services.

Administration on Aging. (2010c). A statistical profile of Hispanic older Americans aged 65+. Washington, DC: U.S. Department of Health & Human Services.

Agree, E. M. & Glaser, K. (2009). Demography of informal caregiving. In P. Uhlenberg (ed.), *International Handbook of Population Aging,* vol. 1 (647–668). New York: Springer.

Ahn, S., Smith, M. L., & Dickerson, J. B. (2012). Health and health care utilization among obese and diabetic baby boomers and older adults. *American Journal of Health Promotion* 27 (2): 123–132.

Akamigbo, A. B. & Wollensky, F. D. (2007). New evidence of racial differences in access and their effects on the use of nursing homes among older adults. *Medical Care* 45 (7): 672–679.

Alba, R. (2009). *Blurring the Color Line: The New Challenge for a More Integrated America.* Cambridge: Harvard University Press.

Alba, R., Jimenez, T. R., & Marrow, H. B. (2013). Mexican Americans as a paradox for contemporary intra-group heterogeneity. *Ethnic and Racial Studies* 37 (3): 446–466.

Aleccia, J. (2012, June 18). Boomers' hep C tests may torpedo insurance chances, experts say. MSNBC. http://vitals.msnbc.msn.com/_news/2012/06/18/12285739. boomers-he. Accessed June 19, 2012.

Alemayehu, B. & Warner, K. E. (2004). The lifetime distribution of health care costs. *Health Services Research* 39 (3): 627–642.

Alexander, M. (2012). *The New Jim Crow: Mass Incarceration in the Age of Color-blindness.* New York: New Press.

Alschuler, G. & Blumin, S. (2009). *The G.I. Bill: The New Deal for Veterans.* New York: Oxford University Press.

Alvarez, L. (2012, November 28). For Latino groups, grass-roots efforts paid off in higher number of voters. *New York Times,* p. A20.

Alzheimer's Association. (2004a). *Minorities Hardest Hit by Alzheimer's.* Washington, DC: Alzheimer's Association.

Alzheimer's Association (2004b). *Hispanic/Latinos and Alzheimer's Disease.* Washington, DC: Alzheimer's Association.

Alzheimer's Association. (2010). *Alzheimer's Disease: Facts and Figures.* Washington, DC: Alzheimer's Association.

Alzheimer's Association. (2012). *Alzheimer's Disease: Facts and Figures.* Washington, DC: Alzheimer's Association.

American Association for Retired Persons. (2004a). *Baby boomers Envision Retirement II: Key Findings.* Washington, DC: American Association for Retired Persons.

American Association for Retired Persons. (2004b). *Hispanic Baby Boomers Envision Retirement: A Special Analysis of the Baby Boomers Envision Retirement II Study.* Washington, DC: American Association for Retired Persons.

American Association for Retired Persons. (2010). *Social Security: A Key Retirement Income Source for Minorities.* Washington, DC: American Association for Retired Persons.

American Federation for Aging Research. (2005). *Boom, Boom, Boom: Obesity Among Baby Boomers and Older Adults.* New York: American Federation for Aging Research.

Ammann, I. & Heckenroth, M. (2012). Innovations for intergenerational neighborhoods. *Journal of Interpersonal Relationships* 10 (3): 228–245.

Anderson, D. & Kennedy, L. (2006). Baby boomer segmentation: Eight is enough. *Consumer Insight* (Fall/Winter): 1–11.

Anderson, K. A. & Dabelko-Schoeny, H. I. (2011). Civic engagement for nursing home residents: A call for social work action. *Journal of Gerontological Social Work* 53 (4): 270–282.

Anderson, K. A., Richardson, V. E., Fields, N. L., & Harotyan, R. A. (2013). Inclusion or exclusion: Exploring barriers to employment for low-income older adults. *Journal of Gerontological Social Work* 56 (4): 318–334.

Angel, J. L. (2008). *Inheritance in Contemporary America: The Social Dimension of Giving Across Generations.* Baltimore: Johns Hopkins University Press.

Angel, J. L. & Angel, R. J. (2006). Minority group status of healthful aging: Social structures still matter. *American Journal of Public Health* 96 (7): 1152–1159.

Angel, J. L. & Mudrazija, S. (2010). Aging, inheritance, and gift-giving. In R. H. Binstock & E. Jarvich (eds.), *Handbook of Aging and the Social Sciences* (pp. 163–173). New York: Academic.

Angel, J. L., Torres-Gil, F., & Markides, K. (2012). Introduction: Aging, health, and longevity in the Mexican-origin population. In I. G. Cook & J. Halsall (eds.), *Aging in Comparative Perspective: Processes and Policies* (pp. 1–11). New York: Springer.

Angel, R. J. (2009). Structural and cultural factors in successful aging among older Hispanics. *Family & Community Health* 32 (1): S46–S57.

Anguelov, C. E. & Tamborini, C. R. (2009). Retiring in debt? Differences between the 1995 and 2004 near-retiree cohorts. *Social Security Bulletin* 69 (2): 13–34.

Anngela-Cole, L. & Hilton, J. M. (2009). The role of attitudes and culture in family caregiving for older adults. *Home Health Care Services Quarterly* 28 (2–3): 59–83.

Anonymous. (2010, October 4). African American baby boomers, what does the future hold. http://africanamericanbabyboomer.com/. Accessed November 25, 2012.

Apesoa-Varano, E. C., Baker, J. C., & Hinton, L. (2011). Curing and caring: The work of primary care physicians with dementia patients. *Qualitative Health Research* 21 (11): 1469–1483.

Arbore, P. (2012). The next big thing: Substance abuse among aging baby boomers. *Aging Today.*

Ariyabuddhiphongs, V. (2011). Lottery gambling: A review. *Journal of Gambling Studies* 27 (1): 15–33.

Arksey, H., Corden, A., Glendinning, A., & Hirts, M. (2008). Managing money in later life: Help from relatives and friends. *Benefits* 16 (1): 47–59.

Armstrong, N. (2012). Historypin: Bringing generations together around a communal history of time and place. *Journal of Interpersonal Relationships* 10 (3): 291–298.

Asheim, G. B. (2010). *Intergenerational Equity: Annual Review of Economics* 2 (4): 197–222.

Asian Development Bank. (2001). *Social Capital, Local Capacity Building, and Poverty Reduction.* Woodland Hills, CA: Office of Environment and Social Development.

Asquith, N. (2009). Positive ageing, neoliberalism and Australian sociology. *Journal of Sociology* 45 (3): 255–269.

Asrani, S. K., Larson, J. J., Yawn, B., Therneau, T. M., & Kim, W. R. (2013). Underestimation of liver-related mortality in the United States. *Gastroenterology* 146 (2): 375–382.

Austin, C. D., Des Camp, E., & Flux, D. (2005). Community development with older adults in their neighborhoods: The Elder Friendly Communities Program. www.calgary.ca/CSPS/CNS/Documents/Social-research-policy-and-resources/elder-friendly-communities.pdf. Accessed December 31, 2011.

Avalong, L. (2004). Cultural variants of caregiving or the culture of caregiving. *Journal of Cultural Diversity* 11 (4): 131–138.

Avery, M. L. (2010). Ecologies of risk and resilience. *Generations* 24 (3): 16–17.

Baby Boomers Generation. (2009). What are the baby boomer statistics? *Baby Boomers Generation.* www.boomersweb.net/Baby-boomers-Statistics.htm. Accessed December 23, 2011.

Bacharach, S., Bamberger, P. A., Somenstuhl, W. J., & Vashdi, D. R. (2008). Retirement and drug abuse: The conditioning role of age and retirement trajectory. *Addictive Behaviors* 33 (12): 1610–1614.

Bailey, S. J., Letiecq, B. L., & Porterfield, F. (2009). Family coping and adaptation among grandparents rearing grandchildren. *Journal of Interpersonal Relationships* 7 (2–3): 144–158.

Baker, D. (2009). *Defaulting on the Social Security Trust Fund: What It Would Mean, and How It Would Be Done.* Washington, DC: Center for Economic and Policy Research.

Baker, D. & Rosnick, D. (2009). *The Housing Crash and the Retirement Prospects of Late Baby Boomers.* Washington, DC: Center for Economic and Policy Research.

Baker, J. C., Herdt, G., & de Vries, B. (2006). Social support in the lives of lesbians and gay men at midlife and later. *Sexuality Research and Social Policy* 3 (2): 1–23.

Banks, S. (2013). Later-life decision-making process of first- and second-generation Latinos in Southern California. Northridge, CA: California State University.

Barondess, J. A. (2008). Toward healthy aging: The preservation of health. *Journal of the American Geriatric Society* 58 (1): 145–148.

Barrett, G. J. & Blackburn, M. L. (2010). The need for caregiver training is increasing as California ages. *California Agriculture* 64 (4): 200–207.

Barry, D. (2010, December 31). Boomers hit new self-absorption milestone: Age 65. *New York Times,* A01.

Bartels, S. J. & Naslund, J. A. (2013). The underside of the Silver Tsunami: Older adults and mental health care. *New England Journal of Medicine* 368:493–496.

Bartley, E. & Bartley, W. J. (2011). Quality-of-life outcomes among Alzheimer's disease family caregivers following community-based intervention. *Western Journal of Nursing Research* 35 (1): 98–116.

Barusch, A. S. (2013). The aging tsunami: Time for a new metaphor? *Journal of Gerontological Social Work* 56 (3): 181–184.

Battaglia, E. (2009, April 2). Baby boomers struggling with addiction. *Drug & Addiction Recovery Magazine,* p. 1.

Baum, C. L. (2007). The effects of race, ethnicity, and age on obesity. *Journal of Population Economics* 20 (6): 687–705.

Beach, E. E. M. & Langeland, K. L. (2010). Boomers' perspective needs for senior centers and related services: A survey of persons 50–59. *Journal of Gerontological Social Work* 51 (1): 116–130.

Becker, J. (2011). Baby boomers and their wallets—financial trends. http://ezinearticles./?Baby-Boomers-and-Their-Wallets-Financial-Trends@id=572362. Accessed December 27, 2011.

Beckley, T. M., Martz, D., Nadeau, S., Wall, E., & Reimer, B. (2008). Multiple capacities, multiple outcomes: Delving deeper into the meaning of community capacity. *Journal of Rural and Community Development* 3 (1): 56–75.

Beden Russonello & Stewart. (2001). In the middle: A report on multicultural boomers coping with family and aging issues: A National survey conducted for AARP. Washington, DC: Beden Russonello & Stewart.

Beinhocker, E. D., Farrell, D., & Greenberg, E. (2008). Why baby boomers will need to work longer. *McKinsey Quarterly,* November.

Beland, D. (2007). Ideas and institutional change in Social Security: Concerns, laying, and policy drift. *Social Science Quarterly* 88 (1): 20–38.

Belluck, P. (2008, October 21). More Alzheimer's risk factors for Hispanics, studies suggest. *New York Times,* pp. A1, A20.

Belluck, P. (2012, February 26). Life with dementia: With few options, prisons use killers to care for killers. *New York Times,* pp. 1, 16.

Belsky, G. (2012, April 18). Why U.S. businesses are nervous about losing boomer retirees. Time. http://business,time.com/2012/04/18/why-u-s-businesses-are-nervous-about-losing-boomer-retirees/#ixzzi1sPGPLesP. Accessed April 30, 2012.

Bengtson, V. L. (2001). Beyond the nuclear family: The increasing importance of multigenerational bonds. *Journal of Marriage and Family* 63 (1): 1–16.

Benjamin, R. J. & Whitaker, B. I. (2011). Boom of bust? Estimating blood demand and supply as the baby boomers age. *Transfusion* 51 (4): 670–673.

Benza, A. T., Calvert, S., & McQuown, C. B. (2010). Prevention BINGO: Reducing medication and alcohol use risks for older adults. *Aging & Mental Health* 14 (8): 1008–1014.

Berger, K. (2010, September 13). If you hate baby boomers, this is the article for you. *Mossback.* crosscut.com/2010/09/13/mossback/20101/If-you-hate-Baby-Boomers-this is-article-for-you/. Accessed June 29, 2013.

Berger, P. & Luckman, T. (1966). *The Social Construction of Reality: A Treatise in the Sociology of Knowledge.* New York: Anchor.

Bergmann, R. F. (2008). Mentoring opportunities abound across the generational divide. *Women's Law Journal.* 93 (3): 19–20.

Bernanke, B. S. (2006, October 4). *The Coming Demographic Transition: Will We Treat Future Generations Fairly?* Washington, DC: Board of Governors of the Federal Reserve System.

Bernard, D. (2011, September 16). Stop blaming the baby boomers. *U.S. News & World Reports,* p. 33.

Bernstein, C. A. (2010). Response to the presidential address. *American Journal of Psychiatry* 167 (10): 1166–1169.

Bernstein, R. & Edwards, T. (2008). An older and more diverse nation by mid-century. Washington, DC: U.S. Census Bureau.

Bertera, E. M. & Crewe, S. E. (2013). Parenthood in the twenty-first century: African American grandparents as surrogate parents. *Journal of Human Behavior and the Social Environment* 23 (2): 178–192.

Bessant, J. (2008). Age and equity: A case for an intergenerational charter. *Journal of Australian Studies* 32 (3): 361–373.

Beveridge, R. N. (2011). Crossing the health care chasm: Health care trends 2011–2015. *Cardia Cath. Lab Director* 1 (1): 6–11.

Bhattacharya, G. & Shibusawa, T. (2009). Experiences of aging among immigrants from India to the United States: Social work practice in a global context. *Journal of Gerontological Social Work* 52 (4): 445–462.

Biehl, A. M., Gurley-Calvez, T., & Hill, B. (2014). Self-employment of older Americans: Do recessions matter? *Small Business Economics* 42 (2): 297–309.

Biggs, S., Phillipson, C., Leach, R., & Money, A. (2007). Baby boomers and adult ageing: Issues for social and public policy. *Quality in Ageing and Older Adults* 8 (3): 32–40.

Binstock, R. H. (2010). From compassionate ageism to intergenerational conflict? *Gerontologist* 50 (5): 574–585.

Binstock, R. H. & Schulz, J. H. (2009). Can threats to social insurance in the United States be repelled? In L. Rogne, C. L. Estes, B. R. Grossman, B. A. Hollister, & E. Solway (eds.), *Social Insurance and Social Justice* (pp. 197–215). New York: Springer.

Birkenmaier, J., Kennedy, T., Kunz, J., Sander, R., & Horwitz, S. (2013). The role of social work in financial capability: Shaping curriculum approaches. In J. Birkenmaier, M. Sherraden, & J. Curley (eds.), *Financial Education and Capability and Asset Development: Research, Education, Policy, and Practice* (pp. 278–301). New York: Oxford University Press.

Birkenmaier, J., Sherraden, M., & Curley, J. (eds.). (2013). *Financial Education and Capability and Asset Development: Research, Education, Policy, and Practice.* New York: Oxford University Press.

Bishop, C. (2009). The looming economic of boomer health care. In R. B. Hudson (ed.), *Boomer Bust? Perspectives on the Boomers* (pp. 95–109). Westport, CT: Praeger.

Bishop, K. & Hudson, S. (2012). Aging with an adult-onset physical disability: A scope review. *International Journal of Integrated Care* 12 (9).

Black, K., Dobbs, D., & Young, T. L. (2012). Aging in community: Mobilizing a new paradigm of older adults as a core source resource. *Journal of Applied Gerontology*, forthcoming.

Blackburn, M. L. (2010). Limited-income seniors report multiple chronic diseases in quality-of-life study. *California Agriculture* 64 (4): 195–200.

Blackburn, M. L., Gillory, B., & Hausett, P. (2010). Research is needed to assess the unique nutrition and wellness needs of aging Californians. *California Agriculture* 64 (4): 1–8.

Blair, T. & Minkler, M. (2009). Participatory action research with older adults: Key principles in practice. *Gerontologist* 49 (5): 651–662.

Blazer, D. G. & Wu, L.-T. (2009). Nonprescription use of pain relievers by middle-aged and elderly community-living adults: National Survey of Drug Use and Health. *Journal of the American Geriatric Society* 57 (7): 125–157.

Bloom, D. E. & McKinnon, R. (2010). Social Security and the challenge of demographic change. *International Social Security Review* 63 (3–4): 3–21.

Bocian, D. G., Li, W., & Ernst, K. S. (2010). Forecloses by race and ethnicity: The demographics of a crisis. Washington, DC: Center for Responsible Lending.

Boerner, K., & Jope, R. (2010). Basic dimensions of resilience. In J. W. Reich, A. J. Zutra, & J. S. Hall (eds.), *Handbook of Adult Resilience* (126–145). New York: Guilford.

Bonastia, C. (2010). *Knocking on the Door: The Federal Government's Attempts to Desegregate the Suburbs.* Princeton: Princeton University Press.

Bonnet, F., Ehmke, E., & Hagemejer, K. (2010). Social security in times of crisis. *International Social Security Review* 63 (2): 47–70.

Bonvalet, C., Clement, C., & Ogg, J. (2013). Baby boomers and their entourage. *International Review of Sociology* 23 (1): 123–140.

Bonvalet, C. & Ogg, J. (2007). Ageing in the inner cities: The residential dilemmas of the baby boomer generation. *International Journal of Ageing and Later Life* 2 (2): 61–90.

Booth, H. (2006). Demographic forecasting: 1980 to 2005 in review. *International Journal of Forecasting* 22 (3): 547–581.

Borger, C., Smith, S., Truffer, C., Keehan, S., Sisko, A., Poisal, J., & Clemens, M. K. (2006). Health spending projections through 2015: Changes on the horizon. *Health Affairs* 25 (2): w61–w73.

Boston Globe. (2011, November 22). Gingrich unveils plan for personal Social Security accounts. *Boston Globe*, p. A8.

Bourdieu, P. (1986). The forms of capital. In J. G. Richardson (ed.), *Handbook of Theory and Research for the Sociology of Education* (pp. 241–258). New York: Greenwood.

Boustan, L. & Shertzer, A. (2011). Population trends as a counterweight to central city declines, 1950–2000. http://164.67.163.139/Documents/areas/ctr/ziman/2011–14WP.pdf. Accessed June 12, 2013.

Boyce, J. K. (2000). "Let them eat risk?" Wealth, rights, and disaster vulnerability. *Disaster* 24 (3): 254–261.

Boyd-Seale, D. L. (2008). Cultural competency in nursing homes' activities programs. Minneapolis: Capella University.

Braubach, M. & Power, A. (2011). Housing conditions and risk: Reporting on a European study of housing quality and risk of accidents for older people. *Journal of Housing for the Elderly* 25 (3): 288–305.

Bridgeland, J. M., Putnam, R. D., & Wofford, H. L. (2008). More to give: Tapping the talents of the Baby Boomers, silent, and greatest generation. Washington, DC: AARP.

Briggs, W. P., Magnus, V. A., Lassiter, P., Patterson, A., & Smith, L. (2011). Substance use, misuse, and abuse among older adults: Implications for clinical mental health counselors. *American Journal of Mental Health Counseling* 33 (2): 112–127.

Brondolo, E., Gallo, L. C., & Myers, H. F. (2009). Race, racism and health: Disparities, mechanisms, and interventions. *Journal of Behavorial Medicine* 32 (1): 1–8.

Brondolo, E., Love, E. E., Pencille, M., Schoenther, A., & Ogedegbe, G. (2011). Racism and hypertension: A review of the empirial evidence and implications for clinical practice. *American Journal of Hypertension* 24 (5): 518–529.

Brønn, P. S. (2008). Intangible assets and communication. In *Public Relations Research*, part 3, 281–291. VS Verlag für Sozialwissenschaften.

Brooke, L. (2005). Here come the baby boomers and their hypertension—but does hypertension really exist. *Medscape Cardiology.* http://medscape.org/viewarticle/520169. Accessed December 17, 2012.

Browdie, R. (2011). Health reform, politics, and conflict: Is this any way to serve America's elders? *Generations* 35 (1): 6–10.

Brown, E. (1999). The scope of volunteering actions and public service. *Law and Contemporary Problems* 62 (4): 17–42.

Brown, M. T. (2010). Early-life characteristics, psychiatric history, and cognition trajectories in later life. *Gerontologist* 50 (5): 646–656.

Brown, R. (2012, July 19). Facing foreclosure after 50: Mortgage problems surge for a once-secure age group. *New York Times,* p. A14.

Brown, T. (2012). The intersection and accumulation of racial and gender inequality: Black women's wealth trajectories. *Review of Black Political Economy* 39 (2): 239–258.

Brown, W. M., Consedine, N. A., & Magai, C. (2005). Altruism relates to health in an ethnically diverse sample of older adults. *Journals of Gerontology Series B: Psychological Sciences and Social Sciences* 60B (3): 143–152.

Brown, A. S., Novak, J. L., & Kitchener, A. (2008). Cultural engagement in California's inland regions. WolfBrown. www.southarts.org/atf/cf/%7B15E1E84E-C906-4F67-9851-A195A9BAAF79%7D/Arts%20Part%20-%20Cultural%20Engagement_FullReport.pdf. Accessed January 1, 2012.

Brown, T. H. & Warner, D. F. (2008). Divergent pathways? Racial/ethnic differences in older women's labor force withdrawal. *Journals of Gerontology Series B: Psychological Sciences and Social Sciences* 63 (3): S122–S134.

Brownell, P. A. (2013). *Ageism and Mistreatment of Older Workers: Current Reality, Future Solutions.* New York: Springer.

Brownstein, R. (2010, July 24). The gray and the brown: The generational mismatch. *National Journal,* pp. 1–4.

Brucker, E. & Leppel, K. (2013). Retirement planning: Planners and nonplaners. *Educational Gerontology* 39 (1): 1–11.

Bruin, M. J., Lien, L. L., Yust, B. L., & Imbertson, K. (2011). Baby boomers: What is the literature missing? In G. Peek (ed.), *Housing Education and Research Association Proceedings.* Baton Rouge, Annual Conference.

Bryant, A. N. & Kim, G. (2013). The relation between acculturation and alcohol consumption patterns among older Asian and Hispanic immigrants. *Aging & Health* 17 (2): 147–156.

Buchanan, N. H. (2007). Social Security and government deficits: When should we worry? *Cornell Law Review* 92:257.

Buckley, J. (2008). Baby boomers, obesity, and social change. *Obesity Research & Clinical Practice* 2 (2): 73–82.

Buckley, J., Tucker, G., Hugo, G., Wittert, G., Adams, R. J., & Wilson, D. H. (2013). The Australian baby boomer population—factors influencing changes to health-related quality of life outcome. *Journal of Aging and Health* 25 (1): 29–55.

Budrys, G. (2003). Unequal health: How inequality contributes to health or illness. New York: Rowman & Littlefield.

Bugental, D. B. & Hehman, J. A. (2007). Ageism: A review of research and policy implications. *Social Issues and Policy Review* 1 (1): 173–218.

Bullock, K. (2011). The influence of culture on end-of-life decision-making. *Journal of Social Work in End-of-Life & Palliative Care* 7 (1): 83–98.

Burney, T. (2012, December 18). All the lonely people: Creating communities where boomer buyers want to live. Builderonline.

Burns, C. M., Abernethy, A. P., Dal Grande, E., & Curran, D. C. (2013). Uncovering an invisible networks of direct caregivers at the end of life: A population study. *Palliative Medicine* 27 (7): 600–615.

Burr, J. A., Gerst, K., Kwan, N., & Mutchler, J. E. (2008–2009). Economic wellbeing and welfare program participation among older immigrants to the United States. *Generations* 32 (4): 53–60.

Burr, J. A. & Mutchler, J. E. (2007). Employment in later life: A focus on race/ethnicity and gender. *Generations* 31 (1): 37–44.

Burr, J. A., Mutchler, J. E., & Gerst, K. (2010). Public policies and older populations of color. In R.B. Hudson (ed.), *The New Politics of Old Age Policy,* 2d ed. (pp. 160–182). Baltimore: Johns Hopkins University Press.

Business Wire. (2005, May 24). Estimated annual spending power of baby boomers is more than $2 trillion. *Business Wire.* www.businesswire.com/news/home/20050524005040/en/Estimated-Annual-Spending-Power-Baby-Boomers-2#.UyFF70XY-Ao.

Business Wire. (2007, May 23). As baby boomers begin transfer of economic influence, echo boomers display practical and mature spending habits. *Business Wire.* www.businesswire.com/news/home/20070523005918/en/Baby-Boomers-Transfer-Economic-Influence-Echo-Boomers#.UyFGN4XY-Ao.

Butler, R. (1976). *Why Survive? Growing Old in America.* New York: Harper & Row.

Butler, R. N. (2011). Preface. Media takes on aging. Sacramento: International Longevity Center.

Butler, S. S. (2013). Older women doing home care: Exploitation or ideal job. *Journal of Gerontological Social Work* 56 (4): 299–317.

Butler, T. H. & Barret, B. A. (2012). A generation lost: The reality of age discrimination in today's hiring practices. *Journal of Management and Market Research* 9:1–11.

Butrica, B. A., Iams, H. M., Smith, K. E., & Toder, E. J. (2009). The disappearing defined benefit pension and its potential impact on the retirement incomes of baby boomers. *Social Security Bulletin* 69 (3): 1–27.

Butrica, B. A. & Johnson, A. J. (2010). Racial, ethnic, and gender differentials in empower-sponsored pensions. Washington, DC: Urban Institute.

Butrica, B. A. & Smith, K. E. (2012). Racial and ethnic differences in the retirement prospects of divorces women in the baby boom generation X cohorts. *Social Security Bulletin* 72 (1): 23.

Butrica, B. A., Smith, K. E., & Iams, H. (2012). This is not your parents' retirement: Comparing retirement income across generations. *Social Security Bulletin* 72 (1): 37–58.

Butrica, B. A., Smith, K. E., & Steurele, C. E. (2006). Working for a good retirement. The Levy Economics Institute Working Paper Series No. 463.

Butrica, B. A. & Uccello, C. E. (2004). How will boomers fare at retirement? Washington, DC: Urban Institute.

Butts, D. M. & Lent, J. P. (2009). Better together: Generational reciprocity in the real world. In R. B. Hudson (ed.), *Boomer Bust? Economic and Political Issues of the Graying Society* (pp. 145–165). Westport, CT: Praeger.

Byers, T. (2006, August 24). Overweight and mortality among baby boomers—now we're getting personal. *New England Journal of Medicine* 355:758–760.

Cahill, S. & Valadez, R. (2013). Growing older with HIV/AIDS: New public health challenges. *American Journal of Public Health* 103 (3): e7–e15.

Calvo, E., Haverstick, K., & Sass, S.A. (2009). Gradual retirement, sense of control, and retirees' happiness. *Research on Aging* 31 (1): 112–135.

Cameron, K. A., Song, J., Manheim, L. M., & Dunlop, D. D. (2010). Gender disparities in health and healthcare use among older adults. *Journal of Women's Health* 19 (9): 1643–1650.

Campbell, A. L. & King, R. (2010). Social Security: Political resilience in the face of conservative strides. In R. B. Hudson (ed.), *The New Politics of Old Age Policy,* 2d ed. (pp. 233–253). Baltimore: Johns Hopkins University Press.

Campbell, K. (2005, January 26). The many faces of the baby boomers. *Christian Science Monitor,* p. 1.

Campbell, R. J. (2004). Older women and the Internet. *Journal of Women & Aging* 16 (1–2): 161–174.

Campbell, R. J. (2009). Internet-based health information seeking among low-income, minority seniors living in urban residential centers. *Home Health Care Management & Practice* 21 (3): 195–202.

Campbell, R. J., Nolfi, D. A., & Bowen, D. (2005). Teaching elderly adults to use the Internet to access health care information: Before-after study. *Journal of Health Care Management & Practice* 7 (2): e19.

Canda, E. & Furman, L. D. (2009). *Spiritual Diversity in Social Work Practice: The Heart of Helping*. New York: Oxford University Press.

Cangelosi, P. R. (2011). Baby boomers: Are we ready for their impact on health care? *Journal of Psychosocial Nursing & Mental Health Services* 49 (9): 15–17.

Capers, M. (2003). More older Americans will need substance abuse treatment by 2020. *SAMHSA News* 11 (1): 1–2.

Caren, N., Ghoshal, R. A., & Ribas, V. (2011). A social movement generation: Cohort and period trends in protest attendance and petition signing. *American Sociological Review* 71 (1): 125–151.

Carlton-LaNey, I. & Washington, T. (2009). Naturally evolving aging-friendly businesses: A special service to African-American elders. *Generations* 33 (2): 68–70.

Carr, D. C. (2005). Changing the culture of aging: A social capital framework for gerontology. *Hallym International Journal of Aging* 7 (2): 81–93.

Carrion, I. V. (2010). When do Latinos use hospice services? Studying the utilization of hospice services by the Hispanic/Latino community. *Social Work in Health Care* 49 (3): 197–210.

Carrion, I. V. & Bullock, K. (2012). A case study of Hispanics and hospice care. *International Journal of Humanities and Social Science* 2 (4): 9–16.

Carter, V. B. & Marx, J. (2007). What motivates African-American charitable giving? *Administration in Social Work* 31 (1): 67–85.

Carter-Edwards, L., Johnson, J., Whitt-Glover, M., Bruce, M., & Goldman, M. (2011). Health promotion for the elderly: Training Black clergy in entrepreneurial spirituality. *Journal of Religion, Spirituality & Aging* 23 (1–2): 139–154.

Casado, E. & Sacco, P. (2012). Correlates of caregiver burden among family caregivers of older Korean-Americans. *Journal of Gerontology Series B: Psychological and Social Sciences* 67B (3): 331–336.

Cashell, B. W. (2010). *Automatic Cost of Living Adjustments: Some Economic and Practical Considerations*. Washington, DC: Congressional Research Service.

Castro, D. (2010). Stigma and disclosure issues experienced by older gay Latino men living with HIV/AIDS. Long Beach: California State University.

Catalano, L. & Lazaro, C. (2010). Financial abuses of elderly investors: Protecting the vulnerable. *Journal of Securities Law, Regulation & Compliance* 3 (1): 5–23.

Cataldo, J. K. & Malone, R.E. (2008). False promises: The tobacco industry, "low tar" cigarettes, and older adult smokers. *Journal of the American Geriatric Society* 56 (9): 1716–1723.

Cawthon, P. & Harrison, S. (2006). Alcohol intake and its relationship with bone mineral density, falls, and fracture risk in older men. *Journal of the American Geriatric Society* 54 (11): 1649–1657.

Cawthorne, A. (2009). Elderly poverty: The challenge before us. Washington, DC: Center for American Progress.

CBS (2011, November 11). Poll: Boomers anxiety about retirement grows. www. cbsnews.com/2102–201_162–57322835.html?tag=contentMain;conentBody. Accessed November 11, 2011.

CBS (2012, July 11). Baby boomers face mental health crisis, Institute of Medicine says. CBS News. www.cbsnews.com/news/baby-boomers-face-mental-health-care-crisis-institute-of-medicine-says/. Accessed January 12, 2013.

Centers for Disease Control and Prevention. (2005). *Obesity, High Blood Pressure Impacting Many U.S. Adults Ages 55–64*. Atlanta: Centers for Disease Control and Prevention.

Centers for Disease Control and Prevention. (2007). *The State of Aging and Health in America 2007*. Atlanta: Centers for Disease Control and Prevention.

Centers for Disease Control and Prevention. (2008). *HIV/AIDS Among Persons Ages 50 and Older*. Atlanta: Centers for Disease Control and Prevention.

Centers for Disease Control and Prevention. (2010a). *No Health Insurance Among Persons Under 65 years of Age, 1984–2009*. Atlanta: Centers for Disease Control and Prevention.

Centers for Disease Control and Prevention. (2010b). *Death Rates by Suicide, 1950–2007*. Atlanta: Centers for Disease Control and Prevention.

Centers for Disease Control and Prevention. (2010c). *Death Rates for Firearms, 1970–2007*. Atlanta: Centers for Disease Control and Prevention.

Centers for Disease Control and Prevention. (2012). *Home & Recreational Safety*. Atlanta: Centers for Disease Control and Prevention.

Centers for Disease Control and Prevention. (2013). *High Blood Pressure Facts*. Atlanta: Centers for Disease Control and Prevention.

Center for a Responsible Federal Budget. (2011). *Third Way Introduces New Social Security Reform Plan*. Washington, DC: Center for a Responsible Federal Budget.

Charise, A. (2012). "Let the reader think of the burdens": Old age and the crisis of capacity. OC.CA.SION, http://arcade.standord.edu/occasion/%E2 %80%9Clet-reader-think-burden%E2%80%9D-old-age-and-crisis-capacity.

Chaskin, R. J. (2013). Theories of community. In M. Weil, M. Reisch, & M. L. Olmer (eds.), *The Handbook of Community Practice* (pp. 105–121). Thousand Oaks, CA: Sage.

Chaudhuri, S. & Ghosh, R. (2012). Reverse mentoring: A social exchange tool for keeping boomers engaged and Millennials committed. *Human Resource Development Review* 11 (1): 55–76.

Chen, S. (2009). Aging with Chinese characteristics: A public policy perspective. *Ageing International* 34 (2): 172–188.

Chernew, M., Goldman, D., & Axeen, S. (2011). How much savings can we wring from Medicare? *New England Journal of Medicine* 365 (e29).

Choi, N. G. (2013). The Digital Divide among low-income homebound older adults: Internet use patterns, eHealth literacy, and attitudes towards computers. *Internet Use: Journal of Medical Information Research* 15 (3): e93.

Christie, L. (2009, February 26). 30 percent of boomers are underwater in their homes. CNN Money.Com. http://money.cnn.com/2012/05/24/real_estate/underwater-mortgages/. Accessed May 10, 2013.

Cianciolo, P. K. (2009). Teaching collaborative learning and continuing education strategies about Social Security and Medicare. In L. Rogne, C. L. Estes, B. R. Grossman, B. A. Hollister, & E. Solway (eds.), *Social Insurance and Social Justice* (pp. 399–416). New York: Springer.

Clark, C. (2008, April 24). Falling feared as baby boomers age. *Union-Tribune* (San Diego), p. 12.

Clark, K. & Glicksman, A. (2012). Age-friendly Philadelphia: Bringing diverse networks together around aging issues. *Journal of Housing for the Elderly* 26 (3): 121–136.

Clark, R. J. (2006). Differences in disability among Black and White elderly. Washington, DC: Georgetown University.

Clarke, L. H. (2011). Facing age: Women growing older in anti-aging culture. Lanham, MD: Rowman & Littlefield.

Clay, S. W. (2010). Treatment of addiction in the elderly. *Aging Health* 6 (2): 177–189.

Coates, D. (2011). *Making the Progressive Case.* New York: Continuum.

Coffman, D. D. (2002). Music and quality of life in older adults. *Psychomusicology, Music, Mind and Body* 18 (1–2): 1–9.

Cohn, D.'V. (2007). The divergent paths of baby boomers and immigrants. Washington, DC: Population Reference Bureau.

Cohn, D.'V. & Taylor, P. (2010). Baby boomers approach age 65—glumly. Washington, DC: Pew Research Center.

Coile, C. & Gruber, J. (2007). Future Social Security entitlements and the retirement decision. *Review of Economics and Statistics* 89 (2): 234–246.

Coins, R. T., Spencer, S. M., McGuire, L. C., Goldberg, J., Wen, Y., & Henderson, J. A. (2011). Adult caregiving among American Indians: The role of cultural factors. *Gerontologist* 51 (3): 310–320.

Cole, M. & MacDonald, K. (2010). Retired occupational therapists' experiences in volunteer occupations. *Occupational Therapy International* 18 (1): 18–31.

Coleman, M., Ganong, L. H., & Rothrauf, T. C. (2006). Racial and ethnic similarities in beliefs about intergenerational assistance to older adults after divorce and remarriage. *Family Relations* 55 (5): 576–587.

Collins, J. M. & Birkeimaier, J. (2013). Building the capacity of social work to enhance financial capability and assets development. In J. Birkenmaier, M. Sherraden, & J. Curley (eds.), *Financial Education and Capability and Asset Development: Research, Education, Policy, and Practice* (pp. 302–321). New York: Oxford University Press.

Collins, S., Davis, K., Schoen, C., Doty, M. M., & Kriss, J. L. (2006). Health coverage for aging baby boomers: Findings from the Commonwealth Survey of Older Adults. New York: Commonwealth Fund.

Collins, S., Doty, M. M., & Garber, T. (2010). Realizing health reforms potential: Adults 50–64 and the Affordable Care Act of 2010. New York: Commonwealth Fund.

Colliver, J. D., Compton, W. M., Gfroerer, J. C., & Condon, T. (2006). Projecting drug use among aging baby boomers in 2020. *Annals of Epidemiology* 16 (4): 257–265.

Commission to Modernize Social Security. (2011). Plan for a new future: The impact of Social Security reform on people of color. Washington, DC: Commission to Modernize Social Security.

Conaboy, C. (2012, December 24). A generation at risk? *Boston Globe,* pp. G12–G13.

Connell, C., Roberts, S., McLaughlin, S., & Akinleye, D. (2009). Racial differences in knowledge and beliefs about Alzheimer Disease. *Alzheimer Disease & Associated Disorders* 23 (2): 110–116.

Connolly, M.-T., Breckman, R., Callahan, J., Lachs, M., Ramsey-Kiawsnik, H., & Solomon, J. (2013). The sexual revolution's last frontier: How silence about sex undermines health, well-being, and safety in old age. *Generations* 36 (3): 43–52.

Connor, K. O. & Rosen, D. (2008). "You're nothing but a junkie": Multiple experiences of stigma in an aging methadone maintenance population. *Journal of Social Work Practice in the Addictions* 8 (2): 244–264.

Consumer Federation of the Southeast. (2012, February 1). New poll 2012: What baby boomers want. Tallahassee: Consumer Federation of the Southeast.

Cook, I. G. & Halsall, J. (2012). Aging in the United States. In I. G. Cook & J. Halsall (eds.), *Aging in Comparative Perspective: Processes and Policies* (pp. 7–16). New York: Springer.

Cook, J. M., Dinnen, S., & O'Donnell, C. (2011). Older women survivors of physical and sexual violence: A systematic review of quantitative literature. *Journal of Women's Health* 20 (7): 1075–1081.

Cote, J. E. A. & Allahar, A. L. (2007). *Ivory Tower Blues: A University System in Crisis.* Toronto: University of Toronto Press.

Cox, C. (2008). Empowerment as an intervention with grandparent caregivers. *Journal of Interpersonal Relationships* 6 (4): 465–477.

Cox, C. (2009). Custodial grandparents: Policies affecting care. *Journal of Interpersonal Relationships* 7 (2–3): 177–190.

Cox, E. O. (2008). Aging in the United States: Challenges to social policy and policy practice. In K. M. Sowers & C. N. Dulmas (eds.), *Comprehensive Handbook of Social Work and Social Welfare.* New York: Wiley.

Cresci, M. K., & Jarosz, P. A. (2010).Bridging the digital divide for urban seniors: Community partnership. *Geriatric Nursing, 31*(6): 455–463.

Cresci, M. R., Yarandi, H. N., & Morrell, R. W. (2010a). The Digital Divide and urban olders. *Computer Information & Nursing* 28 (2): 88–94.

Cresci, M. R., Yarandi, H. N., & Morrell, R. W. (2010b). Pro-nets verses no-nets: Differences in urban older adults' predictions for Internet use. *Educational Gerontology* 36 (6): 500–520.

Cravey, T. & Mitra, A. (2011). Demographics of the sandwich generation by race and ethnicity in the United States. *Journal of Socio-Economics* 40 (3): 306–311.

Crewe, S. E. (2004). Ethnogerontology: Preparing culturally competent social workers for the diverse facing of aging. *Journal of Gerontological Social Work* 43 (4): 45–58.

Crippen, D. & Barnato, A. E. (2011). The ethical implications of health spending: Death and other expensive conditions. *Journal of Law, Medicine & Ethics* 39 (1): 121–129.

Crogan, C. F., Moone, R. P., & Olson, A. M. (2014). Friends, family, and caregiving among midlife and older lesbian, gay, bisexual, and transgendered adults. *Journal of Homosexuality* 61 (1): 79–102.

Croker, R. (2007). *The Boomer Century, 1946–2046: How America's Most Influential Generation Changed Everything.* New York: Springboard.

Cronan, J. J. (2009). Retirement: It's not about the finances! *Journal of the American College of Radiology* 8 (4): 242–245.

Cruce, T. M. & Hillman, N. N. (2012). Preparing for the Silver Tsunami: The demand for higher education among older adults. *Research in Higher Education* 53 (6): 593–613.

Coutts, C., Basmajian, C., & Chapin, T. (2011). Projecting landscapes of death. *Landscape and Urban Planning* 102 (4): 254–261.

Culhane, D. P., Metraux, S., Byrne, T., Stino, M., & Bainbridge, J. (2012). The age structure of contemporary homelessness: Evidence and implications for public policy. *Analysis of Social Issues and Public Policy* 13 (1): 43–52.

Culp III, K. (2009). Recruiting and engaging baby boomer volunteers. *Journal of Extension* 47 (2): 1–8.

Cummings, M. R., Hernandez, V. A., Rockeymoore, M., & Shepard, M. M. (2011). *The Latino Age Wave.* New York: Hispanics in Philanthropy.

Czaja, S., Beach, S., Cherness, N., & Schutz, R. (2013). Older adults and the adoption of healthcare technologies: opportunities and challenges. *Technologies for active aging: International Perspective* 9 (1): 27–46.

Dahmen, N. S. & Cozma, R. (eds.). (2008). *Media Takes: On Aging.* Sacramento: International Longevity Center.

Daley, S. & Kulish, N. (2013, August 14). Germany fights population drop: Takes steps to avoid a shortage of labor. *New York Times,* pp. A1, A6.

Daniel, R., Smith, M. L., & Reynolds, C. F. (2008). The prevalence of mental and physical health disorders among older methadone patients. *American Journal of Geriatric Psychiatry* 16 (6): 488–487.

Davis, G. L. & Roberts, W. L. (2010). The healthcare burden imposed by liver disease in ageing baby boomers. *Current Gastroenterology Reports* 12 (1): 1–6.

Davis, M. E. & Waites, C. (2008). Intergenerational caregiving: Family and long-term care. In C. Waites (ed.), *Social Work Practice with African American Families: An Intergenerational Perspective* (pp. 143–168). New York: Routledge.

Davis, N. S. (2013). A heavenly collaboration: Social workers and churches working to increase advance directive completion among African American elderly. *Journal of Human Behavior and the Social Environment* 23 (4): 462–474.

DeLamater, J. & Karraker, A. (2009). Sexual functioning in older adults. *Current Psychiatric Reports* 11 (1): 6–11.

Delaney, C. R. (2012). The influence of the "Power to Ask" on volunteer rates in the United States. Washington, DC: Georgetown University.

Delanty, G. (2003). *Community.* London: Routledge.

Delgado, M. (ed.). (1998). *Latino Elders and the Twenty-First Century: Issues and Challenges for Culturally Competent Research and Practice*. New York: Haworth.

Delgado, M. (1999). *Social Work Practice in Nontraditional Urban Settings*. New York: Oxford University Press.

Delgado, M. (2007). *Social Work Practice with Latinos: A Cultural Assets Paradigm*. New York: Oxford University Press.

Delgado, M. (2008). *Older Adult-Led Health Promotion in Urban Communities: A Special Focus on Urban Older Adults of Color*. Lanham, MD: Rowman & Littlefield.

Delgado, M. (2011). *Latino Small Businesses and the American Dream*. New York: Columbia University Press.

Delgado, M. (2012). *Prisoner Reentry at Work: Adding Business to the Mix*. Boulder: Lynne Rienner.

Delgado, M. (2013). *Social Justice and the Urban Obesity Crisis: Implications for Social Work*. New York: Columbia University Press.

Delgado, M. & Humm-Delgado, D. (2009). *Health and Health Care in the Nation's Prisons: Issues, Challenges, and Policies*. Lanham, MD: Rowman & Littlefield.

Delgado, M. & Humm-Delgado, D. (2013). *Asset Assessments and Community Social Work Practice*. New York: Oxford University Press.

Delgado, M. & Staples, L. (2008). *Youth-Led Community Organizing: Theory and Action*. New York: Oxford University Press.

Delwiche, A. A. & Henderson, J. J. (2013). The players they are a-changin': The rise of older MMO gamers. *Journal of Broadcasting & Electronic Media* 57 (2): 205–223.

Denmark, F. L. & Williams, D. A. (2012). The older woman as sage: The satisfaction of mentoring. *Women & Therapy* 35 (3–4): 261–278.

Denton, D. & Robertson, T. (2010). A kaleidoscope of innovation: Designing community impact in the Waterloo region. *Philanthropist* 23 (3): 283–302.

Desmette, D. & Gaillard, M. (2008). When a "worker" becomes an "older worker": The effects of age-related social identity on attitudes towards retirement and work. *Career Development International* 13 (2): 168–185.

DeVas-Walt, C., Proctor, B. D., & Smith, J. C. (2012). *Income, Poverty, and Health Insurance Coverage in the United States*. Washington, DC: U.S. Census Bureau.

Devi, S. (2008). U.S. health care still failing ethnic minorities. *Lancet* 371 (9628): 1903–1904.

Dew, J. & Yorgason, J. (2009). Economic pressure and marital conflict in retirement-aged couples. *Journal of Family Issues* 31 (2): 164–188.

Diamond, P. A. & Orszag, P. R. (2003). *Reforming Social Security: A Balanced Plan*. Washington, DC: Urban Institute.

Diamandis, M., Diamandis, E. P., McLaurin, J., Holzman, D. M., Schmitt-Ulms & Quirion, R. (2011). Alzheimer Disease: Advances in pathogenesis, diagnosis, and therapy. *Clinical Chemistry* 57 (5): 664–669.

Dickerson, B.J. & Rousseau, N. (2009). Ageism through omission: The obsolesce of Black women's sexuality. *Journal of African American Studies* 13 (3): 307–326.

Dietz, T. L. (2009). Drug and alcohol use among homeless older adults. *Journal of Applied Gerontology* 28 (2): 235–255.

DiGiacomo, M., Davidson, P. M., Byles, J., & Nolan, M. T. (2013). An integrative and socio-cultural perspectives for health, wealth, and adjustment in widowhood. *Health Care for Women International* 34 (12): 1067–1083.

Dillaway, H. E. & Byrnes, M. (2009). Reconsidering successful aging: A call for renewed and expanded academic critiques and conceptualizations. *Journal of Applied Gerontology* 28 (6): 702–722.

Dillon, P. J., Roscoe, L. A., & Jenkins, J. J. (2012). African Americans and decisions about hospice care: Implications for health message design. *Howard Journal of Communication* 23 (2): 175–193.

Dilworth-Anderson, P., Gibson, B. E., & Burke, J. D. (2006). Working with African-American families. In G. Yeo and D. Gallagher-Thompson (eds.), *Ethnicity and the Dementias,* 2d ed. (pp. 127–144). New York: Routledge.

DiNitto, D. & Choi, N.vG. (2011). Marijuana use among older adults in the U.S.A.: User characteristics, patterns of use, and implications for intervention. *International Psychogeriatrics* 23 (5): 732–741.

Diwan, S., Lee, S. E., & Sen, S. (2011). Expectations of filial obligations and their impact on preferences for future living arrangements of middle-aged and older Asian Indian immigrants. *Journal of Cross-Cultural Gerontology* 26 (1): 55–69.

Diworth-Anderson, P. & Cohn, M. D. (2010). Beyond diversity to inclusion: Recruitment and retention of diverse groups in Alzheimer research. *Alzheimer Disease & Associated Disorders* 14 (1): S14–S18.

Dobbs, B. M. (2008). Aging baby boomers—a blessing or challenge for driver licensing authorities. *Traffic Injury Prevention* 9 (4): 379–386.

Dolan, T. G. (2010, October 18). Latino baby boomers a new and unexpected challenge. *The Hispanic Outlook in Higher Education* 21 (2): 23–27.

Donahue, J. J. (2009). Tobacco smoking among incarcerated individuals: A review of the nature of the problem and what is being done in response. *Journal of Offender Rehabilitation* 48 (7): 589–604.

Donaldson, L. P. & Daughtery, L. C. (2011). Introducing asset-based models of social justice into service learning: A social work approach. *Journal of Community Practice* 19 (1): 80–99.

Doolan, D. M. & Froelicher, E. S. (2008). Smoking cessation interventions and older adults. *Progress in Cardiovascular Nursing* 23 (3): 119–127.

Dornelas, E., Stepnowski, R., Fischer, E., and Thompson, P. (2006). Urban ethnic minority women's attendance at health clinic vs. church based exercise programs. *Journal of Cross Cultural Gerontology* 22 (1): 129–136.

Doukas, N. (2011). Older adults in methadone maintenance treatment: A literature review. *Journal of Social Work Practice in Addictions* 11 (3): 230–244.

Dowling, G. J., Weiss, S. R. B., & Condon, T. P. (2008). Drugs of abuse and the aging brain. *Neuropsychopharmacology* 33 (3): 209–218.

Doyle, R. (2005, July 1). Baby boomer origins: Confluence of forces may have led to post war births. *Scientific American* 293 (1): 25–30.

Draper, B. & Anderson, D. (2010). The baby boomers are nearly here—but do we have sufficient workforce in old age psychiatry. *International Psychogeriatrics* 35:947–948.

Dreher, H. M. D. (2008). A dearth of geriatric specialists: Will invention and gerotechnology save us? *Holistic Nursing Practice* 22 (5): 255–260.

Dumas, A. & Turner, B. S. (2009). Aging in post-industrial societies: Intergenerational conflict and solidarity. In J. Hendricks & J. Powell (eds.), *The Welfare State in Post-industrial Society* (pp. 41–56). New York: Springer.

Duncan, C. (2008). The dangers and limitations of equality agendas as means for tackling old-age prejudice. *Ageing and Society* 28 (8): 1133–1158.

Duncan, D. F., Nicholson, T., White, J. B., Bradley, D. B., & Bonaquro, J. (2010). The baby boomer effect: Changing patterns of substance abuse among adults 55 and older. *Journal of Aging & Social Policy* 22 (3): 237–248.

Dunlap. D. D., Song, J., Manheim, L. M., Davigius, M. L., & Chang, R. W. (2007). Racial/ethnic differences in the development of disability among older adults. *American Journal of Public Health* 97 (12): 2209–2215.

Dychtwald, K. (1999). Age power: How the twenty-first century will be ruled by the new old. New York: Tarcher/Putnam.

Eastman, M. (2013). Baby boomers and the big society. *Working with Older People* 17 (1): 41–42.

Eccleston, M. & Priestman, S. (2007). *Leading with Experience: Engaging Older Adults as Community Leaders.* Washington, DC: Experience Corps National Office.

Ecker, E. (2012, September 17). Retirement savings at 2004 levels, baby boomer "culture" to blame. *Reverse Mortgage Daily.* http://reversemortgagedaily. com/w-content/plugins/google-sitemap-generator/sitemap.xsl. Accessed July 13, 2013.

Economist. (2012, September 29). Sponging boomers: The economic legacy left by the baby boomer is leading to a battle between the generations. www.economist.com/node/21563725. Accessed December 1, 2012.

Eden, J., Maslow, K., Le, M. & Blazer, D. (2012). The mental health and substance use workforce for older adults: In whose hands? Washington, DC: Institute of Medicine, National Academy of Sciences.

Edgerly, E. & Sullivan, T. (2006). Reaching diverse caregiving families through community partnerships. In G. Yeo & D. Gallagher-Thompson (eds.), *Ethnicity and the Dementias,* 2d ed. (pp. 361–377). New York: Routledge.

Edlin, M. (2010, November 1). Baby boomers trend toward higher drug utilization. *Managed Healthcare Executive,* pp. 1–2.

EducationNews. (2010, December 31). Baby boomers to turn 65: 16 statistics about the coming retirement crisis that will drop your jaw. www.educationnews.org/health/105296.html. Accessed August 20, 2011.

Edlund, B., Lufkin, S., & Franklin, B. (2003). Long-term care and planning for baby boomers: Addressing an uncertain future. *Online Journal of Issues in Nursing* 8 (2).

Eggenberger, S. K., Meiers, S. J., Krunwiede, N., Bliesmer, M., & Earle, P. (2011). Reintegration within families in the context of chronic illness: A family health promotion process. *Nursing and Healthcare of Chronic Illness* 3 (3): 283–292.

Eisner, D., Grimm, R. T. Jr., Maynard, S., & Washburn, S. (2009). The new volunteer workforce. *Stanford Social Intervention Review* 53 (1): 30–37.

El Nazzar, H. (2010, December 3). Boomer divide: Generation gap spans 19 years. *USA Today,* p. A3.

El Nazzar, H. & Overberg, P. (2011, May 5). After 50 years of decline, household size is growing. *USA Today,* p. A2.

Elcott, D. M. (2010). *Baby Boomers, Public Service, and Minority Communities: A Case Study of the Jewish Community in the United States.* New York: New York University's Berman Jewish Policy Archive.

Elmendof, D. W. (2011). Four observations about the Federal Budget. *Business Economics* 46 (1): 139–143.

Elnolf, C. J. (2008). Will the boomers volunteer during retirement? Comparing the baby boom, silent, and long civic cohorts. *Nonprofit and Voluntary Sector Quarterly* 38 (2): 181–199.

Emanuel, E. J. (2014, January 19). Sex and the single senior. *New York Times*, p. 8.

Endres, T. & Holmes, C. A. (2006). RespectAbility in America: Guiding principles for civic engagement among adults 55+. Washington, DC: National Council on Aging.

Eng, E., Moore, K. S., Rhodes, S. D., Griffith, D. M., Allison, L. L., Shirah, R., & Mebane, E. M. (2005). Insiders and outsiders assess who is "the community." In B. A. Israel, E. Eng, A. J. Schutz, & E. A. Parker (eds.), *Methods in Community-Based Participatory Research for Health* (pp. 77–100). San Francisco: Jossey-Bass.

Eskildsen, M. & Price, T. (2009). Nursing home care in the USA. *Geriatrics & Gerontology International* 9 (1): 1–6.

Estes, C. L., Biggs, S., & Phillipson, C. (2003). Social theory, social policy, and ageing: A critical introduction. Berkshire: Open University Press.

Estes, C. L., Rogne, L., Grossman, B. R., Hollister, B. A., & Solway, E. (2009a). Epilogue: From the audacity of hope to the audacity of action. In L. Rogne, C. L. Estes, B. R. Grossman, B. A. Hollister, & E. Solway (eds.), *Social Insurance and Social Justice* (pp. 435–439). New York: Springer.

Estes, C. L., Rogne, L., Grossman, B. R., Solway, E., & Hollister, B. A. (2009b). Introduction: We're all in this together: Social insurance, social justice, and social change. In L. Rogne, C. L. Estes, B. R. Grossman, B. A. Hollister, & E. Solway (eds.), *Social Insurance and Social Justice* (pp. xxv–xxxiii). New York: Springer.

Ethnic Technologies. (2012). Asian baby boomers by state. South Hackensack, NJ: Ethnic Technologies.

Evans, J. (2008, October 1). Illicit drug use dips in youth, spikes in boomers. *Family Practice News,* p. 26.

Evans, S. R. (2011). Uncovering risky sexual behaviors: HIV-positive female baby boomers speak out. Minneapolis: Capella University.

Experience Corps. (2003). Boston. www.experiencecorps.org/cities/boston/. Accessed September 29, 2011.

Fabrikant, G. (2013, May 15). Back to school, but for the degree, not just the fun. *New York Times,* p. F8.

Favreault, M. M. (2009). Revitalizing Social Security: Effectively targeting benefit enhancements for low lifetime earners and the oldest of the old. Washington, DC: Urban Institute.

Favreault, M. M. (2010). *Workers with Low Social Security Benefits: Implications for Reform.* Washington, DC: Urban Institute.

Favreault, M. M. & Nichols, A. (2011). *Immigrant Diversity and Social Security: Recent Patterns and Future Prospects.* Chestnut Hill, MA: Center for Retirement Research of Boston College.

Fears, D. (2004, December 17). Black baby boomers' income gap cited. *Washington Post,* p. A02.

Fehring, T. K., Odum, S. M., Troyer, J. L., Lorio, R., Kurtz, S. M., & Lau, E.C. (2010). Joint replacement access in 2016: A supply side crisis. *Journal of Anthroplasty* 25 (8): 1175–1181.

Fennell, M. L., Clark, M., Feng, Z., Mor, V., Smith, D. B., & Tyler, B. D. (2012). Separate and unequal access and quality of care in nursing homes: Transformation of the long term care industry and implications of the research program for aging Hispanics. In J. L. Angel, F. Torres-Gil, & K. Markides (eds.). Aging, health, and longevity in the Mexican-origin population (pp. 259–275). New York: Springer.

Feng, Z., Fennell, M. L., Tyler, D. A., Clark, M., & Mor, V. (2011). Growth of racial and ethnic minorities in U.S. nursing homes driven by demographics and possible disparities in options. *Health Affairs* 30 (7): 1358–1365.

Ferguson, A. J. & Shriver, J. (2012). The future of gerontological social work: A case for structural lag. *Journal of Gerontological Social Work* 55 (4): 304–320.

Ferguson, J. (2009, November 11). Drug-addicted boomers: The new burden. *Herald Sun* (Australia), p. 1.

Fernandez-Kelly, P. (2008). The back pocket map: Social class and cultural capital as transferable assets in advancement of second-generation immigrants. *American Academy of Political and Social Science* 620 (1): 116–137.

Ferrara, P. (2011, March 17). A winning plan for Social Security reform. *Forbes Magazine.* www.forbes.com/sites/peterferrara/2011/03/17/a-winning-plan-for-social-security-reform/. Accessed November 22, 2011.

Fingerman, K. L., Pillemer, K. A., Silverstein, M., & Sultor, J. J. (2012). The baby boomers' intergenerational relationships. *Gerontologist* 52 (2): 199–209.

Finke, M. S., Howe, J. S., & Huston, S. J. (2011). Old age and the decline in financial literacy. http://ssrn.com/abstract=1948627 or http://dx.doi.org/10.2139/ssrn.1948627. Accessed March 1, 2012.

Finkelstein, E. S., Reid, M. C., Kleppinger, A., Pillemar, K., & Robison, J. (2012). Are baby boomers who care for their older parents planning for their own future long-term care needs? *Journal of Aging & Social Policy* 24 (1): 29–45.

Finkelstein, L. & Truxilla, D. (2013). Age discrimination research is alive and well: Even if it doesn't live where you'd expect. *Industrial and Organizational Psychology* 6 (1): 100–102.

Flatt, J. D. & Hughes, T. F. (2013). Participation in social activities in later life: Does employment have important implications for cognitive health? *Aging & Health* 9 (2): 149–158.

Fleck, C. (2011). Social Security benefit crucial to African Americans. Washington, DC: AARP.

Flores, D. V. et al. (2013). Sangre Buena, sangre mala: Good blood, bad blood: The role of familismo as risk and protective factors in heroin-injecting Mexican-Americans. Society for Social Work Research Annual Conference, January San Diego.

Flores, Y. G. (2013). Latina sexuality: De (re) constructing gender and cultural expectations in midlife. *Women, Gender, and Families of Color* 1 (1): 85–101.

Flynn, M. (2010). Who would delay retirement? Typologies of older workers. *Personal Review* 39 (3): 308–324.

Fong, C. (2001). The changing face of seniors: Ethnic diversity in the aging baby boomer population. *Marquette Elder's Advisor* 3 (1): 43–45.

Fox, S. (2006). Online health search 2006: Most Internet users start a search engine when looking for health information. Washington, DC: Pew Internet and American Life Project.

Fram, A. (2011, April 5). Poll reveals baby boomers' retirement fears. Associated Press. www.msnbc.msn.com/id/42436897/ns/business-personal_finance/t/poll-reveals-bab. Accessed November 11, 2011.

Franklin, C. & Hopson, L. M. (2007). Promoting and sustaining evidence-based practice. *Journal of Social Work Education* 43 (3): 377–404.

Fredrikson-Goldsen, K. L., Kim, H.-J., Muraco, A., & Mincer, S. (2009). Chronically ill midlife older lesbians, gay men, and bisexuals and their informal caregivers: The impact of the social context. *Sexual Research & Social Policy* 6 (4): 52–64.

Freedman, M. (1999). How Baby Boomers will revolutionize retirement and transform America. New York: Public Affairs.

Freedman, M. (2006–2007). The social purpose encore career: Baby boomers, civic engagement, and the next stage of work. *Generations* 30 (1): 43–46.

Fremstad, S. (2011). *Maintaining and Improving Social Security for Poorly Compensated Workers.* Washington, DC: Center for Economic and Policy Research.

Frey, W. H. (2007). *Mapping the Growth of Older America: Seniors and Boomers in the Early Twenty-first Century.* Washington, DC: Brookings Institute.

Frey, W. H. (2009). America's regional demographics in the 'oos decade: The role of seniors, boomers and new minorities. Research Institute for Housing America Research Paper No. 06–01.

Frey, W. H. (2010). Baby boomers and the new demographics of America's seniors. *Generations* 34 (3): 28–37.

Frey, W. H. (2011). The uneven aging and "younging" of America: State and metropolitan trends in the 2010 census. Washington. DC: Brookings Institute.

Frey, W. H. (2012, June 8). Baby boomers better embrace change. *Washington Post.*

Friedman, D., Laditka, S., Laditka, J., Wu, B., Liu, R., Price, A., and Sharkey, J. (2011). Ethnically diverse older adults' beliefs about staying mentally sharp. *International Journal of Aging & Human Development* 73 (1): 27–52.

Froelich, K., McKee, G., & Rathge, R. (2011). Succession planning in nonprofit organizations. *Nonprofit Management and Leadership* 22 (1): 3–20.

Frolik, C. (2012, February 12). Falls kill more than car accidents: Numbers expected to grow as baby boomer population ages. *Middletown Journal* (Ohio), p. 1.

Fry, R., Kochlar, R., Passel, J., & Suro, R. (2005). Hispanics and the Social Security debate. Washington, DC: Pew Hispanic Center.

Fuller, F. T., Johnson-Tubes, A., Hall, M. A., & Osuji, T. (2012). Promoting brain health for African Americans: Evaluating the healthy brains initiative, a community-level demonstration project. *Journal of Health Care for the Poor and Underserved* 23 (1): 99–113.

Furman, R. & Gibelman, M. (2013). Navigating human service organizations, third edition. Chicago: Lyceum.

Gabriel, T. (2011, November 22). A Gingrich alternative to Social Security. *New York Times,* p. A15.

Gabrielson, M. L. (2011). "We have to create family": Aging support issues and needs among older lesbians. *Journal of Gay & Lesbian Social Services* 23 (3): 322–334.

Gamble, J. L., Hurley, B. J., Schultz, P. A., Jaglom, W. S., Krishman, N., & Harris, M. (2013). Climate change and older adults: State of the Science. *Environmental Health Perspectives* 121 (1): 15–22.

Gambling News. (2009, May 25). Baby boomers and seniors the main land gamblers. www.casinomeister.com/news/may2009/online_casino_news5/BABY-BOOMERS-AND-SENIORS-THE-MAIN-LAND-GAMBLERS.php. Accessed April 4, 2013.

Garcia, G. M., Romero, R. A., & Maxwell, A. E. (2010). Correlates of smoking cessation among Filipino immigrant men. *Journal of Immigrant and Minority Health* 12 (2): 259–202.

Garrett, N. & Martini, E. M. (2007). The boomers are coming: A total cost of care model of the impact of population aging on the cost of chronic conditions in the United States. *Disease Management* 10 (2): 51–60.

Garson, A. (2009, September 28). The grandparents corps: A new primary care model. Health Affairs Blog. http://healthaffairs.org/blog/2009/09/28/the-grandparents-corps-a-new-primary-care-model/. Accessed January 21, 2012.

Garstka, T. A., Hummert, M. L., & Branscombe, N. R. (2005). Perceiving age discrimination in response to intergenerational inequity. *Journal of Social Issues* 61 (2): 321–342.

Gassoumis, Z. D., Lincoln, K. D., & Vega, W. A. (2011). How low-income minorities get by in retirement: Poverty levels and income sources. USC Edward R. Roybal Institute on Aging.

Gassoumis, Z. D., Wilber, K. H., Baker, L. A., & Torres-Gil, F. M. (2010). Who are the Latino baby boomers? Demographic and economic characteristics of a hidden population. *Journal of Aging & Social Policy* 22 (1): 53–68.

Gelfaud, D. E., Balcazar, H., Parzuchowski, J., & Lenox, S. (2004). Issues in hospice utilization by Mexicans. *Gerontologist* 23 (1): 3–19.

Gelman, C. R. (2010). "La lucha": The experiences of Latino family caregivers of patients with Alzheimer's Disease. *Clinical Gerontologist* 22 (2): 181–193.

Gelman, C. R. (2014). Familismo and its impact on the family caregiving of Latinos with Alzheimer's disease: A complex narrative. *Research on Aging* 36 (1): 40–71.

General Accounting Office. (2003). *Social Security and Minorities: Earnings, Disability Incidence, and Mortality Are Key Factors That Influence Taxes Paid and Benefits Received.* Washington, DC: General Accounting Office.

General Accountability Office. (2011). *Older Adults and the 2007–2009 Recession.* Washington, DC: General Accountability Office.

Gerard, J., Landy-Meyer, L., & Roe, J. (2006). Grandparents raising grandchildren: The role of social support in coping with caregiving challenges. *International Journal of Aging & Human Development* 62 (4): 359–383.

Geyman, J. (2006). *Shredding the Social Contract: The Privatization of Medicare.* Monroe, ME: Common Courage.

Gfroerer, J., Penne, M., Pemberton, M., & Folsom, R. (2003). Substance abuse treatment need among older adults in 2020: The impact of the aging baby-boomer cohort. *Drug & Alcohol Dependence* 69 (2): 127–135.

Ghilarducci, T. (2008). The future of retirement in aging societies. *International Review of Applied Economics* 24 (3): 319–331.

Ghilarducci, T. (2012, July 22). Our ridiculous approach to retirement. *New York Times,* p. 5.

Gibson, R. (2007). *What Is Cultural Assets?* Sydney: University of Sydney College of Arts.

Gilleard, C. & Higgs, P. (2007). The third age and the baby boomer: Two approaches to the social structuring of later life. *International Journal of Ageing and Later Life* 2 (2): 13–30.

Gillick, M. R. (2007). *The Denial of Aging: Perpetual Youth, Eternal Life, and Other Dangerous Fantasies.* Cambridge: Harvard University Press.

Gillick, M. R. (2009). Shades of gray. *Hastings Center Report* 39 (no. 2): pp. 46–47.

Gillon, S. (2004). *Boomer Nation: The Largest and Richest Generation Ever and How It Changed America.* New York: Free Press.

Gilmour, J. A. (2007). Reducing disparities in the access and use of Internet health information: A discussion paper. *International Journal of Nursing Studies* 44 (7): 1270–1278.

Gilroy, R. (2006). Taking a capabilities approach to evaluating supportive environments for older people. *Applied Research in Quality Life* 1 (4): 343–356.

Ginieniewicz, J. (2010). *The Accumulation and Transfer of Civic and Assets by Argentinean Migrants in Spain.* Manchester: Global Urban Research Centre, University of Manchester.

Gist, J. (2009). Population aging, entitlement growth, and the economy. In R. B. Hudson (ed.), *Boomer Bust? Perspectives on the Boomers* (pp. 173–196). Westport, CT: Praeger.

Gist, J., Figueiredo, C., & Verma, S. K. (2012). Boom and bust: Housing equity withdrawal and consumption decisions and their impacts on household wealth. *Journal of Aging & Social Policy* 24 (1): 1–28.

Gitlin, L. N. & Wolff, J. (2011). Familial involvement in care transitions of older adults: What do we know and where do we go from here? *Annual Review of Gerontology and Geriatrics* 31 (1): 31–64 (34).

Gittell, R. & Tebaldi, E. (2006). Charitable giving: Factors influencing giving in U.S. states. *Nonprofit and Voluntary Sector Quarterly* 35 (4): 721–736.

Giunta, N., Morano, C., Parikh, N. S., Friedman, D., Fahs, M. C., & Gallo, W. T. (2012). Racial and ethnic diversity in senior centers: Comparing participant characteristics in more and less multicultural settings. *Journal of Gerontological Social Work* 55 (6): 467–483.

Gokhale, J. (2005). Social Security status quo versus reform: What's the tradeoff? Cato Institute Social Security Choice Paper No. 25.

Gokhale, J. (2011). Social Security's financial outlook and reforms: An independent evaluation. Washington, DC: Cato Institute

Goldsmith, J. (2008). The long baby boom: An optimistic vision for a graying population. Baltimore: Johns Hopkins University Press.

Golick, T. (2008). Demographics, trends, and a call to action. *Journal of Poverty Law and Policy,* September–October.

Gonyea, J. G. (2005). The economic well-being of older Americans and the persistent divide. *Public Policy and Aging Report* 15(3): 1–16.

Gonyea, J. G. (2009). Multigenerational bonds, family support, and baby boomers: Current challenges and future prospects for elder care. In R. B. Hudson (ed.), *Boomer Bust? Perspectives on the Boomers* (pp. 213–232). Westport, CT: Praeger.

Gonzalez, H. M., Tarrar, W., Whitfield, K. E., & Vega, W. A. (2010). The epidemiology of major depression and ethnicity in the United States. *Journal of Psychiatric Research* 44 (15): 1043–1051.

Goodheart, C. D. (2012). The impact of health disparities on cancer caregivers. In R. C. Talley et al. (eds.), *Cancer Caregivers in the United States, Caregiving: Research, Practice, Policy* (pp. 63–77). New York: Springer.

Goodman, J. C., Herrick, D., & Moore, D. (2006). Ten steps to reforming baby boomer retirement. Dallas: National Center for Policy Analysis.

Goodroad, B. K. (2003). HIV and AIDS in people older than 50: A continuing concern. *Journal of Gerontological Nursing* 29 (4): 18–24.

Goss, S. (2010). The future financial status of the Social Security Program. *Social Security Bulletin* 70 (3): 111–125.

Gould, E. & Hertel-Fernandez, A. (2010). Early retiree and near-elderly health insurance in recession. *Journal of Aging & Social Policy* 22 (2): 172–187.

Grandich, P. (2010, July 7). Baby boomer blues. www.demodirt.com/index.php/baby-boomer-trends/consumer-spending/402-baby-boomer-blues. Accessed December 27, 2011.

Gray, J. I. & Kakadaki, K. (2005). A strengths perspective for assessing older adults: Curriculum enrichment in a human behavior course. *Journal of Baccalaureate Social Work* 1(1): 55–66.

Gray, M. (2011). Back to basics: A critique of the strengths perspective in social work: Families in society. *Journal of Contemporary Social Services* 92 (1): 5–11.

Gray, S. L., Elliott, D., & Semla, T. (2009). Implications for pharmacy from the Institute of Medicine's Report on Health Care Workforce and an Aging America. *Annals of Pharmacotherapy* 43 (6): 1133–1138.

Green, A. E. (2009). Older people and transitions from employment to nonemployment: International perspectives and policy issues. *Professional Geographer* 61 (1): 46–58.

Greenblatt, A. (2007). Aging baby boomers: Will the "youth" generation' redefine old age? *CQ Researcher* 17 (37): 867–888.

Greenblatt, A. (2011). Aging population: Can the U.S. support its growing ranks of elderly. *CQ Researcher* 15 (25): 577–600.

Greenfield, J.C., Morrow-Howell, N., & Teufel, J. (2012). Do caregivers benefit more from educational and volunteer activities than their noncaregiving peers? *Journal of Gerontological Social Work* 55 (8): 738–744.

Greer, T. M., Brondobo, E., & Brown, P. (2014). Systematic racism moderts effects of provider racial biases on adherence to hypertension treatment for African Americans. *Health Psychology* 33 (1): 35–42.

Griffith, D. M., Ellis, K. R., & Allen, J. O. (2013). An intersectional approach to social determinants of stress for African American men: Men's and women's perspectives. *American Journal of Men's Health* 7 (4 Suppl.): 19S–30s.

Grossman, B. R. (2009). Part 1: Social insurance: History, politics, and prospects. In L. Rogne, C. L. Estes, B. R. Grossman, B. A. Hollister, & E. Solway (eds.), *Social Insurance and Social Justice* (pp. 3–24). New York: Springer.

Grossman, B. R., Solway, E., Hollister, B. A., Estes, C. L., & Rogne, L. (2009). One nation, interdependent: Exploring the boundaries of citizenship in the history of Social Security and Medicare. In L. Rogne, C. L. Estes, B. R. Grossman, B. A. Hollister, & E. Solway (eds.). *Social Insurance and Social Justice* (pp. 115–147). New York: Springer.

Guberman, N., Lavoie, J.-P., Blein, L., & Olazabal, I. (2012). Baby boomer caregiver: Care in the age of individualization. *Gerontologist* 52 (2): 210–218.

Gusmano, M. & Okma, K. (2010, August 10). The bridge side of aging: Reframing the debate. APSA Annual Meeting Paper.

Gustman, A. L. & Steinmeier, T. (2009). How changes in Social Security affect recent retirement trends. *Research on Aging* 31 (2): 261–290.

Gutierrez, L. (1990). Working with women of color: An empowerment perspective. *Social Work* 35 (2): 149–154.

Guzzardo, M. T. & Sheehan, N. W. (2012). Puerto Rican elders' knowledge and use of community-based long-term care services. *Journal of Gerontrological Social Work* 56 (1): 26–48.

Haber, D. (2009). Gerontology: Adding an empowerment paradigm. *Journal of Applied Gerontology* 28 (4): 283–297.

Haber, D. (2013). *Health Promotion and Aging: Practical Applications for Health Promotion,* 6th ed. New York: Springer.

Hagemejer, K. (2009). Social security in times of crisis: An international perspective. Expert Group Meeting on Population Aging, International Transfers and Social Protection, Santiago, Chile.

Haines, A. (2009). Asset-based community development. In R. Phillips & R. H. Pittman (eds.), *An Introduction to Community Development* (pp. 38–48). New York: Routledge.

Hakoyama, M. & MaloneBeach, E. E. (2013). Predictors of grandparent-grandchild closeness: An ecological perspective. *Journal of Interpersonal Relationships* 11 (1): 32–49.

Hales, B. D. (2012). Untapped: Elderly civic engagement in the rebuilding of the Mississippi Gulf. *Community Development* 43 (5): 599–613.

Halliwell, P. A., Gassoumis, Z. D., & Wilber, K. H. (2007). Social Security reform: Implications for Latino retirees. Latinos Social Security Policy Brief, 3, 1–4.

Hamilton, A. B. & Grella, C. E. (2009). Gender differences among older heroin users. *Journal of Women & Aging* 21 (2): 111–124.

Hampton, T. (2008). Experts predict visits by baby boomers will soon strain emergency departments. *Journal of the American Medical Association* 299 (22): 2613–2614.

Hank, K. (2011). Societal determinants of productive aging: A multilevel analysis across 11 European countries. *European Sociological Review* 27 (4): 526–541.

Hannon, K. (2012, February 14). Why Latinos aren't saving for retirement. *Forbes.* www.forbes.com/sites/kerryhannon/2012/02/14/why-latinos-arent-saving-for-retirem. Accessed April 10, 2012.

Harahan, M. F. (2010–2011). A critical look at the looming long-term-care workforce crisis. *Generations* 34 (4): 20–26.

Harahan, M. F. & Stone, R. I. (2009). Who will care? Building the geriatric long-term care labor force. In R. B. Hudson (ed.), *Boomer Bust? Economic and Political Issues of the Graying Society* (pp. 233–253). Westport, CT: Praeger.

Hardcastle, D. A., Powers, P. R., & Wenocur, B. (2011). *Community Practice: Theories and Skills for Social Workers,* 3d ed. New York: Oxford University Press.

Harris, A. H. & Thoresen, C. E. (2005). Volunteerism is associated with delayed mortality in older people: Analysis of the longitudinal study of aging. *Journal of Health Psychology* 10 (6): 730–752.

Haroian, B., Ekmekjian, E. C., & Grivoyannis, E. C. (2007). Poverty in the United States: A continuing and growing problem. *Journal of Business & Economic Research* 5 (12): 13–19.

Hartman-Stein, P. E. & Polkanowicz, E. S. (2003). Behavioral determinants of healthy aging: Good news for the baby boomer generation. *Journal of Issues in Nursing* 8 (2): 1–27.

Harvard School of Public Health. (2004). *Reinventing Aging: Baby Boomers and Civic Engagement.* Boston: Harvard School of Public Health.

Hasin, D. S., Keyes, K. M., Alderson, D., Wang, S., Aharonovich, E., & Grant, B. F. (2008). Cannabis withdrawal in the United States: A general population study. *Journal of Clinical Psychiatry* 69 (9): 1354–1363.

Hass, D. R. (2009b). Living and leaving: Financial and estate planning for boomers. In R.B. Hudson (ed.), *Boomer Bust? Economic and Political Issues of the Graying Society* (pp. 63–76). Westport, CT: Praeger.

Haugebrooks, S., Zgoba, K. M., Maschi, T., Morgen, K., & Brown, D. (2010). Trauma, stress, health, and mental health issues among ethnically diverse older adult prisoners. *Journal of Correctional Health Care* 16 (3): 220–229.

Hayslip Jr., B. & Goodman, C. C. (2008). Grandparents raising grandchildren: Benefits and rewards? *Journal of Interpersonal Relationships* 5 (4): 117–119.

Hayes-Bautista, D. E., Chang, C., & Schink, W. (2012). Latino and non-Latino elderly in Los Angeles County: A pilot study of demographic trends for disability and long-term care. In I. G. Cook & J. Halsall (eds.), *Aging in Comparative Perspective: Processes and Policies* (pp. 227–241). New York: Springer Science+Business Media.

Hayes-Bautista, D. E., Schink, W. O., & Chapa, J. (1988). *The Burden of Support: Young Latinos in an Aging Society.* Berkeley: University of California Press.

Health Watch (2002). African Americans and older adults and HIV/AIDS. www.hwatch.org/hivseniors.shtml. Accessed May 2, 2006.

Healy, J. (2004). The benefits of an ageing population. Australian National University. www.tai.org.au/documents/dp_fulltext/DP63.pdf. Accessed November 26, 2011.

Heaphy, D. G., Mitra, M., & Bouldin, E. D. (2011). Disability and health inequity. In *Public Health Perspectives on Disability,* pp. 117–150. New York: Springer.

Heavens, A. J. (2006, July 6). Baby boomers a big component of home ownership. *Chicago Tribune,* p. 1.

Hebert, L. E., Veuve, J., Scherr, P. A., & Evans, D. A. (2012). Alzheimer's in the United States (2010–2050) estimated using the 2010 census. *Neurology* 80 (19): 1778–1783.

Hed, P. (2009). The two-legged stool: The reconfiguration of risk in retirement income security. *Generations* 33 (3): 12–18.

Heliker, D., Chadwick, A., & O'Connell, T. (2001). The meaning of gardening and the effects on perceived well being of gardening project on diverse populations of elders. *Activities, Adaptation & Aging* 24 (1): 35–56.

Hellmich, N. (2010, March 3). Baby boomers by the numbers: Census reveals trends. *USA Today,* p. A1.

Herbold, H. (1994–1995). Never a level playing field: Blacks and the GI Bill. *Journal of Blacks in Higher Education* 6 (Winter): 104–108.

Herrera, A. P., Angel, J. L., Venegas, C. D., & Angel, R. J. (2012). Estimating the demand for long-term care among aging Mexican Americans: Cultural preferences versus economic realities. In J. L. Angel, F. Torres-Gil, & K. Markides (eds.), *Aging, Health, and Longevity in the Mexican-Origin Population* (pp. 259–275). New York: Springer.

Heuberger, R. A. (2009). Alcohol and the older adult: A comprehensive review. *Journal of Nutrition for the Elderly* 28 (3): 203–235.

Hicks, J. & Kingson, E. R. (2009). The economic crisis: How fare older Americans? *Generations* 33 (3): 6–11.

Hicks, P. (2011). The surprisingly large policy implications of changing retirement durations. Hamilton, Ontario: SEDAP Research Paper No. 284, McMaster University.

Higgs, P., Leontowitsch, M., Stevenson, F., & Jones, I. R. (2009). Not just old and sick—the "will to health" in later life. *Ageing & Society* 29 (4): 687–707.

Hill, P. (2012, January 29). Retiring later a tough sell in cutting deficit: Safety net under stress. *Washington Times,* p. 1.

Hilt, M. L. & Lipschultz, J. H. (2005). Mass media, an aging population, and baby boomers. Hillsdale, NJ: L. Erlbaum.

Hilton, J. H., Gonzalez, C. A., Saleh, M., Maitoza, R., & Anngela-Cole, L. (2012). Perceptions of successful aging among older Latinas, in cross cultural context. *Journal of Cross-Cultural Gerontology* 27 (3): 183–199.

Hilton, J. M., Kopera-Frye, K., & Krave, A. (2009). Successful aging from the perspective of family caregivers. *Family Journal: Counseling and Therapy for Couples and Families* 17 (1): 39–50.

Hiltonsmith, R. (2010). *The Failure of the 401(k): How Individual Retirement Plans Are a Costly Gamble for American Workers.* New York: Demos.

Hinrichsen, G. A. (2010). Public policy and the provision of psychological services to older adults. *Professional Psychology: Research and Practice* 41 (2): 97–103.

Hinterlong, J. E. (2006). Race disparities in health among older adults: Examining the role of productive engagement. *Health & Social Work* 31 (4): 275–288.

Hirshorn, B. A. & Settersten, R. A. Jr. (2013). Civic involvement across the life course: Moving beyond age-based assumptions. *Advances in Life Course Research* 18 (3): 199–211.

Hispanic PR Blog. (2011, September 12). Education impacts work-life earnings 5X more than other demographic factors, Census Bureau reports. www.latinoeconomicsecurity.org/news-091211.html. Accessed April 10, 2012.

Ho, A. T. (2008). Asian American giving circles: Building bridges between philanthropy and our communities. Paper presented at the 37th Association for Research on Nonprofit Organizations and Voluntary Action (ARNOVA) Conference, November 20, 2008, Philadelphia.

Hodge, D. R. (2005). Developing a Spiritual Assessment Toolbox: A discussion of the strengths and limitations of five different assessment methods. *Health & Social Work* 30 (4): 314–323.

Hodge, D. R. & Sun, F. (2012). Positive feelings of caregivers among Latino Alzheimer's family caregivers: Understanding the role of spirituality. *Aging Mental Health* 16 (6): 689–698.

Hodge, P. (2006). Baby boomer women: Secure futures or not? Cambridge: Harvard Global Generations Policy Institute.

Hoffman, G. J., Lee, J., & Mendez-Luck, C. A. (2012). Health behaviors among baby boomer caregivers. *Gerontologist* 52 (2): 219–230.

Hofstede, G. (1991). Cultures and organizations: Software of the mind. London: McGraw Hill.

Holahan, J. (2009). Medicaid and entitlement reform. Washington, DC: Urban Institute.

Holden, K. C. (2009). The boomer and their economic prospects. In R. B. Hudson (ed.), *Boomer Bust? Perspectives on the Boomers* (pp. 63–75). Westport, CT: Praeger.

Hollister, B. A. (2009). Part III: The ongoing debates over social insurance programs: Introduction. In L. Rogne, C. L. Estes, B. R. Grossman, B. A. Hollister, & E. Solway (eds.), *Social Insurance and Social Justice* (pp. 193–195). New York: Springer.

Holstein, M. (2009). A normative approach to Social Security: What dignity requires. In L. Rogne, C. L. Estes, B. R. Grossman, B. A. Hollister, & E. Solway (eds.), *Social Insurance and Social Justice* (pp. 233–249). New York: Springer.

Holzer, H. J. (2008). *Economic Costs of Inadequate Investments in Workforce Development.* Washington, DC: Urban Institute.

Hong, S.-J. & Morrow-Howell, N. (2013). Increasing older adults' benefits from institutional capacity of volunteer programs. *Social Work Research* 37 (2): 99–108.

Hooper, M. W., Baker, E. A., Rodriguez de Ubarra, D., McNutt, M., & Abuwalia, J. S. (2012). Acculturation predicts 7-day smoking cessation among treatment-seeking African-Americans in a group intervention. *Annals of Behavorial Medicine* 43 (1): 74–83.

Hooyman, N. P. (ed.). (2009). *Transforming Social Work Education: The First Decade of the Hartford Geriatric Social Work Institute.* Alexandria, VA: Council on Social Work Education.

Hospital Home Health. (2008). Baby boomers may not have specialists needed at age 65. *Hospital Home Health* 25 (1): 83–84

Hosteller, A. T. (2011). Senior centers in the era of the "Third Age": Country clubs, community centers, or something else? *Journal of Aging Studies* 25 (2): 166–176.

Houston, D. K., Cai, J., & Stevens, J. (2008). Overweight and obesity in young and middle-age and early retirement. *Obesity* 7 (1): 143–149.

Howard, C. (2010). Taxation and the elderly. In R. B. Hudson (ed.), *The New Politics of Old Age Policy*, 2d ed. (pp. 337–355). Baltimore: Johns Hopkins University Press.

Howden, L. M. & Meyer, J. A. (2011). *Age and Sex Composition: 2010.* Washington, DC: U.S. Census Bureau.

Hoy, S. (2010, September 11). Undocumented immigrants giving Social Security, baby boomers a big boost. *LA Progress.* www.laprogressive.com/immigration-reform/undocumented-immigrants-giving-soc. Accessed November 17, 2011.

Hudson, R. B. (2009a). Public policy and the boomers: An expanding scope of conflict. In R. B. Hudson (ed.), *Boomer Bust? Perspectives on the Boomers* (pp. 113–134). Westport, CT: Praeger.

Hudson, R. B. (ed.). (2009b). *Boomer Bust? Economic and Political Issues of the Graying Society.* Westport, CT: Praeger.

Hudson, R. B. (2010). Contemporary challenges to aging policy. In R. B. Hudson (ed.), *The New Politics of Old Age Policy,* 2d ed. (pp. 3–20). Baltimore: Johns Hopkins University Press.

Hudson, R. B. & Gonyea, J. G. (2012). Baby boomers and the shifting political construction of old age. *Gerontologist* 52 (2): 1–11.

Huffington Post. (2012, September 9). Grandparents raising grandchildren: Study finds childcare assistance growing. *Huffington Post.* www.huffingtonpost.com/2012/09/09/grandparents-raising-gran_n_1866777.html. August 13, 2013.

Hughes, M. E. & Rand, A. M. (2004). *The Lives Times of the Baby Boomers.* Washington, DC: Population Reference Bureau.

Hughes, S. L., Seymour, R. B., Campbell, R. T., Shaw, J. W., Fabiyi, C., & Sokas, R. (2011). Comparison of two health-promotion programs for older workers. *American Journal of Public Health* 101 (5): 883–890.

Hugo, G., Taylor, A. W., & Del Grande, E. (2008). Are baby boomers booming too much? An epidemiological description of overweight and obese baby boomers. *Obesity Research and Clinical Practice* 2 (3): 203–214.

Human Rights Watch. (2012). *U.S. Number of Aging Prisoners Soaring.* New York: Human Rights Watch.

Hutchison, T., Morrison, P., & Mikhailovich, K. (2006). *A Review of the Literature on Active Ageing.* Canberra: University of Canberra.

Iezzoni, L. I. (2006a). Quality of care for Medicare beneficiaries with disabilities under the age of 65 years. *Expert Panel of Pharmacoeconomics and Outcomes Research* 6 (3): 261–273.

Iezzoni, L. I. (2006b). Going beyond disease to address disability. *New England Journal of Medicine* 355:976–979.

Iezzoni, L. I., Frakt, A. B., & Pizer, S. D. (2011). Uninsured persons with disability confront substantial barriers to health care services. *Disability and Health Journal* 4 (3): 238–244.

Ince, L. (2010). Kinship care: An Afrocentric perspective. Birmingham: University of Birmingham.

Isaacs, J. B. (2009). *Spending on Children and the Elderly.* Washington, DC: Brookings Institute.

Issa, P. & Zedlewski, S. R. (2011). *Poverty Among Older Americans, 2009.* Washington, DC: Urban Institute.

Jackson, K. F. (2010). Living the multiracial experience: Shifting racial expressions, resisting race, and seeking community. *Qualitative Social Work* 11 (1): 42–60.

Jacobs, R. J. & Kane, M. N. (2010). HIV-related stigma in midlife and older women. *Social Work in Health Care* 49 (1): 68–89.

Jacobsen, L. A. & Mather, M. (2011). *A Post-recession Update on U.S. Social and Economic Trends.* Washington, DC: Population Bulletin Update.

Jacobsen, L. A., Kent, M., Lee, M., & Mather, M. (2011). America's aging population. Washington, DC: Population Reference Bureau.

Jacoby, S. (2012). *Never Say Die: The Myth of the New Old Age.* New York: Vintage.

James, S. (2012, February 23). Graying and gay, and finding a home. *New York Times,* p. A22.

Jang, Y., Borenstein, A., Chiriboga, D., Phillips, K., and Mortimer, J. (2006). Religiosity, adherence to traditional culture, and psychological well-being among African American elders. *Journal of Applied Gerontology* 25 (4): 343–355.

Jaslow, R. 92011, July 19). Baby boomers becoming more obese, could result in high Medicare costs. CBS News. www.cbsnews.com/2102-504763_162-20080736. html?tag=contentMain;contentBo. Accessed December 21, 2011.

Jayson, S. (2010, November 18). Other generations growing weary of baby boomers. *USA Today,* p. A1.

Jensen, D. & Little, C. (2008). *San Francisco Baby Boomers—a Breed Apart?* San Francisco: Baby Boomer Task Force of the Advisory Council to the San Francisco Aging and Adult Services Commission.

Jeon, S. M. & Hyun, S. S. (2012). Examining the influence of casino attributes on baby boomers' satisfaction and loyalty in the casino industry. *Current Issues in Tourism* 16 (4): 343–368.

Jervis, L. L., Cullum, J. C. M., & Manson, S. M. (2006). American Indians, cognitive assessment, and dementia. In G. Yeo & D. Gallagher-Thompson (eds.), *Ethnicity and the Dementias,* 2d ed. (pp. 87–101). New York: Routledge.

Jeste, D. V. & Palmer, B. W. (2013). A call for a new positive psychiatry of ageing. *British Journal of Psychiatry* 203 (1): 81–83.

Jimenez, T. R. (2008–9). What different generations of Mexican Americans think about immigration from Mexico. *Generations* 32 (4): 93–96.

Johnson, H. (2013). We will be different: Ageism and the temporal construction of old age. *Gerontologist* 53 (2): 198–204.

Johnson, J. D., Whitlatch, C. J., & Menne, H. L. (2013). Activity and well-being of older adults: Does cognitive impairment play a role? *Research on Ageing*.

Johnson, K. & Wilson, K. (2010a). *Current Economic Status of Older Adults in the United States: A Demographic Profile*. Washington, DC: National Council on Aging.

Johnson, K. & Wilson, K. (2010b). *A Look at Issues Facing Older Adults Ages 55 to 64*. Washington, DC: National Council on Aging.

Johnson, M. (2008). Quality of life expectations: Exploring baby-boomer financial means-end goal structures. *Journal of Financial Services Marketing* 13 (4): 245–258.

Johnson, M. L. (2009). Procession of the generations: Are we still traveling together. In L. Rogne, C. L. Estes, B. R. Grossman, B. A. Hollister, & E. Solway (eds.), *Social Insurance and Social Justice* (pp. 25–45). New York: Springer.

Johnson, R. G. & Borrego, E. (2009). Public administration and the increased need for cultural competence in the twenty-first century. *Administrative Theory & Praxis* 31 (2): 206–221.

Johnson, R. W., Haaga, O., & Simms, M. (2011). *50+ African Americans: A Status Report, Implications, and Recommendations*. Washington, DC: Urban Institute.

Johnson, R. W. & Mommaerts, C. (2009). *Unemployment Rate Hits All-Time High for Adults Age 65 and Older*. Washington, DC: Urban Institute.

Johnson, R. W. & Mommaerts, C. (2010a). *How Did Older Workers Fare in 2009?* Washington, DC: Urban Institute.

Johnson, R. W. & Mommaerts, C. (2010b). *Will Health Care Costs Bankrupt Aging Boomers?* Washington, DC: Urban Institute.

Johnson, R. W., Mommaerts, C., & Park, J. (2011). *Unemployment Statistics on Older Americans*. Washington, DC: Urban Institute.

Johnson, R. W., Toohey, D., & Wiener, J. M. (2007). *Meeting the Long-Term Care Needs of the Baby Boomers: How Changing Families Will Affect Paid Helpers and Institutes*. Washington, DC: Urban Institute.

Jokela, B. H., Hendrickson, L., & Haynes, B. (2013). Teaching financial literacy across the generations. *Journal of Extension* 51 (1): 1–6.

Jones, A. (2011). Disability, health and generation status: How Hispanics in the U.S. fare in late life. *Journal of Immigrant Minority Health* 14 (3): 467–474.

Jones, L. Y. (1980). *Great Expectations: America and the Baby Boomer Generation*. New York: Coward, McCann & Geoghegon.

Jones, G. C. & Sinclair, L. B. (2008). Multiple health disparities among minority adults with mobility limitations: An application of the ICF framework and codes. *Disability and Rehabilitation* 30 (12–13): 901–915,

Joyce, K. & Loe, M. (2010). A sociological approach to ageing, technology and health. *Sociology of Health & Illness* 32 (2): 171–180.

Judd, A. (2007). *The Value of Later Life: Deconstructing the Idea of Aging as Decline.* St Paul, MN: Macalester College.

Kahana, E., Bhatta, T., Lovegreen, L. D., Kahana, B., & Midlarsky, E. (2013). Altruism, helping, and volunteering: Pathways to well-being in late life. *Journal of Aging and Health* 25 (1): 159–187.

Kalache, A. (2012, April 4). How the baby boomers are reinventing old age. *Huffington Post.* www.huffingtonpost.com/dr-alexandre-kalache/how-the-baby-boomers-are-_b_1403431.html. Accessed April 30, 2012.

Kalapatapu, R. K. & Sullivan, M. A. (2010). Prescription use disorders in older adults. *American Journal on Addictions* 19 (6): 515–522.

Kamp, B. J., Wellman, N. S. & Russell, C. (2010). Position of the American Dietetic Association, American Society for Nutrition, and Social for Nutrition Education: Food and nutrition programs for community-residing older adults. *Journal of Nutrition Education & Behavior* 42 (2): 72–82.

Kaplan, R.L. (2008). Top ten myths of Social Security. University of Illinois College of Law: Law and Economics Working Papers.

Kaskie, B., Imhof, S., Cavanaugh, J., & Culp, K. (2008). Civic engagement as a retirement role for aging Americans. *Gerontologist* 48 (3): 368–377.

Katz, M. H. (2011). There's no place like home. *Archives of Internal Medicine* 171 (9): 804–805.

Kawachi, I., Daniels, N., & Robinson, D. E. (2005). Health disparities by race and class: Why both matter. *Health Affairs* 24 (2): 343–352.

Keeter, S. (2008). The aging of the boomers and the rise of the millennials. Washington, DC: Brookings Institution.

Kelley, M., Demiris, G., Nguyen, Oliver, D. P., & Wittenberg-Lyles, E. (2013). Informal hospice caregiver pain management concerns: A qualitative study. *Palliative Medicine* 27 (7): 673–682.

Kelly, C. (2013, January 13). Over 50, and over no illusions. *New York Times* (Sunday business), pp. 1, 4–5.

Kerfoot, K. E., Patrakis, I. L., & Rosenheck, R.A. (2011). Dual diagnosis in an aging population: Prevalence of psychiatric disorders, comorbid substance abuse, and mental health service utilization in the Department of Veterans Affairs. *Journal of Dual Diagnosis* 7 (1–2): 4–13.

Kerr, J. & Biese, A. (2012, April 26). Baby boomer volunteers in demand: Charities, nonprofits eye retirement-age work force. *Daily Record*. www.dailyrecord.com/ricle/20120426/NJNEWS/304260036/Baby-boomer-volunteers-in-demand. Accessed April 30, 2012.

Kerz, M., Teufel, J., & Dinman, M. (2013). OASIS: A community-based model for successful aging. *Ageing International* 38 (2): 122–136.

Killett, K., Shugrue, N., Gruman, C., & Robinson, J. (2010). Care needs of older and middle aged adults with mental illness. *International Review of Modern Sociology* 36 (2): 143–168.

Kim, B. J. & Torres-Gil, F. (2011). Social Security and its impact on older Latinos. *Journal of Applied Gerontology* 30 (1): 85–103.

Kim, G. & Chiriboga, D. A. (2009). Factors affecting nursing home use of older whites and Hispanics: A review of the characteristics of care recipients and caregivers. *Hallym International Journal of Aging* 11 (1): 49–64.

Kim, J. (2011). Socioeconomic inequalities in self-rated health among middle-aged and older adults. *Social Work in Health Care* 50 (2): 124–142.

Kim, K. & Antonopoulos, R. (2011). *Unpaid and Paid Care: The Effects of Child Care and Elder Care on the Standard of Living*. New York: Levy Economic Institute of Bard College.

Kim, S. H., Szabo, R. M., & Madera, R. A. (2012). Epidemiology of humerus fractures in the United States: Nationwide emergency department sample, 2008. *Arthritis Care & Research* 64 (3): 407–414.

Kin, E. et al. (2013). High proportion of hepatitis C virus in community Asian Americans patient's non-liver-related complaints. *Journal of Clinical Gastroenterology* 47 (4): 367–371.

King, D. E., Matheson, E., Chirina, S., Shanker, A., & Broman-Fulks, J. (2013). The status of baby boomers' health in the United States: The healthiest generation? *Journal of the American Medical Association* 173 (5): 385–386.

Kingson, E. R., Cornman, J. W., & Torre-Norton, A. L. (2009). The future of social insurance: Values and generational interdependence. In L. Rogne, C. L. Estes, B. R. Grossman, B. A. Hollister, & E. Solway (eds.), *Social insurance and Social Justice* (pp. 95–108). New York: Springer.

Kinney, J. M. & Kart, C. S. (2012). Family gerontology: An emergent agenda for research, policy, and practice. In R. Blieszner & V. I. Bedford (eds.), *Handbook of Family and Aging* (pp. 431–459). Westport, CT: Praeger.

Kirshenblatt-Gimblett, B., Hufford, M., Hunt, M., & Zeitlin, S. (2006). Grand generation: folklore and the culture of aging. *Generations* 30 (1): 32–37.

Knechtel, R. G. (2007). Productive aging in the Twenty-first century. www.go60owork.htm. Accessed November 26, 2011.

Knickman, J. R. & Snell, E. K. (2002). The 2030 problem: Caring for aging baby boomers. *Health Services Research* 37 (4): 849–884.

Knochel, K. A., Quam, J. K., & Croghan, C. P. (2011). Are old lesbian and gay people well served? Understanding the perceptions, preparation, and experiences of aging services providers. *Journal of Applied Gerontology* 30 (3): 370–389.

Ko, E., Cho, S., Perez, R. L., Yeo, Y., & Palomino, H. (2013). Good and bad death: Exploring the perspectives of older Mexican-Americans. *Journal of Gerontological Social Work* 56 (1): 6–25.

Kochanek, K. D., Xu, J., Murphy, S. L., Minino, A. M., & Kung, H.-C. (2011). Deaths: Preliminary data for 2009. *National Vital Statistics Report* 59 (4): 1–51.

Konetzka, R. T. & Werner, R. M. (2009). Review: Disparities in long-term care: Building equity into market-based reforms. *Medical Care Research and Review* 68 (5): 491–521.

Kotkin, J. & Ozuna, E. (2012). America's demographic future. *Cato Journal* 32 (1): 55–69.

Kozar, J. M. (2010). Women's responses to fashion media images: A study of female consumers aged 30–59. *International Journal of Consumer Studies* 34 (3): 272–278.

Krause, N. & Bastida, E. (2011). Financial strain, religious involvement, and life satisfaction among older Mexican Americans. *Research on Aging* 33 (4): 403–425.

Kroff, N. P. (2012). Increasing community capacity for older residents and their families. *Journal of Gerontonlogical Social Work* 55 (4): 304–320.

Kropf, N. P. & Kolomer, S. (2004). Grandparents raising grandchildren: A diverse population. *Journal of Human Behavior and the Social Environment* 9 (4): 65–83.

Kuhn, T. (1962). *The Structure of Scientific Revolutions*. Chicago: University of Chicago Press.

Kunze, F., Boehm, S. A., & Brunch, H. (2011). Generational leadership—How to manage five different generations in the work force. *Business and Economics* 3:87–100.

Kurtzleben, D. (2011, September 15). 5 ways to reform Social Security: There seems to be no painless way to fix the program. *U.S. News and World Report.* www.usnews.com/news/articles/2011/09/15/5-ways-to-reform-social-security. Accessed November 17, 2011.

Kushel, M. (2012). Older homeless adults: Can we do more? *Journal of General Internal Medicine* 67 (1): 5–6.

Kwate, N. O. A. & Meyer, I. H. (2010). The myth of meritocracy and African American health. *American Journal of Public Health* 100 (10): 1831–1834.

Lai, D. W. L. (2007). Cultural aspects of reminiscence of life. In J. A. Kunz & F. G. Soltys (eds.), *Transformational Reminiscence: Life Story Work* (pp. 143–154). New York: Springer.

Laidlaw, K. & Panchana, N. A. (2009). Aging, mental health, and demographic change: Challenges for psychotherapists. *Professional Psychology: Research and Practice* 40 (6): 601–608.

Lambert, J. (2012). *Digital Storytelling: Capturing Lives, Creating Community.* New York: Routledge.

Landau. L., Brazil, K., Kassalainen, S., & Crawshaw, D. (2013). A model for volunteer spiritual care visitors in long-term care. *Journal of Religion, Spirituality & Aging* 25 (3): 216–237.

Landry-Meyer, L., Gerard, J. M., & Guzell, J. R. (2005). Caregiver stress among grandparents raising grandchildren: The functional role of social support. *Marriage and Family Review* 57 (1–2): 171–190.

Langer, N. (2004). Resiliency and spirituality: Foundations of strengths perspective counseling with the elderly. *Educational Gerontology* 30 (7): 611–617.

Lanier, K. A. (2008). Eliminating health disparities among native-born minority older adults. *North Carolina Medical Journal* 69 (5): 390–391.

Lawrence, D. M. (2010). Healthcare for elders in 2050. *Generations* 34 (3): 82–85.

Leal, D. C. & Trejo, S. J. (eds.). (2010). *Latinos and the Economy: Integration and Impact in Schools, Labor Markets, and Beyond.* New York: Springer.

Lee, J. A. B. (1994). *The Empowerment Approach to Social Work Practice.* New York: Columbia University Press.

Lee, J.S. (2012). The Impact of Urban Form on Older Adults: Focusing on Neighborhood Design and Baby Boomers' Local Behavior. Cambridge: M.I.T. Press.

Lee, R., Tuljapurkar, S., & Edwards, R. D. (2010). Uncertain demographic futures and government budgets in the US. *International Studies in Population* 8 (part 2): 79–100.

Lehning, A. J. (2012). City government and aging in place: Community design, transportation and housing innovation adoption. *Gerontologist* 52 (3): 345–356.

Leland, J. (2013, June 2). Spared death, but struggling to live: Those with H.I.V. have arrived at middle age with a virus that is a constant battle. *New York Times*, pp. 24–25.

Lemish, D. & Muhibauer, V. (2012). "Can't have it all": Representation of older women in popular media. *Women & Therapy* 35 (3–4): 165–180.

Lemke, M. R. & Mendonca, R. J. (2013). A question of accessibility: Understanding lay users of medical devices. *Biomedical Instrumentation & Technology: Home Healthcare* 7 (1): 20–25.

Leveille, S. G., Wee, C. C., & Iezzoni, L. I. (2009). Are baby boomers aging better than their predecessors? Trends in obesity, arthritis, and mobility difficulty. In D. M. Cutter & D. A. Wise (eds.), *Health at Older Ages: The Causes and Consequences of Dealing with Disability Among the Elderly* (pp. 223–235). Chicago: University of Chicago Press.

Levine, L. (2008). Retiring baby-boomers—a labor shortage? Washington, DC: Congressional Research Service, Order Code RL33661.

Levinson, W., Kao, A., Kuby, A., & Thisted, R. A. (2005). Not all patients want to participate in decision making: A national study of public preferences. *Journal of General Internal Medicine* 20 (6): 531–535.

Levitsky, S. K. (2010). Caregiving and the construction of political claims for long-term care policy reform. In R. B. Hudson (ed.), *The New Politics of Old Age Policy,* 2d ed. (pp. 208–230). Baltimore: Johns Hopkins University Press.

Levy, D. S. (2005). HIV/AIDS fifty and older: A hidden and growing population. *Journal of Gerontological Social Work* 46 (2): 37–50.

Lewis, D. C., Medvedev, K., & Seponski, D. M. (2011). Awakening to the desires of older women: Deconstructing ageism within fashion magazines. *Journal of Aging Studies* 25 (2): 101–109.

Lewis, J. P. (2011). Successful aging through the eyes of Alaskan Native elders: What it means to be an elder in Bristol Bay, AK. *Gerontologist* 51 (4): 540–549.

Liburd, L. C. (ed.). (2010). *Diabetes and Health Disparities: Community-Based Approaches for Racial and Ethnic Populations.* New York: Springer.

Light, P. C. (1988). *Baby Boomers.* New York: Norton.

Light, P. C. (1993). *Baby Boomers in Retirement: An Early Perspective.* Washington, DC: Congressional Budget Office.

Ligon, J. (2013). When older adult substance abuse affects others: What helps and what does not? *Journal of Social Work Practice in the Addictions* 12 (4): 223–226.

Lin, I.-F. & Brown, S. L. (2012). Unmarried boomers confront old age: A national portrait. *Gerontologist* 52 (2): 153–165.

Lips, H. M. & Hastings, S. L. (2012). Competing discourses for older women: Agency/leadership vs. disengagement/retirement. *Women & Therapy* 35 (3–4): 145–164.

Lipschultz, J. H., Hilt, M. L., & Reilly, H. J. (2007). Organizing the baby boomer construct: An exploration of marketing, social systems, and culture. *Educational Gerontology* 33 (8): 759–773.

Lipset, S. M. (1996). *American Exceptionalism: A Double-Edged Sword*. New York: Norton.

Littrell, J., Brooks, F., Ivery, J. M., & Ohmer, M. L. (2013). Economic realities, history, and framing inequality and its discontent. In L. Simmons & S. Harding (eds.), *Economic Justice, Labor, and Community Practice* (pp. 11–30). New York: Routledge.

Liu, H. & Zhang, Z. (2013). Disability trends by marital status among older Americans: 1997–2010: An examination by gender and race. *Population Research and Policy Research* 32 (1): 103–127.

Liu, Z. & Spiegel, M. M. (2011, August 22). Boomer retirement: Headwinds for the U.S. equity markets? *FRBSF Economic Letter*.

LivingSenior. (2012, June 9). The spiritual but not religious baby boomer. www.livingsenior.com/blog/the-spiritual-but-not-religious-baby-boomer. Accessed November 29, 2012.

Livingston, G. & Parker, K. (2010). Since the start of the Great Recession, more children raised by grandparents. Washington, DC: Pew Research Center.

Llorente, M. D., Nathaniel, V. I., & McCabe, S. (2012). Older adults. In P. Ruiz & A. Primm (eds.), *Disparities in Psychiatric Care* (pp. 139–148). Riverwoods, IL: Lippincott Williams & Wilkins.

Lodge, A. C. & Umberson, D. (2012). All shook up: Sexuality of mid- to later life married couples. *Journal of Marriage and the Family* 74 (3): 428–443.

Longman, P. (1985). Justice between generations. *Atlantic Monthly* 255 (6): 73–81.

Lopez, J., Romero-Moreno, R., Marquez-Gonzalez, M., & Losado, A. (2012). Spirituality and self-efficacy in dementia family caregiving: Trust in God and in yourself. *International Journal of Psychogeriatrics* 24 (12): 1943–1954.

Lopez, L. M. & Vargas, E. W. (2011). En dos culturas: Group work with Latino immigrants and refugees. In G. L. Greif & P. H. Ephross (eds.), *Group Work with Populations at Risk* (pp. 136–152). New York: Oxford University Press.

Losh, S. C. (2009). Generation, education, gender and ethnicity in America: Digital Divides. In E. Ferrsa, Y. K. Dwinedi, J. R.Gill Garcia, & M. D. Williams (eds.), *Handbook of Research on Overcoming Digital Divides: Constructing an Equitable and Competitive Information Society* (pp. 196–222). Hersey, PA: IGI Global.

Love, D. A., Smith, P. A., & McNair, L. C. (2008). A new look at the wealth adequacy of older U.S. households. *Review of Income and Wealth* 54 (4): 616–642.

Low, J. & Dupuls-Bianchard, S. (2013). From zoomers to gesserade: Representations of the aging body in ageist and consumerist society. *Societies* 3 (1): 52–65.

Lowman, S., Hunter, R., & Reddy, S. (2008). Immigrant elders: New challenges for North Carolina. *North Carolina Medical Journal* 69 (5): 389–392.

Lum, T. Y. & Vanderaa, J. P. (2010). Health disparities among immigrant and non-immigrant elders: The association of acculturation and education. *Journal of Immigrant Minority Health* 12 (5): 743–753.

Lumma-Sandt, K. (2011). Images of ageing in a 50+ magazine. *Journal of Aging Studies* 25 (1), 45–51.

Lusardi, A. (2011). America's financial capability. Cambridge, MA: National Bureau of Economic Research.

Lusardi, A. & Mitchell, O. S. (2007). Baby boomer retirement security: The roles of planning, financial literacy, and housing wealth. *Journal of Monetary Economics* 54(1): 205–224.

Lusardi, A. & Mitchell, O. S. (2011). Financial literacy and retirement planning in the United States. National Bureau of Economic Research, Working paper no. 17108.

Lynch, F. R. (2009). Immigrants and the politics of aging boomers: Renewed reciprocity or "Blade Runner" Society? *Generations* 32 (4): 64–72.

Lynch, F. R. (2010). Political power and the baby boomers. In R. B. Hudson (ed.), *The New Politics of Old Age Policy,* 2d ed. (pp. 87–107). Baltimore: Johns Hopkins University Press.

MacArthur Foundation. (2009). *Facts and Fictions About an Aging America.* Chicago: Author.

Mack, K. A. & Ory, M. G. (2003). AIDS and older Americans at the end of the twentieth century. *Journal of Acquired Immune Deficiency Syndromes* 33:S131–S137.

Macnicol, J. (2009). Differential treatment by age: Age discrimination or age affirmation? In R. B. Hudson (ed.), *Boomer Bust? Perspectives on the Boomers* (pp. 241–252). Westport, CT: Praeger.

Macunovich, D. J. (2000). The baby boomers. New York: Barnard College, Columbia University. http://pdf.thepdfportal.com//&id=53359&nocache. Accessed February 2, 2013.

Maestas, N., & Zissimopoulos, J. (2010). How longer work lives ease the crunch of population aging. *Journal of Economic Perspectives* 24 (1): 139–160.

Magnus, G. (2008). *The Age of Aging: How Demographics Are Changing the Global Economy and Our World.* New York: Wiley.

Mahoney, D. F., Cloutterbuck, J., Neary, S., & Zhan, L. (2005). African American, Chinese, and Latino family caregivers' impressions of the onset of diagnosis of dementia: Cross-cultural similarities and differences. *Gerontologist* 45 (6): 783–792.

Mamo, L. (2008). *Awakening Sleeping Beauty: Promises of Eternal Youth Packaged Through Scientific Innovation.* College Park: University of Maryland.

Marcus, M. B. (2010, March 9). Report: Minorities more likely to suffer Alzheimer's Disease. *USA Today,* p. A1.

Mariotto, A. B., Yabroff, K. R., Feuer, E. J., & Brown, M. L. (2011). Projections of the cost of cancer in the United States: 2010–2020. *Journal of the National Cancer Institute* 103 (2): 117–128.

Markert, J. (2008). The fading dream of retirement: Social and financial considerations affecting the retirement dream. *Sociological Spectrum* 28 (2): 213–233.

Marler, P., & Hadaway, C. K. 2002. Being religious or being spiritual in America: A zero-sum proposition? *Journal for the Scientific Study of Religion* 41 (2): 289–300.

Marquez, D. X. & McAuley, E. (2006). Gender and acculturation influences on physical activity in Latino adults. *Annals of Behavioral Medicine* 31 (2): 138–144.

Marquez, N. J., Fogg, L., Wilson, R. S., Staffileno, B. A., Hovern, R. L., Morris, N. C., Bustamente, E. E., & Manning, A. F. (2012). The relationship between physical activity and cognition in older Latinos. *Journal of Gerontology Series B: Psychological Sciences and Social Sciences* 67 (5): 525–534.

Marler, P. L. & Hadaway, C. K. (2002). "Being religious" or "being spiritual" in America: A zero-sum proposition? *Journal for the Scientific Study of Religion* 41 (2): 289–300.

Martin, L. L. (2008). Black asset ownership: Does ethnicity matter? *Social Science Research* 36 (2): 312–323.

Martin, L. G., Freedman, V. A., Schoeni, R. F., & Andreski, P. M. (2009). Health and functioning among baby boomers approaching 60. *Journals of Gerontology Series B: Psychological Sciences and Social Sciences* 64B (3): 369–377.

Martin. L. G., Freedman, V. A., Schoeni, R. F., & Andreski, P. M. (2010). Trends in disability and related chronic conditions among people ages fifty to sixty-four. *Health Affairs* 29 (4): 725–731.

Martin, S. S., Kosberg, J. I., Sun, F., & Durkin, K. (2012). Social work professions in an aging world: Opportunities and perspectives. *Education Gerontology* 38 (3): 166–178.

Martin, R. & Pardini, A. (2009). Booming opportunity: Philanthropy, aging, and recognizing that the glass is half full. In R. B. Hudson (ed.), *Boomer Bust? Perspectives on the Boomers* (pp. 113–123). Westport, CT: Praeger.

Martinez, B. O. (2009). *Diabetes Among Older Latino Adults.* Long Beach: California State University.

Martinez, I. L., Crooks, D., Kim, K. S., & Tanner, E. (2011). Invisible civic engagement among older adults: Valuing the contributions of informal volunteering. *Journal of Cross-Cultural Gerontology* 26 (1): 23–37.

Martini, E. M., Garrett, N., Linquist, T., & Isham, G. J. (2007). The boomers are coming: A total cost of care model of the impact of population aging on health care costs in the United States by major practice category. *Health Services Research* 42 (1): 201–218.

Martinson, M. & Minkler, M. (2006). Civic engagement and older adults: A critical perspective. *Gerontologist* 46 (3): 318–324.

Matthews, D. C., Brilliant, M. G., Clovis, J. B., McNally, M. E., Filiaggi, M. J., Kotzer, R. D., & Lawrence, H. P. (2012). Assessing the oral health of an ageing population: Methods, challenges and predictors of survey participation. *Gerodontology* 29 (2): e656–e666.

Mausbach, B. T., Chattilion, B. A., Roepke, S. K., Patterson, T. L., & Grant, I. (2013). A comparison of psychosocial outcomes in elderly Alzheimer's caregivers and noncaregivers. *American Journal of Geriatric Psychiatry* 21 (1): 5–13.

McCann, L. A. & Ventrell-Monsees, C. (2010). Age discrimination in employment. In R. B. Hudson (ed.), *The New Politics of Old Age Policy,* 2d ed. (pp. 356–372). Baltimore: Johns Hopkins University Press.

McCarthy, M., Ruiz, E., Karam, C., & Moore, N. (2004). The meaning of health: Perspectives of Anglo and Latina older women. Health Care for Women International 25 (10): 950–969.

McCleary, R. (2009). The great American crime decline. *Contemporary Sociology: A Journal of Reviews* 38 (1): 44–45.

McCombs, J. S., Yuan, Y., Shin, J., & Saab, S. (2011). Economic burden associated with patients diagnosed with hepatitis C. *Clinical Therapeutics* 33 (9): 1268–1280.

McCourt, S. B. (2008). A Phenomenological Study of Anticipated Housing, Healthcare, and Biopsychosocial Needs of Aging Female Baby Boomers. Phoenix: University of Phoenix.

McCoy, R. (2011). African American elders, cultural traditions, and the family reunion. *Generations* 35 (3): 16–21.

McCullion, P., Ferretti, L. A., & Park, J. (2013). Financial issues and an aging population: Responding to an increased potential for financial abuse and exploitation. In J. Birkenmaier, M. Sherraden, & J. Curley (eds.), *Financial Education and Capability and Asset Development: Research, Education, Policy, and Practice* (pp. 278–301). New York: Oxford University Press.

McCulloch, B. J., Lassig, S., & Barnett, A. (2012). Older White adults and mental health. In E. C. Chang & C. A. Downey (eds.), *Handbook of Race and Development in Mental Health* (pp. 243–257). New York: Springer Science+Business Media.

McDaniel, J. G. & Clark, P. G. (2009). The new adult orphan: Issues and considerations for health care professionals. *Journal of Gerontological Nursing* 35 (12): 44–49.

McDonald, L. (2011). Theorizing about ageing, family and immigration. *Ageing and Society* 31 (7): 1180–1201.

McDonough, K. E. & Davitt, J. K. (2011). It takes a village: Community practice, social work, and aging-in-place. *Journal of Gerontological Social Work* 54 (5): 528–541.

McGarry, K. & Skinner, J. (2008). *Out-of-Pocket Medical Expenses and Retirement Security.* Hanover, NH: Dartmouth College.

McHugh, M. C. (2012). Aging, agency, and activism: Older women as social change agents. *Women & Therapy* 35 (3–4): 279–295.

McKee, M. & Stucker, D. (2013). Older people in the UK: Under attack from all directions. *Age and Ageing* 42 (1): 11–13.

McKernan, S.-M., Steuerle, C. E., & Lei, S. (2010). *Opportunity and Ownership Over the Life Cycle.* Washington, DC: Urban Institute.

McLaren, P. (1998). *Life in Schools: An Introduction to Critical Pedagogy in the Foundations of Education.* 3d ed. New York: Longman.

McManus, T., Anderberg, J., & Lazarus, H. (2007). Retirement—an unaffordable luxury. *Journal of Management Development* 2 (5): 484–492.

McNamara, T. K., & Gonzales, E. (2011). Volunteer transitions among older adults: the role of human, social, and cultural capital in later life. *Journals of Gerontology, Series B: Psychological Sciences and Social Sciences* 66:490–501.

McNamara, T. K. & Williamson, J. B. (2012). Is age discrimination acceptable? *Public Policy & Aging Report* 22 (3): 9–13.

Mehta, K. M. & Chang, V. W. (2009). Mortality attributable to obesity among middle-aged adults in the United States. *Demography* 46 (4): 851–872.

Mehta, K. M., Yaffe, K., Perez-Stable, E. A., Stewart, A., Barnes, D., Kurland, B. F., & Miller, B. L. (2008). Race/ethnic differences in AD survival in United States Alzheimer's Disease Centers. *Neurology* 70 (14): 1163–1170.

Mencke, B. K. B. (2010). *Education, Racism, and the Military: A Critical Race Theory Analysis of the GI BILL and Its Implications for African Americans.* Washington State University Research Exchange.

Mendes de Leon, C. F., Eschbach, K., & Markides, K. S. (2011). Population trends and late-life disabilities in Hispanics from the Midwest. *Journal of Aging and Health* 23 (7): 1166–1188.

Mendez-Bustos, P., Lopez-Castroman, J., Baca-García, E., & Ceverino, A. (2013). Life cycle and suicidal behavior among women. *Scientific World Journal* (online) 485851.

Mermin, G. B. T., Johnson, R. W., & Toder, E. J. (2008). Will employers want aging boomers? Washington, DC: Urban Institute.

Meschede, T., Shapiro, T. M., Sullivan, L., & Wheary, J. (2011). *Severe Financial Insecurity Among African-American and Latino Seniors.* New York: Demos.

MetLife Mature Market Institute. (2010). *Demographic Profile: America's Younger Boomers.* New York: MetLife Mature Market Institute.

MetroSouth Medical Center. (2011, December 21). Obesity in baby boomers. MetroSouth Medical Center. http://healthconnect.metrosouthmedicalcenter.com/2011/08/obesity-in-baby-boomers/. Accessed December 21, 2011.

Meyer, M. H. (2009). Why all women (and most men) should support universal rather than privatized Social Security. In L. Rogne, C. L. Estes, B. R. Grossman, B. A. Hollister, & E. Solway (eds.), *Social Insurance and Social Justice* (pp. 149–164). New York: Springer.

Meyers, D. & Ryu, S. (2008). Aging baby boomers and the generational housing bubble: Foresight and mitigation of an epic transition. *Journal of the American Planning Association* 74 (1): 17–33.

Miech, R., Koester, S., & Dorsey-Holliman, B. (2011). Increasing U.S. mortality due to accidental poisoning: The role of the baby boomer cohort. *Addiction* 106 (4): 806–815.

Migliorino, P. (2010). The ageing of the post-war migrants: A challenge for health promotion and service delivery. *Healthy Voices: Journal of the Consumers Health Forum of Australia* 6 (1): 1–3.

Miller, D. K., Wolmsky, F. D., Malmstrom, T. K., Andersen, B. M., & Miller, J.P. (2005). Inner city, middle-aged African Americans have excess frank and subclinical disability. *Journals of Gerontology Series A: Biological Sciences and Medical Sciences* 60 (2): 207–212.

Miller, N. H., Berra, K., & Long, J. (2010). Hypertension 2008—awareness, understanding, and treatment of previously diagnosed hypertension in baby boomers and seniors. *Journal of Clinical Hypertension* 12 (5): 328–334.

Minkler, M. (1986). Generational equity and the new blaming the victim: An emerging public policy issue. *International Journal of Health Services* 16 (4): 539–551.

Minkler, M. & Holstein, M. B. (2008). From civil rights to . . . civic engagement? Concerns of two older critical gerontologists about a "new social movement" and what it portends. *Journal of Aging Studies* 22 (2): 196–204.

Mirowsky, J. (2011). Cognitive decline and the default American lifestyle. *Journals of Gerontology Series B: Psychological Sciences and Social Sciences* 66B (Suppl 1): i50–i58.

Mitchell, O. S., Lusardi, A., & Curto, V. (2009). Financial literacy and financial sophistication among older Americans. Social Science Research Network: Pension Research Council Working Paper No. 25.

Miyawaki, C. E. (2013). Generational differences in Japanese-American baby boomers and senior service environments. *Journal of Gerontological Social Work* 56 (5): 388–406.

Molestina, K. (2012, April 25). LeNelle Mozell, addiction specialist, of Arlington County, Va., sees rising numbers of baby boomers abusing drugs. *9 News Now.* http://wusa9.com/news/article/203683/373/Buzzing-Boomers-Study-Shows-50-60-year-olds-Battle-Addiction. April 16, 2013.

Monahan, D. J. (2013). Family caregivers for seniors in rural areas. *Journal of Family Social Work* 16 (1): 116–128.

Monholton, R. (2010). *Baby Boom: People and Perspectives.* Santa Barbara: Greenwood.

Montero-Rodriguez, J., Small, J. A., & McCallum, A. T. (2006). With Hispanic/Latino American families with focus on Puerto Ricans. In G. Yeo & D. Gallagher-Thompson (eds.), *Ethnicity and the Dementias,* 2d ed. (pp. 287–309). New York: Routledge.

Moody, H. R. (2008). Aging America and the boomer wars. *Gerontologist* 48 (6): 839–844.

Moon, J. R., Glymour, M. H., Subramanion, S. V., Avendano, M., & Kawachi, I. (2012). Transition to retirement and risk of cardiovascular disease: Prospective analysis of the U.S. health and retirement study. *Social Science & Medicine* 75 (3): 626–630.

Moon, M. (1993). "Measuring intergenerational equity." In L. Cohen (ed.), *Justice Across Nations: What Does It Mean?* (pp. 111–138). Washington, DC: Public Policy Institute, AARP.

Moon, P. & Floods, S. (2013). Women's and men's work/volunteer time in the encore life course stage. *Social Problems* 60 (2): 206–233.

Moore, J. H. (2006). Projected pension income: Equality or disparity. *Monthly Labor Review.* www.thefreelibraryfor the baby-boom-a0145882415. Accessed October 15, 2011.

Morgan, K. J. (2010). Medicare: Deservingness encounters cost containment. In R. B. Hudson (ed.), *The New Politics of Old Age Policy,* 2d ed. (pp. 254–274). Baltimore: Johns Hopkins University Press.

Morrell, R. W., Echt, K. V., & Caramagno, J. (2008). *Older Adults, Race/Ethnicity and Mental Health Disparities: A Consumer-Focused Research Agenda.* Alexandria, VA: Human Resources Research Organization.

Morrow-Howell, N. (2010). Volunteering in later life: Research frontiers. *Journal of Gerontology: Social Sciences* 65B (4): 461–469.

Morrow-Howell, N. & Greenfield, J. C. (2010). Productive engagement of older adults. *China Journal of Social Work* 3 (2–3): 153–164.

Morrow-Howell, N. & Wang, Y. (2013). Productive engagement of older adults: Elements of a cross-cultural research agenda. *Ageing International* 13 (2): 159–170.

Moxley, D. P. & Washington, O. G. M. (2013). Helping older African American homeless women get and stay out of homelessness: Reflections on lessons learned from long-haul developmental action research. *Journal of Progressive Human Services* 24 (2): 140–161.

Mui, A. C., Glajhon, M., Chen, H., & Sun, J. (2012). Developing an older adult volunteer program in a New York Chinese community: An evidence-based approach. *Ageing International* 38 (2): 108–121.

Mui, A. C. & Kang, S.-Y. (2006). Acculturation stress and depression among Asian immigrant elders. *Social Work* 51 (3): 243–255.

Mui, A. C. & Shibusawa, T. (2008). *Asian American Elders in the Twenty-First Century: Key Indicators of Well-Being.* New York: Columbia University Press.

Mujtaba, B. G., Hinds, R. M., & Oskal, C. (2004). Cultural paradigms of age discrimination and unearned privileges. *Clute Institute Journal of Business & Economics Research* 2 (12): 31–44.

Mulbauer, V. & Christer, J. C. (2012). Women, power, and aging: An introduction. *Women & Therapy* 35 (304): 137–144.

Mungas, D. (2006). Neuropsychological assessment of Hispanic elders: Challenges and psychometric approaches. In G. Yeo & D. Gallagher-Thompson (eds.), *Ethnicity and the Dementias,* 2d ed. (pp. 71–86). New York: Routledge.

Munnell, A. H. (2008). "A reappraisal of Social Security financing" revisited. *Journal of Economics and Finance* 32 (4): 394–408.

Munnell, A. H., Webb, A., & Golub-Sass, F. (2009). *The National Retirement Index: After the Crash.* Chestnut Hill, MA: Boston College Center for Retirement Research.

Munnell, A. H., Webb, A., Karamcheva, Z., & Eschtruth, A. (2011). *How Important Are Intergenerational Transfers for Baby Boomers?* Chestnut Hill, MA: Boston College Center for Retirement Research.

Munro, D. & Zeisberger, C. (2010). Demographic forecasting stock market and housing trends in Japan and the United States over the past 50 years and a forecast for the next 20 years. INSEAD Working Paper No. 2010/90/DS.

Muracz, A. R. & Akinsulure-Smith, A. M. (2013). Older adults and sexuality: Implications for counseling ethnic and sexual minority clients. *Journal of Mental Health Counseling* 35 (1): 1–14.

Murphy, D., Johnson, R. W. & Mermin, G. (2007). *Racial Differences in Baby Boomers' Retirement Expectations.* Washington, DC: Urban Institute.

Murray, M. (2008). When war is work: The G.I. Bill, citizenship, and the civic generation. *California Law Review* 96 (4): 967–998.

Musich, S., McDonald, T., & Chapman, L. S. (2009). Health promotion strategies for the "boomer" generation: Wellness for the mature worker. *American Journal of Health Promotion* 23 (3): Suppl., 1–9.

Mutchler, J. E., Baclgalupe, G., Coppin, A., & Gottlieb, A. (2007). Language barriers surrounding medication use among older Latinas. *Journal of Cross-Cultural Gerontology* 22 (1): 101–114.

Mutchler, J. E. & Burr, J. (2009). Boomer diversity and well-being: Race, ethnicity, and gender. In R. B. Hudson (ed.), *Boomer Bust? Perspectives on the Boomers* (pp. 23–46). Westport, CT: Praeger.

Muzacz, A. K. & Adeyinke-Smith, A. M. (2013). Older adults and sexuality: Implications for counseling ethnic and sexual minority clients. *Journal of Mental Health Counseling* 35 (1): 1–14.

Myers, D. (2007). *Immigrants and Boomers: Forging a New Social Contract for the Future of America.* New York: Russell Sage Foundation.

Myers, D. (2009). Aging baby boomers and the effect of immigration: Rediscovering the intergenerational social contract. *Generations* 32 (4): 18–23.

Mykytyn, C. E. (2010). A history of the future: The emergence of contemporary anti-ageing medicine. *Sociology of Health & Illness* 32 (2): 181–196.

Myles, J. (2010). What justice requires: Normative foundations for U.S. pension reform. In R. B. Hudson (ed.), *The New Politics of Old Age Policy,* 2d ed. (pp. 64–86). Baltimore: Johns Hopkins University Press.

National Council on Aging. (2010). *The Boomer Solution: Skilled Talent to Meet Nonprofit Needs.* Washington, DC: National Council on Aging.

Neary, S. R. & Mahoney, D. F. (2005). Dementia caregiving: The experiences of Hispanic/Latino caregivers. *Journal of Transcultural Nursing* 16 (2): 163–170.

Neergaard, L. (2011a, July 18). Poll: Baby boomers not as young as they think they are. www.dailynews.com/fdcp?unique=1324501695828. Accessed December 21, 2011.

Neergaard, L. (2011b, July 18). Baby boomers obesity problem. www.wwlp.com/dpp/health/healthy_living/baby-boomers-obesity-problem. Accessed December 21, 2011.

Neergaard, L. (2012, February 21). Boomers most at risk for hepatitis c, study says. *Boston Globe,* p. A12.

Nelson, P. B., Lee, A. W., & Nelson, L. (2009). Linking baby boomer and Hispanic migration streams into rural America—a multi-scaled approach. *Population, Space and Place* 15 (3): 277–293.

Nelson, T. (2002). Ageism: Stereotyping and prejudice against older persons. Cambridge: MIT Press.

Nersisyan, Y. & Wray, L. R. (2010). Deficit hysteria redux? Why we should stop worrying about U.S. government deficits. Levy Economic Institute, Public Policy Brief, No. 111.

Netting, F. E. (2011). Bridging critical feminist gerontology and social work to interrogate the narrative on civic engagement. *Affilia* 26 (3): 239–249.

Neumark, D. (2009). The Age Discrimination in Employment Act and the challenge of population aging. *Research on Aging* 31 (1): 41–68.

Neumark, D., Johnson, H. P., & Mejia, M. C. (2011). Future skill shortages in the U.S. economy. National Bureau of Economic (NBER) Working Paper No. 17213.

Neumark, D. & Song, J. (2011). Do stronger age discrimination laws make Social Security reforms more effective? National Bureau of Economic (NBER) Working Paper No. 17467.

Neustifter, R. (2008). Common concerns faced by lesbian elders: An essential context for couple's therapy. *Journal of Feminist Family Therapy* 20 (3): 251–267.

Neville, S. & Henrickson, M. (2010). "Lavender retirement": A questionnaire survey of lesbian, gay, and bisexual people's accommodation plans for old age. *International Journal of Nursing Practice* 16 (4): 586–594.

New America Media. (2010). Hispanic baby boomers hit hard by recession. San Francisco: New America Media.

Newton, J. P. (2011). Anti-ageing—fact, fiction or faction? *Gerontology* 28 (3): 163–164.

New York Times. (2012, December 18). Hypertension. http://health.nytimes.com/health/guides/disease/hypertension/pverview.html. Accessed December 18, 2012.

New York Times editorial. (2012, September 16). The road to retirement: The recession and its aftermath spell insecurity and hardship for millions of Americans. *New York Times,* p. 10.

New York Times editorial. (2013a, January 13). Misguided Social Security reform. *New York Times,* p. 10.

New York Times editorial. (2013b, June 10). What's next for Social Security? *New York Times,* p. A20.

Ng, J. (2010). Disparities in quality of care for midlife adults (45–64) versus older adults (ages > 65). Washington, DC: National Committee for Quality Assurance.

Ngo-Metzger, Q., Phillips, R. S., & McCarthy, E. P. (2008). Ethnic disparities in hospice use among Asian-American and Pacific Islander patients dying with cancer. *Journal of the American Geriatric Society* 56 (1): 139–144.

Ngo-Metzger, Q., Ward, J. W., & Valdiserri, R. O. (2013). Expanded Hepatitis C virus screening recommendations promote opportunities for care and cure. *Annals of Internal Medicine* 159 (3): 364–365.

Nielsen Holdings. (2012). *African-American Consumers: Still Vital, Still Growing.* New York: Nielsen Holdings.

Nitta, H. (2006). Capitalizing on retirement of Japan's first baby boomers. JETRO Japan Economic Report, April–May.

Nolan, E. (2009). Picking up after the baby boomers: Can immigrants carry the load. *Georgetown Immigration Law Journal* 24:77–96.

Norris, S. L., High, K., Gill, T. M., Hennessy, S., Kulner, J. S., Reuben, D. B., Unutzer, J., & Landefeld, C. S. (2008). Health care for older Americans with multiple chronic conditions: A research agenda. *Journal of the American Geriatric Society* 56 (1): 149–159.

Nusbaum, N. J. (2011). An anticipatory geriatric strategy: To better care for those Americans not yet old. *Current Gerontological & Geriatric Research, Open Access Journal,* 4 pages.

Nyce, S.A. (2007). The aging workforce: Is demography destiny? *Generations* 31 (1): 9–15.

O'Brien, S. (2007). More seniors face injury and death from falling down. About. com.Senior Living. http://seniorliving.about.com/od/healthnutrition/a/fall-study.htm. Accessed June 13, 2013.

Odden, M. C., Coxson, P. G., Moran, A., Lightwood, J. M., Goldman, L., & Bibbins-Domingo, K. (2011). The impact of the aging population on coronary heart disease in the United States. *American Journal of Medicine* 124 (9): 827–833.

Ohlemacher, S. (2011, August 22). Layoffs, baby boomers strain Social Security disability. *Boston Globe,* p. A2.

Okoro, C. A., Young, S. L., Strine, T. W., Balluz, L. S. & Mokdad, A. H. (2005). Uninsured adults aged 65 years and older: Is their health at risk? *Journal of Health Care for the Poor and Underserved* 16 (3): 453–463.

Oliver, T. R. & Lee, P. R. (2009). The Medicare Modernization Act: Evolution or revolution in social insurance. In L. Rogne, C. L. Estes, B. R. Grossman, B. A. Hollister, & E. Solway (eds.), *Social Insurance and Social Justice* (pp. 63–93). New York: Springer.

Olshansky, S. J., Goldman, D. P., Zheng, Y., & Rowe, J. W. (2009). Aging in America in the twenty-first century: Demographic forecasts from the MacArthur Foundation Network on an Aging Society. *Milbank Quarterly* 87 (4): 842–862.

Olson, Z. (2013, May 15). Turning hobbies into profits, with a little help. *New York Times,* p. F2.

O'Malley, P. A. (2012). Baby boomers and substance abuse: The curse of youth again in old age: Implications for the clinical nurse specialist. *Clinical Nurse Specialist* 26 (6): 305–307.

O'Neill, D. (2013). 2012—that was the year that was. *Age and Ageing* 42 (2): 140–144.

O'Neill, G. (2009). The baby boom age wave: Population success or tsunami? In R. B. Hudson (ed.), *Boomer Bust? Perspectives on the Boomers* (pp. 23–45). Westport, CT: Praeger.

Onkst, D. H. (1998). "First a Negro . . . Incidentally a Veteran": Black World War Two Veterans and the G. I. Bill of Rights in the Deep South, 1944–1948. *Journal of Social History* 31 (3): 517–543.

O'Rand, A. & Shuey, K. M. (2007). Gender and the devolution of pension risks in the U.S. *Current Sociology* 55 (2): 287–304.

Orel, N. A. & Fruhauf, C. A. (2013). Lesbian, gay, bisexual, and transgender grand-parents. In A. E. Goldberg & K. R. Allen (eds.), *Lesbian, Gay, Bisexual, and Transgender Grandparents* (pp. 177–192). New York: Springer.

Ortman, J. M. & Guarneri, C. E. (2009). United States population projections: 2000 to 2050. Washington, DC: U.S. Census Bureau.

Osborn, C. (2012, April 25). Aging with pride: The call for boomer consciousness. *Huffington Post.* www.huffingtonpost.com/carol-osborn/aging-with-prode-the-call_b_1429906.html. April 30, 2012.

Ouwehand, C., de Ridder, D. T., & Bensing, J. M. (2007). A review of successful aging models: Proposing proactive coping as an important additional strategy. *Clinical Psychology Review* 27 (8): 873–884.

Ozawa, M. & Lee, Y. S. (2011). Generational inequity in social spending: The United States in comparative perspective. *International Social Work* 15 (2): 162–179.

Painter, J. A., Elliott, S., & Hudson, S. (2009). Falls in community-dwelling adults age 50 years and older: Prevalence and contributing factors. *Journal of Allied Health* 38 (4): 201–207.

Painter, G. & Lee, K. (2009). Housing tenure transitions of older households: Life cycle, demographic, and familial factors. *Regional Science and Urban Economics* 39 (4): 749–760.

Papadimitriou, D. B. (2007). Economic perspectives on aging. New York: Bard College-Levy Economics Institute Working Paper No. 500.

Park, H.-O. H. (2009). Factors associated with the psychological health of grand-parents as primary caregivers: An analysis of gender. *Journal of Interpersonal Relationships* 7 (2–3): 191–208.

Parker, E., Meiklejohn, B., Patterson, C., Edwards, K., Preece, C., Shuter, P., & Gould, T. (2006). Our games our health: A cultural asset for promoting health in indigenous communities. *Health Promotion Journal of Australia* 17 (2): 103–108.

Parker, R. M., Wolf, M. S., & Kirsch, I. (2008). Preparing for an epidemic of lim-ited health literacy: Weathering the perfect storm. *Journal of General Internal Medicine* 23 (8): 1273–1276.

Parker, V. A. (2010–2011). The importance of cultural competence in caring for and working in a diverse America. *Generations* 34 (4): 97–102.

Parker, V. A. & Geron, S. M. (2007). Cultural competency in nursing homes' activities programs. *Gerontology Geriatric Education* 69 (2): 37–54.

Parker-Pope, T. (2013, May 3). Suicide rates in middle age soared in U.S. *New York Times,* pp. A1, A12.

Parry, C., Kent, E. E., Mariotto, A. B., Alfano, C. M., & Rowland, J. H. (2011). Cancer survivors: A booming population. *Cancer Epidemiology Biomarkers & Prevention* 20 (10): 1996–2005.

Passel, J. & Cohn, D.'V. (2008). Immigration to play lead role in future U.S. growth: 2005–2050. Washington, DC: Pew Research Center.

Pavel, M., Jimison, H. B., Wactlar, H. D., & Hayes, T. L. (2013). The role of technology and engineering models in transforming healthcare. *Biomedical Engineering, IEEE Reviews* 6 (2): 156–177.

Pavkov, M. E., Geiss, L. S., Beckles, G. L., & Williams, D. E. (2010). Overview and epidemiology of diabetes in racial/ethnic minorities in the United States. In L. C. Liburd (ed.), *Diabetes and Health Disparities: Community-Based Approaches for Racial and Ethnic Populations* (pp. 23–59). New York: Springer.

Pear, R. (2012, January 28). Medicare seen as battleground issue in congressional races. *New York Times,* p. A11.

Pellerin, L. A. & Stearns, E. (2001). Status honor and the valuing of cultural and material capital. *Poetics* 29 (1): 1–24.

Penner, R. G. (2008a). *Can Faster Economic Growth Bail Out Our Retirement Programs?* Washington, DC: Urban Institute.

Penner, R. G. (2008b). *Are Baby Boomers Saving Enough for Their Retirement?* Washington, DC: Urban Institute.

Perez-Escanilla, R. & Putnik, P. (2007). The role of acculturation in nutrition, lifestyle, and incidence of Type 2 diabetes among Latinos. *Journal of Nutrition* 137 (4): 860–870.

Perlman, B., Kenneally, K., & Boivie, I. (2011). Pensions and retirement security 2011: A roadmap for policy makers. Washington, DC: National Institute on Retirement Security.

Perry, D. P. (2009). In the balance: Silver tsunami or longevity divided? *Quality in Ageing and Older Adults* 10 (2): 15–22.

Perry, S. (2007, May 17). Baby boomers seek a purposeful direction in later life, study finds. *Chronicle of Philanthropy* 19:32.

Perry, V. G. & Wolburg, J. M. (2011). Aging gracefully: Emerging issues for public policy and consumer welfare. *Journal of Consumer Affairs* 45 (3): 365–371.

Perkins, E. A. & Haley, W. E. (2010). Compound caregiving: When lifelong caregivers undertake additional caregiving roles. *Rehabilitation Psychology* 55 (4): 409–417.

Perkins, K. & Tire, C. (1995). A strengths perspective in practice: Older people and mental health challenges. *Journal of Gerontological Social Work* 23 (3–4): 83–98.

Peters, R. M. (2004). Racism and hypertension among African Americans. *Western Journal of Nursing Research* 26 (6): 812–831.

Pethokoukis, J. M. & Brandon, E. (2006). Going your own way. *U.S. News & World Report* 140:52–55.

Pew Hispanic Center. (2013). *Mexican-Origin Hispanics in the United States.* Washington, DC: Pew Hispanic Center.

Pew Research Center. (2009). *Public Looks Back at Worst Decade in 50 years.* Washington, DC: Pew Research Center.

Phillips, J. A., Robin, A. V., Nugent, C. N., & Idler, E. L. (2010). Understanding recent changes in suicide rates among the middle-aged: Period of cohort effects. *Public Health Reports* 125 (5): 680–688.

Phillipson, C. (2007). Understanding the baby boom generation: Comparative perspectives. *International Journal of Ageing and Later Life* 2 (2): 7–11.

Phillipson, C. (2009). Pensions in crisis: Aging and inequality in a global age. In L. Rogne, C. L. Estes, B. R. Grossman, B. A. Hollister, & E. Solway (eds.), *Social Insurance and Social Justice* (pp. 319–339). New York: Springer.

Phillipson, C., Bernard, M., Phillips, J., & Ogg, J. (2001). Family and community life of older people a: Social networks and social support in three urban areas. London: Routledge.

Phillipson, C., Leach, R., Money, A., & Biggs, S. (2008). Social and cultural constructions of ageing: The case of the baby boomers. *Sociological Research Online.* www.socresonline.org.uk/13/3/5.html. Accessed August 19, 2011.

Physical Activity Resource Center. (2013). *Physical Activity for Older Adults: A Step-by-Step Guide.* Ontario: Physical Activity Resource Center.

Piercy, K. W., Cheek, C., & Teemant, B. (2011). Challenges and psychosocial growth for older volunteers giving intensive humanitarian service. *Gerontologist* 51 (4): 550–560.

Pinazo, S. & Montoro, J. (2004). La relacion entre los abuelos=as y metos=las factores que predicen la calidad de la relación intergeneracional. *Revista Internacional de Sociología* 37 (1): 7–28.

Pinazo-Hernandis, S. & Tompkins, C. J. (2009). Custodial grandparents: The state of the art and the many faces of this contribution. *Journal of Interpersonal Relationships* 7 (2–3): 137–143.

Piven F. F. (2004). The politics of retrenchment: The U.S. case. www.brynmawr.edu/socialwork/GSSW/schram/piveninstitutionalism.htm. Accessed December 4, 2011.

Poindexter, C. & Shippy, R. A. (2008). Networks of older New Yorkers with HIV: Fragility, resilience, and transition. *AIDS Patient Care and STDS* 22 (9): 723–733.

Pol, L. G., Mueller, K. J., & Adidam, P. T. (2002). Racial and ethnic differences in health insurance for the near elderly. *Journal of Health Care for the Poor and Underserved* 13 (2): 229–240.

Polivka, L. (2006). Gerontology for the 21st century. *Gerontologist* 46 (4): 558–563.

Polivka, L. (2011). Neoliberalism and postmodern cultures of aging. *Journal of Applied Gerontology* 30 (2): 173–184.

Polivka, L. & Estes, C. L. (2010). The economic meltdown and old-age politics. *Generations* 33 (3): 56–62.

Pollmann, A. (2013). Intercultural capital: Toward conceptualization, operationalization, and empirical investigation of a rising marker of sociocultural distinction. *Sage Open* 3 (2). 2158244013486117.

Pope, R.C., Wallhagen, M., & Davis, H. (2010). The social determinates of substance abuse in African American baby boomers: Effects of family, media images, and environment. *Journal of Transcultural Nursing* 21 (3): 246–256.

Portner, J. (2011, October 18). Minority nursing home residents increase, whites decline. *California Watch.* http://californiawatch.org/search/node/Minority%20nursing%20home%20residents%20increase%2C%20whites%20decline.%20California%20Watch.

Postigo, J. & Honrubia, R. (2010). The co-residence of elderly people with their children and grandchildren. *Educational Gerontology* 36 (4): 330–349.

Potetz, L. & Cubanski, J. (2009). *A Primer on Medicare Financing.* Menlo Park, CA: Henry J. Kaiser Family Foundation.

Potter, J. F. (2010). Aging in America: Essential considerations in shaping senior care policy. *Aging Health* 6 (3): 289–299.

Powel, S. K. (2013). The Affordable Care Act, Medicare spending, and the case manager. *Professional Case Manager* 18 (4): 163–165.

Powell, L. A., Williamson, J. B., & Branco, K. J. (1996). *The Senior Rights Movement: Framing the Policy Debate in America.* New York: Twayne.

Poytheway, B. (2012). Age discrimination, work, and retirement. *Public Policy & Aging Report* 22 (3): 14–16.

Preston, S. (1984). Children and the elderly: Divergent paths for America's dependents. *Demography* 21 (1): 81–86.

Price, C. A. (2006). *Aging Inmate Population Study.* North Carolina Department of Correction Division of Prisons.

Pritchard, R. F. & Potter, G. C. (2011). Senior citizens, Social Security. And healthcare costs. *Journal of Business & Economics Research* 9 (1): 23–28.

PRLOG. (2011, July 26). Obesity is baby boomers's greatest health risk. www.prlog.org/11600535-obesity-is-baby-boomers-greatest-health-risk.html Accessed May 27, 2013.

Pruchno, R. (2012). Not your mother's old age: Baby boomers at age 65. *Gerontologist* 52 (2): 149–152.

Pruchno, R. A. & Smyer, M. A. (eds.). (2007). *Challenges of an Aging Society: Ethical Dilemmas, Political Issues.* Baltimore: Johns Hopkins University Press.

Prudential. (2011). *The African American Financial Experience: A Study.* Newark, NJ: Prudential.

Pumariega, A. J. & Rothe, E. (2010). Leaving no children or families outside: The challenges of immigration. *American Journal of Orthopsychiatry* 80 (4): 505–515.

Prynoos, J. & Liebig, P. (2009). Changing work, retirement, and housing patterns. *Generations* 33 (3): 20–25.

Quine, S. and Carter, S. (2006), Australian baby boomers' expectations and plans for their old age. *Australasian Journal on Ageing* 25:3–8. doi: 10.1111/j.1741–6612.2006.00147.x.

Quinn, M., and Guion, K. W. (2010). A faith-based and cultural approach to promoting self-efficacy and regular exercise in older African American women. *Gerontology & Geriatrics Education* 31 (1): 1–18.

Rabb, C. (2010). *Invisible Capital: How Unseen Forces Shape Entrepreneurial Opportunity.* San Francisco: Berret-Koehier.

Rabin, R. C. (2013, August 13). A glut of antidepressants. *New York Times,* p. D4.

Rahn, D. W. & Wartman, S. A. (2007, November 2). For the health-care work force, a critical prognosis. *Chronicle of Higher Education.* www.careerladdersproject.org/docs/Health%20Care.pdf. Accessed August 12, 2013.

Reisch, M., Ife, J., & Weil, M. (2013). Social justice, human rights, values, and community practice. In M. Weil, M. Reisch, & M. L. Olmer (eds.), *The Handbook of Community Practice* (pp. 73–103). Thousand Oaks, CA: Sage.

Reisenwitz, T. & Lyer, R. (2007). A comparison of younger and older baby boomers: Investigating the viability of cohort segmentation. *Journal of Consumer Marketing* 24 (4): 202–213.

Reuteman, R. (2010, February 8). Will baby boomers bankrupt Social Security? CNBC. www.cnbc.com/id/34941334/.

Rexbye, H. & Povlen, J. (2007). Visual signs of ageing: What are we looking at? *International Journal of Ageing and Later Life* 2 (1): 61–83.

Reynolds, S. L. & McIlvane, J. M. (2009). The impact of obesity and arthritis on active life expectancy in older Americans. *Obesity* 17 (2): 363–369.

Rice, N. E., Lang, I. A., Henley, W., & Melzer, D. (2010). Baby boomers nearing retirement: The healthiest generation? *Rejuvenation Research* 13 (1): 105–114.

Richardson, K.A. (2011). The impact of retiring baby boomers on nursing short-age. *Journal of Global Health Care Systems* 1 (1): 1–13.

Richman, K., Barboza, G., Ghilarducci, T., & Sun, W. (2008). La tercera edad: Latinos' pensions, retirement and impact on families. Terre Haute, IN: University of Notre Dame Institute for Latino Studies.

Rikard, R. V. & Rosenberg, E. (2007). Aging inmates: A convergence of trends in the American criminal justice system. *Journal of Correctional Health Care* 13 (3): 150–162.

Ristau, S. (2011). People do need people: Social interaction boosts brain health in older age. *Generations* 35 (2): 70–76.

Rix, S. E. (2009). Will the boomers revolutionize work and retirement? In R. B. Hudson (ed.), *Boomer Bust? Perspectives on the Boomers* (pp. 77–94). Westport, CT: Praeger.

Robbins, W. L. (2012). *A Place for Us? Baby Boomers, Their Elders, and the Public Library.* Ottawa: University of Ottowa.

Robert Wood Johnson Foundation. (2007). *Findings Brief: Meeting the Future Long-term Care Needs of the Baby Boomers.* Princeton, NJ: Robert Wood Johnson Foundation.

Roberts, S. (2008, August 14). In a generation minorities may be the majority. *New York Times,* p. A1.

Robinson, K. M. (2010). Policy issues in mental health among the elderly. *Nursing Clinic of North America* 45 (4): 627–634.

Robinson, M. W. (2010–2011). The current economic situation and its impact on gender, race, and class: The legacy of raced (and gendered) employment. *Journal of Gender, Race & Justice* 14:431.

Rockeymoore, M. & Maitin-Shepard, M. (2010). *Tough Times Require Strong Social Security Benefits: Views on Social Security Among African Americans, Hispanic Americans, and White Americans.* Washington, DC: National Academy of Social Insurance.

Rodriguez, D. A. (2011). *A Future for the Latino Church: Models for Multilingual, Multigenerational Hispanic Congregations.* Downers Grove, IL: IVP Academic.

Rogerson, P. A. & Kim, D. (2005). Population distribution and redistribution of the baby-boom cohort in the United States: Recent trends and implications. *Proceedings of the American Academy of Sciences of the United States* 102 (43): 15319–15324.

Rogne, L. (2009). Part V. Teaching social insurance: Critical pedagogy and social justice. In L. Rogne, C. L. Estes, B. R. Grossman, B. A. Hollister, & E. Solway (eds.), *Social Insurance and Social Justice* (pp. 379–382). New York: Springer.

Rosales, S. (2011). Home: Mexican American Veterans and the 1944 GI Bill of Rights. *Pacific Historical Review* 80 (4): 597–627.

Rosanova, J. (2010). Discourse of successful aging in *The Globe & Mail:* Insights from critical gerontology. *Journal of Aging Studies* 24 (4): 213–222.

Roscigno, V. J. (2010). Ageism in the American workplace. *Contexts* 9 (1): 16–21.

Roseland, A.-M., Heisley, M., & Piette, J. D. (2012). The impact of family behaviors and communication patterns on chronic illness outcomes: A systematic review. *Journal of Behavioral Medicine* 35 (2): 221–239.

Rosen, D., Goodkind, S., & Smith, M. L. (2011). Using photovoice to identify service needs of older African American methadone clients. *Journal of Social Service Research* 37 (5): 526–538.

Rosen, D., Hunsaker, A., Albert, S. M., Corenlius, J. R., & Reynolds III, J. R. (2011). Characteristics and consequences of heroin use among older adults in the United States: A review of the literature, treatment implications, and recommendations for further research. *Addictive Behaviors* 36 (4): 279–285.

Rosenberg, M. (2011, May 2). Baby boomers: The population baby boom of 1946–1964 in the United States. About.com Guide. Accessed February 2, 2013.

Rosenfeld, D., Bartlam, B., & Smith, R. D. (2012). Out of the closet and into the trenches: Gay male baby boomers, aging, and HIV/AIDS. *Gerontologist* 52 (2): 255–264.

Ross, B. H. & Levine, M. A. (2012). Urban politics: Cities and suburbs in a golden age. Armonie, NY: Sharpe.

Rosnick, D. & Baker, D. (2009). *The Wealth of the Baby Boom Cohorts After the Collapse of the Housing Bubble.* Washington, DC: Center for Economic and Policy Research.

Rosnick, D. & Baker, D. (2010). The impact of the housing crash on the wealth of the baby boom cohorts. *Journal of Aging & Social Policy* 22 (2): 117–128.

Rotegard, A. K., Moore, S. M., Fagermoen, M. S., & Ruland, C. M. (2010). Health assets: A concept analysis. *International Journal of Nursing Studies* 47 (4): 513–525.

Roth, E. C., Keimig, L., Rubenstein, R. L., Morgan, L., Eckert, J. K., Goldman, S., & Peeples, A. D. (2012). Baby boomers in an active adult retirement community: Comity interrupted, *Gerontologist* 52 (2): 189–198.

Rothstein, M. A. (2011). Who will treat Medicaid and uninsured patients? Retire providers can help. *Journal of Law, Medicine and Ethics* 39 (1): 91–95.

Roux, A. V. D. (2012). Conceptual approaches to the study of health disparities. *Annual Review of Public Health* 33 (1): 41–58.

Rowan, N. L., Faul, A. C., & Birkenmeier, J. (2011). Social work knowledge of community-based services for older adults: An educational model for social work students. *Journal of Gerontological Social Work* 54 (2): 189–202.

Rozario, P. A. (2006–2007). Volunteering among current cohorts of older adults and baby boomers. *Generation* 30 (4): 31–36.

Rubin, R. M. & White-Means, S. L. (2009). Informal caregiving: Dilemmas of sandwiched caregivers. *Journal of Family Economic Issues* 30 (4): 252–267.

Rudman, D. L. & Molke, D. (2009). Forever productive: The discursive shaping of later life workers in contemporary Canadian newspapers. *Work* 32 (4): 377–389.

Rudolph, K. E., Glass, T. A., Crum, R. M., & Schwartz, B. S. (2013). Neighborhood psychosocial hazards and binge drinking among late middle-aged adults. *Journal of Urban Health* 90 (5): 970–982.

Ruiz, D. S. & Carlton-LaNey, I. B. (2008). The increase in intergenerational African-American families headed grandmothers. In C. Waites (ed.), *Social Work Practice with African American families: An Intergenerational Perspective* (pp. 89–104). New York: Routledge.

Ruiz, M. E &. Ransford, H. E. (2012). Latino elders reframing familismo: Implications for health and caregiving support. *Journal of Cultural Diversity* 19 (2): 50–57.

Ryan, L. H., Smith, J., Antonucci, T. C., & Jackson, J. S. (2012). Cohort differences in the availability of informal caregivers: Are the boomers at risk? *Gerontologist* 52 (2): 177–188.

Ryan, P. & Sawin, K. J. (2009). The individual and family self-management theory: Background and perspectives on context, process, and outcomes. *Nursing Outlook* 57 (4): 217–225.

Ryter, J. C. (2008, July 18). Baby boomer Armageddon. NewsWithViews.com. www.newswithviews.com/Ryter/jon245.htm. Accessed October 1, 2011.

Saegert, S., Fields, D., & Libman, K. (2011). Mortgage foreclosures and health disparities: Serial displacement as asset extraction in African American populations. *Journal of Urban Health* 88 (3): 390–402.

Saenz, R. (2010). *Latinos in the United States*. Washington, DC: Population Reference Bureau.

Saint Paul Foundation. (2007). The civic engagement of Baby Boomers: Preparing for a new wave of volunteers. St. Paul: Saint Paul Foundation.

Saleebey, D. (ed.). (1992). *The Strengths Perspective in Social Work Practice*. New York: Longman.

Saleebey, D. (1996). The strengths perspective in social work practice: Extensions and cautions. *Social Work* 41 (4): 296–305.

Salkin, P. (2009). Quiet crisis in America: Meeting the affordable housing needs of the invisible low-income healthy seniors. *Georgetown Journal on Poverty Law & Policy* 16:285.

Sander, T. H. & Putnam, R. D. (2006). Social capital and civic engagement of individuals over age fifty in the United States. In L. B. Wilson & S. P. Simon (eds.), *Civic Engagement and the Baby Boomer Generation: Research, Policy, and Practice Perspectives* (pp. 21–39). New York: Haworth.

Sanders, D. G. & Fortinsky, R. H. (2012). *Dementia Care with Blacks and Latino families: A Social Work Problem-Solving Approach*. New York: Springer.

Sanjek, R. (2009). *Gray Panthers*. Philadelphia: University of Pennsylvania Press.

Satcher, D. (1996). The aging of America. *Journal of Health Care for the Poor and Underserved* 7 (3): 179–182.

Sawhill, I. V. & Monea, E. (2008). *Revising the Intergenerational Contract*. Washington, DC: Brookings Institution.

Schaefer, J. L. (2009). Voices of older baby boomer students: Supporting their transitions back into college. *Educational Gerontology* 36 (1): 67–90.

Scharlach, A. E. & Sanchez, E. (2010). From interviewers to friendly visitors: Bridging research and practice to meet the needs of low-income Latino seniors. *Journal of Gerontological Social Work* 54 (1): 73–91.

Schieber, S. J. (2012). *The Predictable Surprise: The Unraveling of the U.S. Retirement System*. New York: Oxford University Press.

Schrauf, R. W. (2009). English use among older bilingual immigrants in linguistically concentrated neighborhoods: Social proficiency and internal speech as intracultural variation. *Journal of Cross Cultural Gerontology* 24 (2): 157–179.

Schulz, R., Beach, S. R., Matthews, J. T., Courtney, K., Dabbs, A. D., Mecca, L. P., & Sankey, S. S. (2013). Willingness to pay for quality of life technologies to enhance independent functioning among baby boomers and the elderly adults. *Gerontologist,* gnt016.

Schumacher-Matos, E. (2010, September 3). How illegal immigrants are helping Social Security. *Washington Post,* p. 24.

Schwab, S. J. & Glissman, G. (2011). Age and disability within the scope of American discrimination law. In *Disability and Aging Discrimination* (pp. 145–155). New York: Springer.

Schwartz, M. D. (2012). Health care reform and the primary care workforce bottleneck. *Journal of General Internal Medicine* 27 (4): 469–472.

ScienceDaily. (2009, November 27). Diabetes cases to double and costs to triple by 2034. *ScienceDaily.* www.sciencedaily.com/releases/2009/11/091127102038.htm. Accessed December 21, 2011.

Scommegna, P. (2013). *Aging U.S. Baby Boomers Face More Disability.* Washington, DC: Population Reference Bureau.

Seaman, P. M. (2012). Time for my life now: Early boomer women's anticipation of volunteering in retirement. *Gerontologist* 52 (2): 245–254.

Seeman, T. E., Merkin, S. S., Crimmins, E. M., & Karlamangla, A. S. (2010). Disability trends among older Americans: National Health and Nutrition Examination Survey, 1988–1994 and 1999–2004. *American Journal of Public Health* 100 (1): 100–107.

Senzon, S. A. (2010). Seeds of meaning, transformations of health care, and the future. *Journal of Alternative and Complementary Medicine* 16 (12): 1239–1241.

Sexton, S. (2006). Too many grannies? The politics of population aging. *Differen-Takes* 42 (1): 1–4. www.global-sisterhood-network.org/content/view/1486/59/.

Sharpe, D. L. (2009). Economic status of older Asians in the United States. *Journal of Family and Economic Issues* 29 (4): 570–583.

Sheffrin, K. (2013). Establishing an international organ exchange through the General Agreement on Trade in Services. *Brooklyn Journal International Law* 38:829.

Shim. J. K. (2010). Cultural health capital: A theoretical approach to understanding health care interactions and the dynamics of unequal treatment. *Journal of Health and Social Behavior* 51 (1): 1–15.

Silverstein, M. C. (2007). Benefits of grandparents raising grandchildren. *Journal of Interpersonal Relationships* 5 (3): 131–134.

Silverstein, M. C. & Giarusso, R. (2010). Aging and family life: A decade of review. *Journal of Marriage and the Family* 72 (5): 1039–1058.

Simoni-Wastila, L. & Yang, H. K. (2006). Psychoactive drug abuse in older adults. *American Journal of Geriatric Pharmacotherapy* 4 (4): 380–394.

Singleton, J. K., Levin, R. F., Feldman, H. R., & Truglio-Londrigan, M. (2005). Evidence for smoking cessation: Implications for gender-specific strategies. *Worldviews on Evidence-Based Nursing* 2 (2): 63–74.

Sisko, A., Truffer, C., Smith, S., Keehan, S., Cylus, J., Poisal, J. A., Clemens, K., & Lizonitz, J. (2008). Health spending projections through 2018: Recession effects add uncertainty to the outlook. *Health Affairs* 28 (2): w346–w357.

Skinner, J. (2007). *Are You Sure You're Saving Enough for Retirement?* Cambridge, MA: National Bureau of Economic Research.

Skinner, J. (2009). Comment. In J. Brown, J. Liebman, & D. A. Wise (eds.), *Social Security Policy in a Changing Environment* (pp. 379–384). Chicago: University of Chicago Press.

Smedley, B. D. (2008). Moving beyond access: Achieving equity in state health reform. *Health Affairs* 27 (2): 447–455.

Smirnova, M. A. (2012). A will to youth: The woman's anti-aging elixir. *Social Science & Medicine* 76 (7): 1236–1243.

Smith, D. (2010). Volunteer patterns of mid- and later life American couples. *Journal of Sociology & Social Welfare* 37 (3): 131–154.

Smith, D. B. & Feng, Z. (2010). The accumulated challenges of long-term care. *Health Affairs* 29 (1): 29–34.

Smith, S. K., Rayer, S., & Smith, E. A. (2008). Aging and disability: Implications for the housing industry and housing policy in the United States. *Journal of the American Planning Association* 74 (3): 289–306.

Smith, W. T., Roth, J. J., Okoro, O., Kimberlin, C., & Odedina, F. T. (2011). Disability in cultural competency pharmacy education. *American Journal of Pharmaceutical Education* 75 (2): 1–9.

Smokowski, P. R., Rose, R., & Bacallao, M. L. (2008). Acculturation and family processes: How cultural involvement, and acculturation gaps influence family dynamics. *Family Relations* 57 (3): 295–308.

Smyer, M. A., & Pitt-Catsouphes, M. (2007). The meanings of work for older workers. *Generations* 31 (1): 23–30.

Social Security Administration. (2011a). *Never beneficiaries: Aged 62–84, 2010.* Washington, DC: Social Security Administration.

Social Security Administration. (2011b). Fact Sheet: Social security is important to Hispanics. Washington, DC: Social Security Administration.

Social Security Administration. (2011c). Fact Sheet: Social security is important to African Americans. Washington, DC: Social Security Administration.

Social Security Administration. (2011d). Fact Sheet: Social security is important to Asian Americans and Pacific Islanders. Washington, DC: Social Security Administration.

Social Security Administration. (2011e). Social security is important to American Indians and Alaska Natives. Washington, DC: Social Security Administration.

Solomon, B. B. (1976). *Black Empowerment: Social Work in Oppressed Communities*. New York: Columbia University Press.

Sommers, A. R. (2007). Mortality of Americans age 65 and older: 1980 to 2004. Washington, DC: Congressional Research Report for Congress.

Sorocco, D. C., Kasi-Godley, J., Thompson, L., Rabinowitz, Y., & Gallagher-Thompson, D., (2005). Caregiver self-efficacy, ethnicity, and kinship differences in dementia caregivers. *American Journal of Geriatric Psychiatry* 13 (9): 787–794.

Sowards, S. K. & Pineda, B. D. (2013). Immigrant narratives and popular culture in the United States: Border spectacles, unmotivated sympathies, and individualized responsibilities. *Western Journal of Communication* 77 (1): 72–91.

Sperling, G. (2005). *A Progressive Framework for Social Security Reform*. Washington, DC: Center for American Progress,

Spira, M. (2006). Mapping your future—a proactive approach to aging. *Journal of Gerontological Social Work* 47 (1–2): 71–87.

Stanford, E. P., Yee, D. L., & Rivas, E. E. (2009). Quality of life for communities of color. In L. Rogen, C. Estes, B. R. Grossman, B. Hollister, & E. Solway (eds.), *Social Insurance and Social Justice* (pp. 179–189). New York: Springer.

Star, P. (2005, February). Why we need Social Security. *American Prospect*. www.princeton.edu/~starr/articles/articles05/Starr-SocSec-2-05.htm. Accessed October 1, 2013.

Steel, N., Clark, A., Lang, I. A., Wallace, R. B., & Melzer, D. (2008). Racial disparities in receipt of hip and knee joint replacements are not explained by need: The Health and Retirement Study 1998–2004. *Journals of Gerontology Series A: Biological Sciences and Medical Sciences* 63 (6): 629–634.

Stein, G. (2008). The economic, political and financial implications of ageing populations. *Economic Affairs* 28 (1): 23–28.

Stelle, C., Fruhauf, C. A., Orel, N., & Landry-Meyer, L. (2010). Grandparenting in the 21st century: Issues of diversity in grandparenting-grandchild relationships. *Journal of Gerontological Social Work* 53 (8): 682–701.

Stephens, C. & Flick, U. (2010). Health and ageing—challenges for health psychology research. *Journal of Health Psychology* 15 (5): 643–648.

Steuerle, C. E. (2010). America's related fiscal problems. *Journal of Policy Analysis and Management* 29 (10): 876–883.

Steuerle, C. E. (2011, February 17). The progressive case against subsidizing middle-age retirement. *American Prospect.* www.urban.org/url.cfm?ID=901414& renderforprint=1. Accessed November 17, 2011.

Steuerle, C. E. & Rennane, S. (2010). *Social Security and the Budget.* Washington, DC: Urban Institute.

Stevenson, J. S. (2005). Alcohol use, misuse, abuse, and dependence in later adulthood. *Annual Review of Nursing Research* 23:245–280.

Stewart, D. W. (2006). Generational mentoring. *Journal of Continuing Education in Nursing* 37 (3): 113–120.

Stice, B. D. & Canetto, S. S. (2008). Older adult suicide: Perceptions of participants and protective factors. *Clinical Gerontology* 31 (4): 4–30.

Stipp, D. (2013, July 23). Meaning markers of aging. *New York Times,* p. D3.

Strack, R., Baier, J., & Fahlander, A. (2008). Managing demographic risk. *Harvard Business Review* (February): 1–12.

Strand, P. J. (2010). Inheriting inequality: Wealth, race, and the laws of succession. *Oregon Law Review* 89:453–504.

Street, D. (2009). Social justice and tax expenditures. In L. Rogne, C. L. Estes, B. R. Grossman, B. A. Hollister, & E. Solway (eds.), Social insurance and social justice (pp. 359–375). New York: Springer.

Street, D. & Cossman, J. S. (2006). Greatest generation or greedy geezer? Social spending preferences and the elderly. *Social Problems* 53 (1): 75–96.

Su, B. W. (2007). The U.S. economy to 2016: Slower growth as boomers begin to retire. *Monthly Labor Review* 130:13–32.

Suarez, A. V. (2013, February 9). Baby boomers aren't sold on retirement communities. *Miami Herald,* p. 1.

Sullivan K., Lynch, A., Artesani, A., & Seed, S. (2007). Medication and alcohol misuse among older adults. *U.S. Pharmacist* 32 (6): HS20–HS30.

Sun, F. & Hodge, D. R. (2012). Latino Alzheimer's Disease caregivers and depression: using the stress coping model to examine the effects of spirituality and religion. *Journal of Applied Gerontonlogy* 16 (6): 689–698.

Sundeen, R. A., Raskoff, S. A., & Garcia, C. (2007). Differences in perceived barriers to volunteering to formal organizations: Lack of time versus lack of interest. *Nonprofit Management and Leadership* 17 (3): 279–300.

Sussman, N. M. & Truong, N. (2011). "Please extinguish all cigarettes": The effects of acculturation and gender on smoking attitudes and smoking prevalence of

Chinese and Russian immigrants. *International Journal of Intercultural Relations* 36 (2): 163–178.

Sutherland, J.-A., Poloma, M. M., & Pendleton, B. F. (2005). Religion, spirituality, and alternate health practices: The baby boomers and cold war cohorts. *Journal of Religion and Health* 42 (4): 315–338.

Svihula, J. & Estes, C. L. (2006). Social Security politics: Ideology and reform. *Journals of Gerontology Series B: Psychological Sciences and Social Sciences* 62 (2): S79–S89.

Svihula, J. & Estes, C. L. (2009). Social Security privatization: The institutionalization of an ideological movement. In L. Rogne, C. L. Estes, B. R. Grossman, B. A. Hollister, & E. Solway (eds.), *Social Insurance and Social Justice* (pp. 217–231). New York: Springer.

Swinson, J. L. (2006). Focusing on the health benefits of volunteering as a recruitment strategy. *International Journal of Volunteer Administration* 24 (2): 25–30.

Szinovacz, M. E. & Davey, A. (2013). Changes in adult children's participation in parent care. *Ageing and Society* 33 (4): 667–697.

Talavera-Garcia, L., Ghadder, S., Valerio, M., & Garcia, C. (2013). Health care access and utilization among Hispanic manufacturing workers across the Texas-Mexico border. *Journal of Health Care for the Poor and Underserved* 24 (2): 656–670.

Talley, R. C. & Crews, J. E. (2007). Caring for the most vulnerable: Framing the public health of caregiving. *American Journal of Public Health* 97 (2): 224–228.

Tan, E. J., Rebok, G. W., Yu, Q., Frangakis, C. E., Carlston, M. C., Wang, T., Ricks, M., Tanner, E. K., McGill, S., & Fried, L. P. (2009). The long-term relationship between high-intensity volunteering and physical activity in older African American women. *Journals of Gerontology Series B: Psychological and Social Sciences* 64B (2): 304–311.

Tang, F., Choi, E., & Goode, R. (2013). Older Americans employment and retirement. *Ageing International* 38 (1): 82–94.

Tang, F., Choi, E., & Morrow-Howell, N. (2010). Organizational support and volunteering benefits for older adults. *Gerontologist* 50 (5): 603–612.

Tang, F., Copeland, V. C., & Wexler, S. (2012). Racial differences in volunteering engagement by older adults: An empowerment perspective. *Social Work Research* 36 (2): 89–100.

Tang, F., Morrow-Howell, N., & Hong, S. (2008). Inclusion of diverse older populations in volunteering: The importance of institutional facilitation. *Nonprofit and Voluntary Sector Quarterly* 38 (5): 810–827.

Tangredi, T., Danvers, K., Molony, S. L., & Williams, A. (2008). New CDC recommendations for HIV testing in older adults. *Nurse Practitioner* 33 (6): 37–44.

Tankersley, J. (2012, October 10). General warfare: The case against parasitic baby boomers. *National Journal.* www.nationaljournal.com/features/restoration-calls/my-father-the-parasite-20121004. Accessed January 13, 2013.

Tanner, M. (2001). *Disparate Impact: Social Security and African Americans.* Washington, DC: Cato Institute.

Tavernise, S. (2013, May 30). For Medicare, immigrants offer surplus, study finds: A crucial balance to an aging population. *New York Times,* pp. A12, A15.

Taylor, A. (2007). Mentoring across generations: Engaging age 50+ adults as mentors. Research in Action. *MENTOR,* no. 8.

Taylor, P., Fry, R., & Kochhar, R. (2011). *Wealth Gaps Rise to Record Highs Between Whites, Blacks, Hispanics.* Washington, DC: Pew Research Center.

Taylor, P., Livingston, G., Parker, K. Wang, W., & Dockterman, D. (2010). *Since the Start of the Great Recession, More Children Raised by Grandparents.* Washington, DC: Pew Research Center.

Thaker, S. N. (2008). Understanding the role of culture in the health-related behaviors of older Asian Indian immigrants. Athens: University of Georgia.

Thompson, M. (2008, September 22). Who coined the phrase baby boomers? www.lifewhile.com/family/17530056/detail.html. Accessed August 26, 2011.

Three Degrees of Acculturation. (2005). Entrepreneur.com. www.entrepreneur.com/article/0.4621.228754–3.00.html. Accessed March 29, 2012.

Tienda, M. (2007). Hispanics at the age crossroads: Opportunities and risks. *Forces* 25 (1): 27–32.

Tierney, E. P. & Hanke, C. W. (2009). Recent trends in cosmetic and surgical procedure volumes in dermatologic surgery. *Dermatologic Surgery* 35 (9): 1324–1333.

Tilly, J. (2010). The Administration on Aging's experiences with health, prevention, and wellness. *Generations* 34 (1): 20–25.

Tippett, R. M. (2010). Household debt across the life course: An analysis of the late baby boomers. Durham, NC: Duke University Dissertations.

Toder, E. J. & Smith, K. E. (2011). Do low-income workers benefit from 401(K) plans? Boston College: Center for Retirement Research at Boston College Working Paper No. 2011–14.

Tone, A. & Watkins, E. S. (eds.). (2007). *Medicating Modern America: Prescription Drugs in History.* New York: New York University Press.

Toossi, M. (2009). Labor force projections to 2018: Older workers staying more active. *Monthly Labor Review* 132 (11).

Tootelian, D. H. & Varshney, S. B. (2010). The grandparent consumer: A financial "goldmine" with gray hair? *Journal of Consumer Marketing* 27 (1): 57–63.

Torres, L. R., Kaplan, C., & Valdez, A. (2011). Health consequences of long-term injection heroin use among aging Mexican American men. *Journal of Aging Health* 23 (6): 312–332.

Torres-Gil, F. & Lam, D. (2012). The evolving nexus of policy, longevity and diversity: Agenda setting for Latino health and aging. In J. L. Angel, F. Torres-Gil, & K. Markides (eds.), *Aging, Health, and Longevity in the Mexican-Origin Population* (pp. 327–336). New York: Springer.

Toseland, R. W., Hagler, D. H., & Monahan, D. J. (2011). Current and future directions of education and support programs for caregivers. In R. W. Toseland, D. H. Hagler, & D. J. Monahan (eds.), *Education and Support Programs for Caregivers and Caregiving: Research, Practice, Policy* (pp. 149–158). New York: Springer.

Toupin, L. & Plewes, B. (2007). Exploring the looming deficit in the voluntary and nonprofit sector. *Philanthropist* 21 (2): 128–136.

Tovar, C. (2011, May 31). The fate of Latino baby boomers. *Being Latino Online Magazine*. http://beinglatino.wordpress.com/2011/05/31/the-fate-of-latino-baby-boomers/. Accessed August 30, 2011.

Transgenerational Design. (2011). The demographics of aging. http://transgenerational.org/viewpoint/transgenerational.htm.

Trawinski, L. (2012). Nightmare on Main Street: Older Americans and the mortgage crisis. Washington, DC: AARP Public Policy Institute.

Treas, J. (2008). Transnational older Americans and their families. *Family Relations* 57 (4): 468–478.

Treas, J. & Carreon, D. (2010). Diversity and our common future: Race, ethnicity, and the older American. *Generations* 34 (3): 38–44.

Trevisan, L. A. (2008). Baby boomers and substance abuse. *Geriatric Psychiatry* 25 (8): 28–31.

Truffer, C. J., Keehan, S., Smith, S., Cylus, J., Sisko, A., Polsal, J. A., Lizonitz, J., & Clemens, M. K. (2010). Health spending projections through 2019: The recession impact continues. *Health Affairs* 29 (3): 522–529.

Truman, B. I., Smith, C. K., Roy, K., Chen, Z., Moonesinghe, R., Zhu, J., Crawford, C. G., & Zaza, S. (2011). *MMWR* 60 (1): 3–10.

Tugend, A. (2013, July 27). Unemployed and older, and facing a jobless future. *New York Times,* p. B4.

Turner, B. S. (2009). *Can We Live Forever? A Sociological and Moral Inquiry.* London Anthem.

Uhlenberg, P. (2009). Children in an aging society. *Journals of Gerontology Series B: Psychological and Social Sciences* 64B (4): 489–496.

Uhlenberg, P. & Cheuk, M. (2010). The significance of grandparents to grandchildren: An international perspective. In D. Dannefer & C. Phillipson (eds.), *The SAGE Handbook on Social Gerontology* (pp. 447–458). Thousand Oaks, CA: Sage.

Unger M. (2010). Cultural dimensions of resilience among adults. In J. W. Reich, A. J. Zutra, & J. S. Hall (eds.), *Handbook of Adult Resilience* (404–426). New York: Guilford.

University of Michigan. (2008, June). Trends in health and disability among adults approaching retirement age. Trends in research Brief. http://trends.psc.isr.umich.edu/pdf/pubs/TRENDSResBrief-02-20-09.pdf.

Urban Institute. (2006). Productive aging: Boom or bust? Washington, DC: Urban Institute.

U.S. Administration on Aging. (2011a). Number of persons 60+ by Race and Hispanic origin—by state—2008. Washington, DC: U.S. Administration on Aging.

U.S. Administration on Aging. (2011b). Population projections by race and Hispanic origin for persons 60 and over: 2000 to 2050. Washington, DC: U.S. Administration on Aging.

U.S. Census Bureau. (2000). All across the USA. Population distribution and composition. Washington, DC: U.S. Census Bureau.

U.S. Census Bureau. (2006). Oldest baby boomers turn 60! Washington, DC: U.S. Census Bureau.

U.S. Census Bureau. (2009). Selected characteristics of baby boomers 42 to 60 years old in 2006. Washington, DC: U.S. Census Bureau.

U.S. Census Bureau. (2010). Black (African-American) History Month February 2011. Washington, DC: U.S. Census Bureau.

U.S. Census Bureau. (2011a). Older Americans Month: May 2011. Washington, DC: U.S. Census Bureau.

U.S. Census Bureau. (2011b). Hispanic Heritage Month 2011: Sept. 15–Oct. 15. Washington, DC: U.S. Census Bureau.

U.S. Census Bureau. (2011c). Asian/Pacific American Heritage Month: May 2011. Washington, DC: U.S. Census Bureau.

U.S. Census Bureau. (2011d). American Indian and Alaska Native Heritage Month: November 2011. Washington, DC: U.S. Census Bureau.

Valle, R., Garrett, M. D., & Velasquez, R. (2013). Developing dementia prevalence rates among Latinos: A locally attuned, data-based, service planning tool. *Population Aging* 6 (3): 211–225.

Valls, A. & Kaplan, J. (2007). Housing discrimination as a nasis for Black reparations. *Public Affairs Quarterly* 21 (3): 255–273.

Van Den Bogaard, L. E. V. I., Henkens, K., & Kalmijn, M. (2013). So now what? Effects of retirement on civic engagement. *Ageing and Society,* pp. 1–23.

Vanderhei, J. L. & Copeland, C. (2009). Private pensions and the boomers: How much is enough? In R. B. Hudson (ed.), *Boomer Bust? Perspectives on the Boomers* (pp. 197–225). Westport, CT: Praeger.

Van der Klaauw, W. & Wolpin, K. I. (2008). Social Security and the retirement and savings behavior of low-income households. *Journal of Econometrics* 145 (1–2): 21–42.

Van Wagenen, A., Driskell, J., & Bradford, J. (2013). "I'm still raring to go": Successful aging among lesbian, gay, bisexual, and transgender older adults. *Journal of Aging Studies* 27 (1): 1–14.

Veciana-Surarez, A. (2011, September 4). Baby boomers face parenting that stretches on and on . . . *Miami Herald,* p. 1.

Vega, W. A. & Gonzalez, H. M. (2012). Latinos "aging in place": Issues and potential solutions. In J. L. Angel, F. Torres-Gil, & K. Markides (eds.), *Aging, Health, and Longevity in the Mexican-Origin Population* (pp. 193–206). New York: Springer.

Vesperi, M. D. (2009b). Evaluating images of aging in print and broadcast media. In R. B. Hudson (ed.), *Boomer Bust? Economic and Political Issues of the Graying Society* (pp. 125–144). Westport, CT: Praeger.

Villa, V. M., Wallace, S. P., Bagdasaryn, S., & Arranda, M. (2012). Hispanic baby boomers: Health inequities likely to persist in old age. *Gerontologist* 52 (2): 166–176.

Villa, V. M., Wallace, S. P., & Huynh-Hohnbaum, A.-L. T. (2005–2006). The aging Hispanic population: Prescriptions for health and economic security in old age. *Harvard Journal of Hispanic Policy* 18 (1): 59–73.

Vincent, G. K. & Velkoff, V. A. (2010). The next four decades: The older population in the United States: 2010 to 2050. Current Population Reports P 25–1138.

Voelker, R. (2010, January 27). Ethnic shifts raise issues in elder care. *Journal of the American Medical Association* 303 (4): 321–324.

von Hoffman, A. (2011). Housing Rights and Inequality in Postwar America. APSA 2011 Annual Meeting Paper. Available at SSRN: http://ssrn.com/abstract=1901931.

Waggoner, J. (2010, July 19). How will baby boomers' retirement affect stocks? *USA Today,* p. A10.

Wagner, J. A., Osborn, C. Y., Mendenhall, E. A., Budris, L. M., Belay, S., & Tennen, H. A. (2011). Beliefs about racism and health among African American women with diabetes: a qualitative study. *Journal of the National Medical Association* 103 (3): 224.

Wagnild, G. M. & Collins, J. A. (2009). Assessing resilience. *Journal of Psychosocial Nursing & Mental Health Services* 47 (12): 28–33.

Waidmann, T. (2009). Estimating the cost of racial and ethnic health disparities. Washington, DC: Urban Institute.

Waidmann, T., Ormond, B. A., & Bovbjerg, R. R. (2011). The role of prevention in bending the cost curve. Washington, DC: Urban Institute.

Waite, L. & Das, A. (2010). Families, social, life, and well-being at older ages. *Demography* 47 (Suppl.): S87–S109.

Waites, C. (2009). Building on strengths: Intergenerational practice with African-American families. *Social Work* 54 (3): 278–287.

Walker, A. (2005). Towards an international political economy of ageing. *Ageing & Society* 25 (6): 815–839.

Walker, A. (2009). Social insurance in Europe. In L. Rogne, C. L. Estes, B. R. Grossman, B. A. Hollister, & E. Solway (eds.), *Social Insurance and Social Justice* (pp. 299–317). New York: Springer.

Walker, A. & Fong, F. (2010). Relations between the generations: Uniting the macro and the micro. *Journal of Intergenerational Relationships* 8 (4): 425–430.

Wallace, G. (2001). Grandparent caregiving. *Journal of Gerontological Social Work* 34 (3): 127–136.

Wallace, S. P. & Villa, V. M. (2009). Healthy, wealthy, and wise? Challenges to income security for elders of color. In L. Rogen, C. Estes, B. R. Grossman, B. Hollister, & E. Solway (eds.), *Social Insurance and Social Justice* (pp. 165–178). New York: Springer.

Walsh, M. W. (2010, March 24). Social Security to see payout exceed pay-in this year. *New York Times,* p. A1.

Wang, D., Ihara, E., Chonody, J., & Krase, K. (2013). Social work faculty interest in aging: Impact of education, knowledge, comfort, and experience. *Gerontology & Geriatrics Education* 34 (3): 257–271.

Wang, M. & Shih, J. (2013). Psychological research on retirement. *Annual Review of Psychology* 000 (00): 000.

Wang, P.-C., Tong, H.-Q., Liu, W., Long, S., Leung, L. Y. I., Yau, E., & Gallagher-Thompson, D. Working with Chinese-American families. In G. Yeo and D. Gallagher-Thompson (eds.), Ethnicity and the dementias, 2d ed. (pp. 173–188). New York: Routledge.

Warburton, J. & McLaughlin, D. (2007). How older Australians from diverse cultural backgrounds contribute to civil society. *Journal of Cross-Cultural Gerontology* 22 (1): 47–60.

Ward, E. G., Disch, W. B., Schensul, J. J., & Levy, J. A. (2011). Understanding low-income, minority older adult self-perceptions of HIV risk. *Journal of the Association of Nurses in AIDS Care* 22 (1): 26–37.

Washington, O. G. M. & Moxley, D. P. (2008). Telling my story: From narrative to exhibit in illuminating the lived experience of homelessness among older African American women. *Journal of Health Psychology* 13 (2): 154–166.

Washko, M. M., Schack, R. W., Goff, B. A., & Pudlin, J. D. (2011). Title V of the Older Americans Act, the Senior Community Service Employment Program: Participant demographics and service to racially/ethnically diverse populations. *Journal of Aging & Social Policy* 23 (2): 182–197.

Wasik, J. F. (2011). *How Safe Are Your Savings? How Complex Derivative Products Imperil Seniors' Retirement Security.* New York: Demos.

Weaver, H. N. (2011). Serving multicultural elders: Recommendations for helping professionals. *Case Management Journals* 12 (2): 42–49.

Weaver, J. D. (2013). Granma in the White House: Legal support for intergenerational caregiving. *Seton Hall Law Review* 43:1.

Webb, M. S., Rodriguez-Esquivel, D., & Baker, E. A. (2010). Smoking cessation interventions among Hispanics in the U.S.: A systematic review and mini meta-analysis. *American Journal of Health Promotion* 25 (2): 109–118.

Weiner, M. E. (2008). Perspectives on race and ethnicity in Alzheimer's disease research. *Alzheimer and Dementia* 4 (4): 233–238.

Welleford, E. A. & Netting, F. E. (2012). Integrating aging and civic engagement into the curriculum. *Educational Gerontology* 38 (4): 243–256.

Wellner, A. S. (2001). The forgotten baby boomers-baby boomer generation. BNET. http://adage.com/article/american-demographics/forgotten-baby-boom/42228. Accessed November 11, 2012.

Whaley, M. & Paul-Ward, A. (2011). Keeping close to home: The ritual of domino playing among older Cuban immigrants in Miami's "Little Havana." *Generations* 35 (3): 22–27.

Wheary, J. (2011). *Rising Economic Insecurity Among Single Women*. New York: Demos.

Wheary, J. & Meschede, T. (2010). *Living Longer on Less pt. 3: Severe Financial Insecurity Among African-American and Latino Seniors*. New York: Demos.

White, B. E. & Beach, P. R. (2012). In the shadows of family-centered care: Parents of ill adult children. *Journal of Hospice & Palliative Nursing* 14 (1): 53–60.

White, J. (2004). "(How) Is aging a health policy problem?" *Yale Journal of Health Policy, Law, and Ethics* 4 (1): article 2.

White, J. (2013). Thinking generations. *British Journal of Sociology* 64 (2): 216–247.

Whitefield, K. E. (2005). Studying biobehavorial aspects of health disparities among older adult minorities. *Journal of Urban Health* 82 (2, Suppl. 3): 103–110.

Wick, J. Y. (2012a). Senior centers: traditional and evolving roles. *Consultant Pharmacists* 27 (9): 664–667.

Wick, J. Y. (2012b). High-stakes gambling: Seniors may be the losers. *Consultant Pharmacists* 27 (8): 544–551.

Wickrama, K. A. S., O'Neal, L. W., & Lorenz, F. D. (2013). Marital functioning from middle to later years: A life course-stress process framework. *Journal of Family Theory & Review* 5 (1): 15–34.

Wickramasinghe, N. & Goldberg, S. (2013). Using wireless to monitor chronic disease patients in urban poor regions. In R. Bali, I. Troshani, S. Goldberg, & N. Wickramasinghe (eds.), *Pervasive Health Knowledge Management: Healthcare Delivery in the Information Age* (pp. 195–208). New York: Springer.

Wild, K., Wiles, J. L., & Allen, R. E. S. (2013). Resiliency: Thoughts on the value of the concept for critical gerontologists. *Ageing & Society* 33 (1): 137–158.

Wilensky, G. R. (2011, May 19). Reforming Medicare—toward a modified Ryan Plan. *New England Journal of Medicine* 364:1890–1892.

Wiles, J. L., Leibing, A., Guberman, N., Reeve, J., & Allen, R. E. S. (2012). The meaning of "Aging in place" to older adults. *Gerontologist* 52 (3): 357–366.

Willcox, D. C., Willcox, B. J., Sokolovsky, J., & Sakihara, S. (2007). The cultural context of "successful aging" among older women. *Journal of Cross-Cultural Gerontology* 22 (2): 137–165.

Willetts, D. (2010). *The Pinch: How the Baby Boomers Took Their Children's Future—and Why They Should Give It Back*. London: Atlantic.

Williams, M. N. (2011). The changing roles of grandparents raising grandchildren. *Journal of Human Behavior and the Social Environment* 21 (8): 948–962.

Williams, S. (2013). Pain disparity: Assessment and traditional medicine. In T. R. Deer et al. (eds.), Comprehensive treatment of chronic pain by medical, intervential, and integrative approaches (pp. 935–946). New York: Springer.

Williams, T. (2012, January 27). Number of older inmates grows, stressing prisons. *New York Times,* p. A12.

Williamson, J. B., McNamara, T. K., & Howling, S. A. (2003). Generational equity, generational interdependence, and the framing of the debate over Social Security reform. *Journal of Sociology & Social Welfare* 30 (3): 3–14.

Williamson, J. B. & Watts-Roy, D. M. (2009). Aging boomers, generational equity, and the framing of the debate over Social Security. In R. B. Hudson (ed.), *Boomer Bust? Perspectives on the Boomers* (pp. 153–169). Westport, CT: Praeger.

Williamson, T. (2008a). From the 60s to their sixties. Baby boomers—challenges and choices for public mental health. *Journal of Public Mental Health* 7 (1): 4–8.

Williamson, T. (2008b). Working with older people. *Pier Professional* 12 (3): 15–18.

Wilmoth, J. M. (2010). Aging policy and structural lag. In R.B. Hudson (ed.), *The New Politics of Old Age Policy,* 2d ed. (pp. 42–63). Baltimore: Johns Hopkins University Press.

Wilmoth, J. M. & Longino Jr., C. F. (2006). Demographic trends that will shape U.S. policy in the twenty-first century. *Research on Aging* 26 (4): 269–288.

Wilson, J. (2012). Volunteering research: A review easy. *Nonprofit and Voluntary Sector Quarterly* 41 (2): 176–212.

Wilson, J. & Dengo, S. (2013, March 6), $245 billion in 2012, up 41% from $174 in 2007. *Diabetes Care* 36 (4):1033–1046. doi: 10.2337/dc12-2625. Accessed June 13, 2013.–

Wilson, J., Tilsa, C., Setterlund, D., & Rosenman, L. (2009). Older people and their assets: A range of roles and issues for social workers. *Australian Social Work* 62 (2): 155–167.

Wilson, L. B. & Harlow-Rosentraub, K. (2009). Providing new opportunities for volunteerism and civic engagement for boomers: Chaos theory redefined. In R. B. Hudson (ed.), *Boomer Bust? Economic and Political Issues of the Graying Society* (pp. 79–98). Westport, CT: Praeger.

Wilson, L. B. & Simson, S. P. (eds.). (2006). *Civic Engagement and the Baby Boomer Generation: Research, Policy, and Practice Perspectives.* New York: Haworth.

Winter, N. J. G. (2006). Beyond welfare: Framing and the racialization of white opinion on Social Security. *American Journal of Political Science* 50 (2): 400–420.

Wirth, C. K. (2010). *Weight Concerns and Weight Loss Problems of Baby Boomer Men.* Gainesville: University of Florida.

Wisensale, S. K. (2009). Aging policy as family policy: expanding family leave and improving flexible work policies. In R. B. Hudson (ed.), *Boomer Bust? Perspectives on the Boomers* (pp. 253–269). Westport, CT: Praeger.

Wister, A. W. (2005). *Baby Boomer Health Dynamics: How Are We Aging?* Toronto: University of Toronto Press.

Wolf, R. (2010, December 12). Medicare to swell with baby boomer onslaught. *USA Today,* p. A1.

Wolff, E. N. (2007). The retirement wealth of the baby boom generation. *Journal of Monetary Economics* 54 (1): 1–40.

Wolff, J. L. & Roter, D. L. (2011). Family presence in routine medical visits: A meta-analysis review. *Social Science & Medicine* 72 (6): 823–831.

Woods II, L. L. (2013). ALMOST "NO NEGRO VETERAN . . . COULD GET A LOAN": AFRICAN AMERICANS, THE GI BILL, AND THE NAACP CAMPAIGN AGAINST RESIDENTIAL SEGREGATION, 1917–1960. *Journal of African American History* 38 (3): 392–417.

World Bank. 1994. *Averting the Old Age Crisis: Policies to Protect the Old and Promote Growth.* Washington DC: World Bank. http://documents.worldbank.org/curated/en/1994/09/698030/averting-old-age-crisis-policies-protect-old-promote-growth

Worsley, A., Wang, W. C., & Hunter, W. (2011). The relationships between eating habits, smoking and alcohol consumption, and body mass index among baby boomers. *Appetite* 58 (1): 74–80.

Wray, L. R. (2006). Social security in an aging society. *Review of Political Economy* 18 (3): 391–411.

Wright, J. D. (2005). The graying of America: Implications for health professionals. *Case Management Journals* 6 (4): 178–184.

Wu, L.-T. & Blazer, D. C. (2011). Illicit and nonmedical drug use among older adults: A review. *Journal of Aging & Health* 23 (3): 481–504.

Wu, S.-W. S. & Wortman, J. (2009). Senior gaming: More than just buffers. *Worldwide Hospitality and Tourism Themes* 1 (4): 344–354.

Yahirun, J., Perreira, K., & Fuligni, A. (2010). *Family Obligation Across Contexts: Latino Youth in North Carolina and Southern California.* Los Angeles: UCLA International Institute.

Yan, T., Silverstein, M., & Wilber, R. H. (2011). Does race/ethnicity affect aging anxiety in American baby boomers? *Research on Aging* 33 (4): 361–378.

Yang, P. & Barrett, N. (2006). Understanding public attitudes towards Social Security. *International Journal of Social Welfare* 15 (1): 95–109.

Yang, F. M. & Levkoff, S. E. (2005). Ageism and minority populations: Strengths in the face of challenge. *Generations* 29 (3): 42–48.

Yankeslov, P. A., Faul, A. C., D'Ambrosio, J. F., Collins, W. L., & Gordon, B. (2013). "Another Day in Paradise": A photovoice journey of rural older adults living with diabetes. *Journal of Applied Anthropology* 00 (00): 00.

Yasar, Y. (2009). It's the prices, stupid: The underlying problems of the U.S. Social Security System. *Journal of Economic Issues* 43 (4): 843–865.

Yeo, G. (2009). How will the U.S. healthcare system meet the challenge of the ethnogeriatric imperative? *Journal of the American Geriatric Society* 57 (7): 1278–1285.

Yeo, G. & Gallager-Thompson, D. (eds.). (2006). *Ethnicity and the Dementias,* 2d ed. New York: Routledge.

Yokohari, M. & Bolthouse, J. (2011). Planning for the slow lane: The need to restore working greenspaces in maturing contexts. *Landscapes and Urban Planning* 100 (4): 421–424.

Yoo, G. J. & Kim, B. W. (2010). Remembering sacrifices: Attitude and beliefs among second generation Korean Americans regarding family support. *Journal of Cross-Cultural Gerontology* 25 (2): 165–181.

Yoon, T. J. (2005). A mixed-method study of Princeville's rebuilding from the flood of 1999: Lessons on the importance of invisible community assets. *Social Work* 54 (1): 19–28.

Yosso, T. J. & Garcia, D. G. (2007). "This is no slum!": A critical race theory analysis of community cultural wealth in culture clash's Chancez Ravine. *Aztlan: A Journal of Chicano Studies* 32 (1): 145–179.

Youmans, S. L., Schillinger, D., Mamary, E., & Stewart, A. (2007). Older African Americans' perceptions of pharmacists. *Ethnicity & Disease* 17 (4): 284–290.

Zemore, S. E. (2007). Acculturation and alcohol among Latino adults in the United States: A comprehensive review. *Alcoholism: Clinical and Experimental Research* 31 (12): 1968–1990.

Zemore, S. E., Mulia, N., & Greenfield, T. K. (2009). Gender, acculturation, and other barriers to alcohol treatment utilization among Latinos in three national alcohol surveys. *Journal of Substance Abuse Treatment* 36 (4): 446–458.

Zhan, L. (2004). Caring for family members with Alzheimer's disease: Perspectives from Chinese-American caregivers. *Journal of Gerontological Nursing* 30 (8): 19–29.

Zhan, D., Hirota, S., Garcia, J., & Ro, M. J. (2008). Valuing families and meeting them where they are. *American Journal of Public Health* 98 (Suppl. 1): S62–S64.

Zhou, M., & Lee, R. (2013). Transnationalism and community building: Chinese immigrant organizations in the United States. *Annals of the American Academy of Political and Social Sciences* 647 (1): 22–49.

Zingmond, D. S., Soohoo, N. F., & Silverman, S. L. (2006). The role of socioeconomic status on hip fracture. *Osteoporos* 17 (10): 1562–1568.

Zink, T. & Fisher, B. S. (2007). Older women living with intimate partner violence. *Aging Health* 3 (2): 257–265.

Zipkin, A. (2013, May 15). Gone, but still linked to the home office. *New York Times,* p. F2.